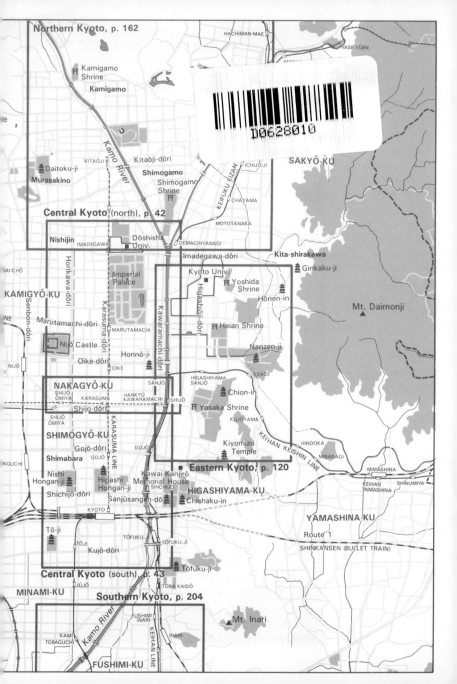

Northern Kyoto, p. 162

HACHIMAN-MAE

YASE YÜEN

Kamigamo
Shrine
Kamigamo

KITAŌJI Kitaōji-dōri

Daitoku-ji
Murasakino

ICHIJŌ JI **SAKYŌ-KU**

Shimogamo
Shimogamo
Shrine

CHAYAMA

MOTOTANAKA

Central Kyoto (north), p. 42

Nishijin IMADEGAWA Dōshisha
Univ.

DEMACHIYANAGI

Imadegawa-dōri **Kita-shirakawa**

BAI-CHŌ

KAMIGYŌ-KU

Horikawa-dōri

Senbon-dōri

NE

Karasuma-dōri

Kyoto Univ.

Yoshida
Shrine **Ginkaku-ji**

Imperial
Palace

Hōnen-in

Higashiōji-dōri

Mt. Daimonji

Marutamachi-dōri

MARUTAMACHI

Heian Shrine

NIJŌ

Nijō Castle

Oike-dōri

Honnō-ji

OIKE

Nanzen-ji

KEAGE

SANJŌ

HIGASHIYAMA
SANJŌ

NAKAGYŌ-KU

SHIJŌ
ŌMIYA

KARASUMA

HANKYŪ
KAWARAMACHI

Chion-in

Shijō-dōri

SHIJŌ

Yasaka Shrine

KUJŌYAMA

SHIJŌ
ŌMIYA

KEIHAN KEISHIN LINE

SHIMOGYŌ-KU

Gojō-dōri

GOJŌ

Kiyomizu
Temple

HINOOKA

MISASAGI

Shimabara

GOJŌ

YAMASHINA

Nishi
Hongan-ji

Higashi
Hongan-ji

Kawai Kanjirō
Memorial House

Eastern Kyoto, p. 120

KEIHAN
YAMASHINA

SHINUMIYA

AGUCHI

KARASUMA LINE

SHICHIJŌ

HIGASHIYAMA-KU

Shichijō-dōri

Sanjūsangen-dō **Chishaku-in**

YAMASHINA-KU

KYOTO

Tō-ji

TŌJI

Kujō-dōri

TŌFUKU-JI

Route 1

SHINKANSEN (BULLET TRAIN)

Tōfuku-ji

Central Kyoto (south), p. 43

JŪJŌ

TOBA KAIDŌ

MINAMI-KU

Southern Kyoto, p. 204

KAMI
TOBAGUCHI

Kamo River

FUSHIMI
INARI

KEIHAN LINE

INARI

Mt. Inari

FUSHIMI-KU

Kamo River

Kitaōji-dōri

Kamo River

KEIFUKU EIZAN

Higashiōji-dōri

Kawaramachi-dōri

10628010

OLD KYOTO

OLD KYOTO

A Guide to Traditional Shops, Restaurants, and Inns

Diane Durston

Photographs by Lucy Birmingham
Foreword by Donald Richie

KODANSHA INTERNATIONAL
Tokyo, New York and San Francisco

Here's to you, Stephen

NOTE: The Japanese personal names of historical figures who lived in or before the Edo period are written in the Japanese manner, surname preceding given name. Post-Edo names follow the Western order.

PHOTO CREDITS: Kenneth Hamm 163, 164, 181, 182, 205, 206, 222, 228, 229. Ito Tsuyoshi 35, 36, 217, 218, 219 (top), 220, 221, 226. Stephen Futscher 111–17, 153–59, 188, 200–202, 225 (bottom). Gekkeikan 208, 209. Kodansha Photo Library 17, 219 (bottom), 223, 224, 225 (top). Bon Color Photo Agency 214.

Maps by Michio Kojima

Distributed in the United States by Kodansha International/USA Ltd., through Harper & Row, Publishers, Inc., 10 East 53rd Street, New York, New York 10022. Published by Kodansha International Ltd., 2-2, Otowa 1-chome, Bunkyo-ku, Tokyo 112, and Kodansha International/USA Ltd., with offices at 10 East 53rd Street, New York, New York 10022 and The Hearst Building, 5 Third Street, Suite 400, San Francisco, California 94103.

Library of Congress Cataloging-in-Publication Data
Durston, Diane, 1950–
  Old Kyoto.
  Bibliography: p.
  1. Kyoto (Japan)—Description—Guide-books. Title.
DS897.K83D87 1986 915.2'18640448 85–45709

ISBN 0–87011–757–2 (U.S.)
ISBN 4–7700–1257–8 (JAPAN)
LCC 771257–x

Contents

Foreword   *by Donald Richie*   7

Beginnings   9

History   13

Kyoto Crafts   23

The Traditional Local Cuisine   28

A Night in a Traditional Inn   31

Machiya: Bedroom of Eels   33

A Few Helpful Notes   39

Central Kyoto, RAKU-CHŪ   41

Eastern Kyoto, RAKU-TŌ   119

Northern Kyoto, RAKU-HOKU   161

Western Kyoto, RAKU-SEI   189

Southern Kyoto, RAKU-NAN   203

Getting Around 214
Walks through Old Kyoto 217
Day Trips to the Countryside 222
A Few Special Places to Hide 225
Nishikikōji Street Market 227

Glossary 230
Shops by Type 233
Alphabetical List of Shops 236
Bibliography 239

Foreword

Kyoto—a fact well publicized—is very special. It holds the imperial past and the cultural best—temples, gardens, cuisine, kimono, crafts.

What is not generally recalled is that Kyoto is what it is because, almost alone among Japanese cities, it was not bombed, remaining undestroyed during World War II. Thus the old capital looks as all Japan might have, had it not been destroyed.

This being so, Kyoto—or at least parts of it—is still made of wood. It is the only city in Japan, perhaps in the world, so made. To walk the backstreets of the old capital is to stroll in a carpentered forest.

Thus Kyoto is more than the official traditional Japan one reads about in ordinary guidebooks and takes guided tours to see; it is also these warrens of backstreets with their inns and restaurants and shops, the buildings still made of wood and stone and tile.

As we walk these streets we see the grain, the hue, the texture of wood, watch its changing color, feel its warmth, sense nature. If you half close your eyes and look at these streets you will see how natural they are—the varied textures, the different shapes, the lines of roofs, all natural, all organic as though growing there.

Here, too, the last of the urban natural. Elsewhere, still, rice paddies harmonize and contrast with the valleys and the hills. The very materials—straw, wood, plaster, paper—are natural; when the dyed cloth was washed in the stream it delineated the current, emphasized the banks, seemed a part of the water itself.

And so even now there are backstreet corners in Kyoto where a harmonious accommodation is made between what man has built and what he found there—the line of a tree reflected in the line of a pillar; the grain of the rock, the grain of the stone wall.

Even now that concrete is cheaper than stone and metal is cheaper than wood and plastic is cheaper than anything, the warrens of old buildings—shops, inns, eateries—have no pretensions, do not aspire to becoming monuments. They can never become a part of the official traditional Kyoto. They are still in use. People live in these old buildings, work in them, always have.

The blank, anonymous postwar look of most Japanese cities is due not only to their having been destroyed by war. They are also being destroyed by the high price of land, the necessity for larger and more efficient buildings, the price of building materials and the necessity of building with cheap prefab modules, by the national preoccupation with the making of money.

Indeed, even sections of Kyoto look like Osaka or Nagoya, and in time the resemblance will be closer still. None of the great sights will go—this or that palace, that pavilion or this. There may well be some who would prefer a useful modern apartment block to a useless ancient temple, no matter how famous, but the official attitude is against them. The Kyoto city government would never permit this.

But there is no one to speak for these old-fashioned streets where the possibly dangerous wooden buildings are so inefficiently occupying valuable land.

Consequently, some of the finest environments, those which speak most truly of living Kyoto—these will vanish. This part of the living fabric of tradition will disappear. "Old Kyoto" will, of course, survive—it is, after all, a city on display where all, Japanese and foreigner alike, come as they would to an exposition.

But traces of the quiet, traditional backstreets of Kyoto will not vanish. One of these is the book you are holding. Here the look, the feel, the smell, the tastes of real traditional Kyoto have been preserved.

In her eight years in Kyoto, Diane Durston has lived with this true, living tradition. With affection and understanding she now gives it to us, the only account of these streets and their inns and shops and places to eat and to drink.

More than any other book it captures with care, with precision, and with love those qualities which make the real Kyoto what it still remains.

Donald Richie

Beginnings

Dusk settles over the backstreets of Kyoto, tucking in the rows of old wooden houses for another peaceful night's sleep. The glow of sunset deepens and hangs between the sagging tile rooftops; telephone lines and pine branches are silhouetted against an indigo sky. Someone's grandfather, bucket and washrag under one arm, clacks down the alley in wooden *geta* on his way to the public bath. The cackle of old women gossiping in doorways echoes in the quiet night air. An old man in white gauze pajamas squats on his doorstep amid a circle of impatient children begging him to light another sparkler to celebrate an ordinary summer night.

One of the only shops left open on the street is the corner saké shop, where a boisterous caucus of day laborers and pensioners wash down the day's grievances with a cold bottle of beer. The reassuring whir of an electric fan (and the shopkeeper's amazing skills of arbitration) temper the injustices of eight hours in the relentless Kyoto heat. "*Oideyasu!*" she calls out in Kyoto dialect, welcoming another weary pilgrim into the fold.

The bathhouse is still open, and their entryway curtains wave enticingly at simmering neighbors with promises of relief. The noodle shop two doors down feeds the last of the day's ravenous boardinghouse students, who sit slurping noodles with the cook in front of the TV set, kibitzing the outcome of the ball game.

The vegetable stand, the tofu shop, and the flower vendor have all closed down for the night. So have the knife sharpener, the seal carver, and the lacquerer—their electric fans the only ones working overtime tonight. An hour past supper and the smell of grilled fish still clings to the air. Lights go on behind the latticed paper windows of the houses, making them glow like a corridor of two-story wooden lanterns in the deepening twilight. A temple bell tolls the passage of another day. The local cop bicycles past on his evening rounds, humming; trouble is still a surprise in old Kyoto neighborhoods like these.

If it weren't for the surveyor's stakes in the vacant lot down the street, the year could as easily be 1887 as 1987. Within two weeks a three-story concrete apartment building will wedge its way between the gray tile rooftops of these "bedrooms of eels," the local nickname for the elongated wood-frame houses whose narrow façades line the streets of Kyoto. The *apaato*, the latest modern addition to the old neighborhood, though a disappointment to some, at least is no longer a surprise.

The old wooden buildings, the homes of craftsmen and merchants whose shop fronts open right onto the streets, are disappearing one by one; extracted hygienically, like aching teeth, leaving cavities in the landscape and the heart of the ancient city. Made simply of wood, clay, and sand, they are easily demolished, gone within hours on any hot Kyoto afternoon. But with them goes much of the history and charm of this thousand-year-old city. The old shops and houses gave shelter to a different world. A poorer world economically—kept down by an oppressive class system, dominated by a long line of tyrants—but one in which the common people learned, if only out of sheer necessity, how to live peacefully in cramped quarters, how to turn disaster into progress and poverty into an aesthetic ideal. During ages in which the aristocrats sank in their own decadence and the samurai fought their way to destruction, it was the common people of Kyoto, the merchants and craftsmen, who kept many of the arts and crafts, customs and traditions, of their civilization alive.

The old shops of Kyoto, some of whose families boast over twenty generations in the same trade, continue to house the spirit of the ancient capital, quietly tending the simple businesses of their grandfathers, as if the essence of what they represent were tucked safely away in the family shrine behind the urn that holds his ashes.

Wooden buckets and paper umbrellas are still made in the old shops as they were in the seventeenth century, but the citizens of twentieth-century Kyoto haven't much use for them anymore, preferring the "advantages" of plastic and nylon. Many homes in Japan now have their own baths, and people no longer relish the pleasures of a soak in the communal tubs of the city's old-fashioned *sentō*, or public baths. *Kyō-ryōri*, the exquisite local cuisine, must now compete with German delicatessens and French cafes for customers among Kyoto's increasingly cosmopolitan populace.

No one begrudges the improvements in the quality of life this last century has brought to Japan—modern transportation, better medical care, more of the luxuries once reserved for the upper classes. But a sigh escapes at times, bemoaning the inevitable loss of old-world charm.

Down Kyoto's narrow, quiet backstreets there are still many glimpses of an elegant past to be found. The luster of a hand-painted vermilion lacquer bowl with an inlaid mother-of-pearl dragonfly carefully removed from a signed wooden box by a solicitous old shopkeeper's wife ... the moment's hesitation before you slice into a sweet bean cake the fragile shape and color of a cherry blossom . . . the unexpected pleasure of discovering the intricately woven pattern on a common house broom. The aura of classical Japanese living does still exist in Kyoto. It can be found in the windows of old fan shops, on the curtains of confectioneries, in the tiny gardens of the neighborhood inns. The spirit of the city lives on in the hearts of its shopkeepers.

Thousands of people flock to Kyoto year after year in search of the old spirit. They take bus tours to famous gardens and ancient temples; they visit museums and read pamphlets on religions and warlords to try to find it. They walk past it without blinking twice on their way to catch the train.

The dark façades of the traditional Kyoto shops at first seem all alike with their curtain veils and no signs in English. Even the seasoned traveler finds it awkward to venture further. But what you'll find inside is often a warm-hearted shopkeeper eager to be at your service. My hope is that this book will help you to find what you're looking for in Kyoto, help you locate the heart of the city.

The traditional shopkeepers of Kyoto have taken great pains to maintain the old wooden buildings with their sagging beams and sinking stone floors. They insist on making the same fine products with the best materials they can buy, as if they were still purveyors to the imperial household, as many of them once were. They stubbornly cling to old wood-burning stoves, convinced as their grandfathers were that they boil a tastier pot of rice. They shun power tools, knowing nothing can match the character of a surface that has been laboriously polished by hand. They are aware that the twentieth century has made many of their products passé and search for ways to show modern customers that the quality of one's life does not depend entirely on the number of electric appliances on the kitchen counter. They hope their children will take over when they die, but live in the knowledge that, for many of them, their shop's legacy will be buried with them as their sons hurry off to Osaka in search of fashionable office jobs.

The famous temples and manicured villas may define the rarefied soul of feudal Japan, but the old noodle shops and inns, the teahouses and bucket makers, are the marrow of its bones. Walk around Kyoto; part the curtains of the old shops; step inside . . . *"Oideyasu!"*

Diane Durston
Kyoto

CHRONOLOGY

NARA
710–94

HEIAN
794–1185

KAMAKURA
1185–1333

MUROMACHI
1333–1568

MOMOYAMA
1568–1600

EDO
1600–1868

MEIJI
1868–1912

TAISHŌ
1912–26

SHŌWA
1926 to present

History

The folk that have been attracted thither and the poets do all with one voice acclaim this Heian-kyō, the capital of peace and tranquility.
—Emperor Kanmu
794, eleventh month, eighth day

When the emperor Kanmu brought his court to this valley in the eighth century, he could not have known that the title he bestowed on the city held an irony that would one day be as classic as the grand imperial city itself. For over a thousand years, Kyoto (as it is known today) was the capital of Japan, and, like most capital cities, was the scene of endless wars and political strife, and the site of more than its share of devastating natural disasters. Although it was indeed the birthplace of one of the most refined and sophisticated cultures on earth, in reality it was far from the peaceful citadel Kanmu originally envisioned. Still considered the center of traditional culture in Japan, Kyoto and the people who live there have a long and difficult history behind them.

Kanmu chose this site for a number of reasons: it was surrounded on three sides by mountains that made it a natural castle, it had an endless (if capricious) supply of water from the river that divides it in half, and, conveniently enough, it had 130,000 members of the Hata clan, who as the descendants of Chinese immigrants could teach his craftsmen how to weave (and lend him the money to build his palace).

His dream was to create an imperial city that would rival the glorious capital of the Tang dynasty, Chang-an. He called for a comprehensive plan for the layout of his city, branding the valley floor with a permanent grid pattern of streets, which divided the area into rectangular blocks, just like the Chinese model he sought to outdo.

During the 390 years of relative calm now known as the Heian period, Kanmu's descendants led a life of luxury and elegance inside the palace walls characterized by languid afternoons sipping saké and breaking romantic promises beneath the willows in an atmosphere of isolated splendor that rivaled the excesses of Versailles. The "Golden Age" also resulted in the weakening of imperial determination to deal with the mundane business of governing the land, a duty which powerful local clans would fight over for the ensuing several centuries. The Fujiwara clan dominated this first age of scrambled Kyoto politics, assuming the role of regents by marrying into the imperial family.

The presence of the emperor and his squabbling entourage made Kyoto not only the center of the political scene, but also a bustling hub of commerce. Artisans, skilled in the sophisticated techniques of Chinese craftsmanship, were called to the new capital to provide the accoutrements and luxuries required to maintain the extravagant lifestyle of the imperial court. Merchants flocked to Heian-kyō to provide the materials, foods, and commodities necessary to build and support the growing city. Two marketplaces were established in the southeast and southwest of the city where merchants could exchange their wares. The markets were lively places where people of all ranks, from noblemen to peasants, walked about examining the latest products and wares. The eastern market, where Kyoto Station now stands, flourished, while the western market died out, establishing the eastern half as the city center as early as the tenth century.

By the twelfth century, however, it had become obvious that the townspeople would have to stick together in order to defend themselves against the endless stream of military and natural disasters that were now in full swing. Neighborhoods formed around shrines and temples in tightly knit communities for self-defense. Some communities even built moatlike ditches around their neighborhoods, not just for protection, but for the purpose of flood control, crop irrigation, and defense against the frequent fires that plagued the city built entirely of wood and thatch.

It was during this era of natural (and man-made) disaster that Kamo no Chōmei, the hermit poet, sat alone in his hut on a mountainside near Ōhara foretelling the fate of the city he loved:

——The flow of the river is ceaseless:

——Its waters never the same . . .

He watched as the torrents of political turmoil swept away the elegance and refinement of what later would be called the Golden Age of Japanese history. He mourned the devastating price the people of Kyoto paid for the honor of inhabiting the ancient capital of Japan. And perhaps he realized that constant "change" would be the only element upon which the populace could depend.

The military government established by the Minamoto clan that took over when the Fujiwara family went into decline was so busy holding down its own fort that it had not the time, inclination, or means to help the commoners rebuild their row houses after every battle, fire, or flood. By the time Minamoto no Yoritomo had himself proclaimed the first shogun in 1192, a large portion of the city had been devastated, and the starving townspeople were left to their own devices when he moved his camp to Kamakura in the east.

The ability of the merchants and craftsmen to band together in mini-townships enabled them to undertake reconstruction on their own. The crisscross pattern of the city streets provided manageable blocks of approximately forty dwellings each in which groups of merchants and craftsmen worked together to rebuild their homes and shops. The unity and self-determination that evolved in these neighborhoods at the beginning of the twelfth century helped them survive the rise and fall of a succession of military leaders over the next four hundred years.

The arrival of Zen from China in the early thirteenth century was an event that had a great impact on Japanese culture. The austere sect of Buddhism with its emphasis on personal training of body and mind was attractive to the shogun and his samurai for the strength and discipline it encouraged, a welcome change from the weak life of luxury they saw as a primary factor in the decline of both the emperor and his regents. The great Zen temples that were built in the following century became centers of culture in Kyoto. Zen priests encouraged continued contact with China, offering Kyoto merchants the opportunity to begin a prosperous trade network that gave them the economic strength, not only to survive, but to flourish while other sectors of the society collapsed. They began to form guilds called *za*, which were under the protection of shrines and temples on whose grounds they held regular markets in return for the payment of special taxes.

Yet another coup took place in the early fourteenth century that brought the Ashikaga shogunate to power, re-establishing Kyoto as the center of political power. The 235 years of Ashikaga reign were characterized by unparalleled cultural development in contrast to equally unmatched political and social disaster. The Ashikaga shogunate, firm followers of Zen, were great patrons of the arts. The Muromachi period, named for the palace they built near the emperor's quarters in Kyoto, was an age in which ink painting, calligraphy, and tea ceremony flourished in Japan. The third shogun, Yoshimitsu, ordered the construction of the magnificent Kinkaku-ji, the Gold Pavilion, in the northwest of Kyoto in 1397.

But by the middle of the fifteenth century, Kyoto was again the scene of a power struggle between warlords from the provinces who flocked to the capital city with cravings for a taste of the notorious life of luxury at court.

The realm Ashikaga Yoshimasa, the grandson of Yoshimitsu, inherited was in a state of total chaos; 1449, the year he was born, marked the beginning of a terrible plague that took the lives of a thousand citizens a day. It was as if the mid fifteenth century had been singled out for disaster by a legion of angry gods. In 1442 the Kamo River had flooded, washing away two major bridges. In 1444, the merchants took over Kitano Shrine in an appeal for just government. The military government slashed their way in, forcing the merchants to commit group suicide, but not before they had set fire to the shrine, burning it to the ground. Throughout the decade before Yoshimasa's birth, the warrior-priests of Enryaku-ji temple on Mt. Hiei stormed down the mountainside on a number of occasions, wielding the feared portable shrine (said to possess the power of life and death) and making demands on the imperial court. The year 1447 saw severe earthquakes and floods, and by the time Yoshimasa was ten years old, a massive famine had left great funerary mounds all over the besieged capital city.

Depressed (though probably not the word for it) by the condition of the kingdom he had inherited, Yoshimasa chose to abandon his duties as shogun at the age of thirty-five. He pined away the rest of his days at Ginkaku-ji, the Silver Pavilion, an exquisite if less glamorous villa than his grandfather's, on the opposite side of the city. The villa "turned its back on the city" and faced the Higashiyama Mountains. The aesthetic ideal it

Bird's-eye view of Kyoto, 1808

represents was named after them—*Higashiyama Bunka*, the "culture of the Eastern Mountains," referring to a wealth of aesthetic endeavors that flourished under the patronage of a timorous warlord who refused to deal with the world outside his exquisite villa.

For the city's craftsmen and merchants, the Muromachi period saw the development of the tea ceremony, a practice whose popularity stimulated the production of ceramic bowls and flower vases, bamboo basketry and utensils, cast-metal teakettles, and lacquerware. It also created a need for skilled carpenters and gardeners capable of building and caring for tearooms and landscape gardens, establishing an aesthetic basis for Japanese architecture from then on.

The succession dispute Yoshimasa left behind started the Ōnin War (1467–77), a disastrous ten years of battles that leveled the city, ruining all parties involved, and ironically failing to settle the original dispute. Hardly a building was left standing. The need for city-wide reconstruction following the Ōnin War provided another (if tragic) source of work for the common people. The merchant townships set about rebuilding their city with little or no help from either the shogunate or the noblemen, who were either disinterested in the fate of the peasants or in nearly as desperate shape themselves. A recorded eighty-two thousand citizens died of starvation in

1480. Even the imperial court fell into a state of poverty, with the emperor himself at one point resorting to the sale of calligraphy to survive.

By this time, the merchants had acquired the acumen to take advantage of the constantly shifting political winds, and had accumulated the wealth to put the city back on its feet by supplying both sides of an endless string of competing armies with food and supplies. For the talent of hiding their true sympathies, Kyoto merchants earned the reputation for being "two-faced"—never answering directly, never giving a clear yes or no—a trait they are still accused of from time to time today.

The inn Kinmata (page 92), ca. 1900

Gion, the entertainment district

By the middle of the sixteenth century, the winds of war had once again begun to blow the wrong way. When St. Francis Xavier arrived in Kyoto in 1551, he was the first Western traveler to see the ancient city, or what was left of it. He wrote: "Today much of Kyoto lies in ruins because of the wars; many people have told us that it once had eighteen thousand houses, and it seems to me that this must have been true, to judge from the very large size of the city." When the Ashikaga shogunate fell, the rough-and-tumble Oda Nobunaga was there to grab power. Although he did much to unify the country that had for so long been at the mercy of warring factions, he did not endear himself to the people of Kyoto. He burned down over four hundred temples at Enryaku-ji on the top of Mt. Hiei, Kyoto's sacred mountain, because of the threat its powerful priests presented to his own regime. He then proceeded to wipe out a large portion of the northeastern sector of the city (not well organized into communities) for their inability to pay his exorbitant taxes. He was not a popular fellow.

Toyotomi Hideyoshi, Nobunaga's successor, did the most to rebuild Kyoto, if only to add to his own power and glory. During this period at the end of the sixteenth century the merchants and craftsmen came to his aid by helping with the reconstruction of the many temples that had been destroyed during the Ōnin War. Hideyoshi had dreams of restoring the capital city to an even higher level of grandeur than Emperor Kanmu himself could have imagined. In 1591, he ordered the construction of the Odoi, a wall that would surround the entire city. Only a few crumbling mementos of the great wall remain standing that survived the centuries that followed. Hideyoshi enlisted the aid of Kyoto merchants and craftsmen, not only in the rebuilding of temples and shrines, but also in the construction of a magnificent pleasure palace, Juraku-dai, which he built on the ruins of the Imperial Palace itself.

During this period groups of townspeople organized in neighborhood communities called *machi* (or *chō*) and undertook much of this reconstruction on their own. The rebuilding of the city proved much to their advantage, and the merchant class became so prosperous that they started to create their own separate world of art and extravagance, the "floating world" depicted in woodblock prints, a world of pleasure and often excess, but a world that existed for the first time for the common people.

With substantial wealth around them now, the townspeople were in a position to begin refining their existence. Aware of the aesthetics of tea, the merchants employed master carpenters (formerly only available to the samurai warriors and nobility) to create a living environment that embodied the finest aspects of all the levels of society whose presence could be felt in Kyoto: the spiritual qualities of the Zen priesthood, the refined tastes of the nobility, the austere restraint of the warriors, the skill of the finest craftsmen, the simplicity of farmers, and the sense of unflagging practicality that had brought the prospering merchant class this far.

The death of Hideyoshi and the rise of Tokugawa Ieyasu may have taken politics to the east when he moved his government to Edo (now Tokyo) in 1603, but it left Kyoto's merchants and craftsmen to spend the next two hundred years developing the arts and crafts for which the city is famous. The merchants aspired to raise their lowly social status by imitating all the trappings of the upper-class samurai, who by then were practically out of work with no wars left to wage. The merchants patronized the arts—pottery, weaving, lacquering, paper-making, painting, gardening, and architecture.

By the middle of the Edo period, the shogunate was feeling the waves of social change resulting from the merchants' rise in power and began legislating every detail of their lives, right down to the size of dolls their children were allowed to own. Not only did they close all traffic with foreign countries by edict in 1639 in the hope of stemming the merchants' access to goods from abroad, but they issued a long list of restrictions intended to keep the merchants down. No elaborate hair combs, no parasols, no silk kimonos, no "selling of peculiar things to hit the public fancy," to name a few. But these at least were based on the assumption that the merchant class was a force to be dealt with. The rules of conduct issued for the peasants were even more abusive: get up early, don't buy saké or tea, don't smoke, and divorce a wife who drinks too much tea and wastes time on casual excursions.

In spite of the rigid codes, it was, by the middle of the eighteenth century, too late for the shogun to control the merchants any longer. They were well on their way to becoming the powerful economic wizards that run the country today. The townhouses, or *machiya*, they lived in grew bigger (sometimes overnight) during the confusion of rebuilding after every fire that plagued the tinderbox city. With each reconstruction, the now powerful merchants extended their property lines farther into the streets (making it a real art for cars to navigate today between telephone poles planted right on the shoulder and children on bicycles with no other place to play). The servants and employees of the merchants were relegated to dwellings much humbler than the grand abodes of their masters that faced the main boulevards. They were set back off the roads on narrow alleys, hidden away behind the *machiya* of their employers. The merchants owned the property on which their employees lived, and at the same time relied upon them to work in their shops and to make the products they sold, establishing a pattern of mutual dependence within each community in Kyoto which has survived to the present day.

The shops of Kyoto and their keepers flourished in the late Edo period . . . until one bone-chilling morning late in the winter of 1788. A wind suddenly blew in from the east, knocking over street stalls, peddlers, even horses with a force unheard of in Kyoto, a city usually thankful for the slightest breeze to break the stillness of its captive basin air. Somewhere along the west bank of the Kamo River, a fire broke out in a moneychanger's shop that gave way to the hurricane gusts. By dawn the next day the entire city was in flames. Three days later 183,000 homes, 909 temples, and 37 shrines had been reduced to ash. Virtually no wooden structure in the city center remains that pre-dates the monstrous Tenmei Fire. Again the townspeople had a city to rebuild.

The end of the eighteenth century was a difficult time not only for the citizens of Kyoto, but for the entire country as well. The military government was in disastrous economic straits, having borrowed the funds to finance the extravagant tastes of the increasing population of samurai who played a nonproductive role during the politically stable Edo period, when the need for their services had all but been eliminated. The samurai had begun to borrow money from the merchants, and fell further and further into debt.

A series of major famines occurred during the end of the eighteenth and

Shintarō Morita, Kagoshin (page 125), in formal dress on the day he was honored by the emperor

Weaving, Kagoshin, ca. 1920

early nineteenth centuries. Over a million peasants died of starvation during the great famine of 1780–86. The Tokugawa shogunate was ineffectual despite the new laws calling for a return to austerity among the samurai, who were by now accustomed to leading an indolent life of luxury. A succession of weak Tokugawa shoguns noted for administrative incompetence assured the decline of the shogunate's power throughout the land. An impoverished and restless populace with the aid of dissatisfied *daimyō* began plotting the overthrow of the shogunate and the restoration of the emperor as ruler of Japan.

When Commodore Perry's ships sailed into port on July 8, 1853, the country was ready for change. His demands for the opening of trade with the United States ended over two hundred years of self-enforced isolation. Renewed commerce with the West was to have a major impact on Japanese culture from then on. Intrigued by the guns and machinery the foreigners brought with them, the Japanese sought to acquire much of the "advanced" accoutrements of Western life. The new word for chic in Japanese was *haikarā*, the Japanese phonetic rendition of "high collar," in vogue among Western men in the late nineteenth century.

For Kyoto, still the home of the emperor, this era of change and confusion meant that it would once again be the site of a major battle. Unrest in the provinces brought vassals to Kyoto to "save the emperor" from the hands of the shogun, who by now was struggling to maintain control. Plotters with hopes of restoring the emperor to power held clandestine meetings at some of the city's famous inns; deep gashes in beams and corner posts in some of those inns today attest to the amount of swashbuckling that preceded the shogunate's surrender. One such skirmish led to a fire in the Kyoto hideout of a provincial clan leader, again leaving much of the city devastated in 1864. But within four short years the people of Kyoto had once again rebuilt the entire city.

Lacking the support of most of the military lords (*daimyō*), the last shogun surrendered power in 1868 and the court of the emperor Meiji moved to Edo in the same year, renaming it Tokyo, the eastern capital.

The loss of their emperor broke the hearts of the people of Kyoto. All their civic pride was bound to an image of Kyoto as the "Imperial City." An air of depression hung over the valley for over a decade, leaving its mark on the local arts and crafts, which suffered a great decline in production in the years that followed.

But 1894 marked the 1000th anniversary of Kyoto, and the people commemorated the event by building Heian Shrine, a replica of the original Imperial Palace and a memorial to the deified soul of Emperor Kanmu, whose dream had created their proud city so long ago.

The period that followed was a time of welcome peace for the people of

Kyoto. Craftsmen continued to hone the skills for which they had become world famous. The caste system prescribed by the Tokugawas was finally abolished, leaving citizens of all classes freer than ever before to pursue the livelihood of their choice; a number of new shops opened around the turn of the century.

World War II was the next (and hopefully the last) catastrophe to disrupt the lives of the citizens of Kyoto. Fortunately, the United States opted to save the ancient capital city, and it was not destroyed in the firebombings that leveled Tokyo and Osaka. Uncertainty, however, caused city fathers to order the widening of Kyoto's most important thoroughfares to act as possible firebreaks if such a tragedy should occur. This resulted in the loss of over eighteen thousand fine old shops and houses. The number of merchants and craftsmen enlisted by the Imperial Army who were lost in the war caused a drastic decline in the number of shops left open when Japan surrendered in 1945. After the war, materials were scarce and difficult to obtain, forcing many craftsmen to seek other employment. Before World War II there were over a hundred bucket makers in Kyoto; today their number can be counted on one hand.

The trend for Americanization after the war also left its mark on Kyoto arts and crafts. Young people preferred American-style products, mass-produced in five shades of plastic, to the studiously handmade breakables their grandfathers crafted. Fast food and fast cars represent the latest hazards to life in Kyoto. What is left of old Kyoto must contend with this latest threat to their existence, a more insidious foe than fire or famine. The old shops must find ways to adjust to changing Japanese tastes, to fit their products to twentieth-century life, or fade away. With luck the strength of will and stubborn determination the shopkeepers of Kyoto have shown over the past eleven centuries will help them through this most recent "minor difficulty."

The prediction of Kamo no Chōmei was not far from wrong. Theirs has always been a legacy of change . . . a history of elegance and disaster . . . always flowing, never the same.

Kyoto Crafts

For years . . . ages . . . the rivers of Kyoto flaunted their brilliant Yūzen colors, the long streamers of hand-painted silk giving up their excess dye to the cold, clear waters. (It was rough on the fireflies.) In the Gojōzaka district near Kiyomizu-dera, the huge climbing kilns puffed and snorted their black smoke into the Kyoto skies, turning the efforts of local potters into gleaming porcelain. The great Thousand-Armed Kannon, the goddess of mercy, and her 1,000 equally-armed companion images stood watch over rows and rows of open fans that were laid out to dry in the courtyard before her. The constant *kattan-kotton* clanking of thirty thousand looms vibrated the wood-frame houses along the narrow streets of Nishijin, the weaving district.

Far to the north, woodsmen carefully trimmed the towering cedar trees, shaving them like the legs of college girls, flawlessly preparing them to decorate the homes of the wealthy. Kyoto bustles today as it did in the seventeenth century; the skies and waters are colored now with a different sort of affliction. The sights, like the sounds of the city, have synthesized.

The crafts of Kyoto have changed, but they have survived. Baskets are still woven, scrolls mounted, incense prepared with formulas that are still family secrets. Knives and fine carving tools are forged, and O-Shaka-sama is still cast in bronze and gilded in Kyoto. What has changed is not so much the objects which are produced, but the role they play in Japanese society. Today the craftsman decorates where once he filled a daily need; his products are costly where once they were commonplace; he has become an artist where once he was a nameless craftsman. There was no word for "art" in the Japanese language until the nineteenth century.

Adjectives like rustic and rough-hewn have no place in the vocabulary of Kyoto crafts; the word is *miyabi,* the elusive element of refinement and elegance that characterizes even the most common of everyday objects produced in the ancient capital city.

Kyoto crafts evolved out of certain cultural phenomena that developed over the centuries and can be grouped accordingly. The presence of the imperial court in Kyoto; the development of the tea ceremony; the position of the ancient capital as the center of Buddhism in Japan; and the lavish entertainment world of geisha and kabuki were some of the primary factors that influenced the extraordinary level of craftsmanship that developed throughout the long history of Kyoto.

Purveyors to the Imperial Household

Ever since the emperor Kanmu arrived in Kyoto in the eighth century, the strongest influence on Kyoto craftsmen has been the presence of the imperial court. From then on the privilege of being selected as *kunaichō-goyōtashi*—a purveyor to the imperial household—was an honor unparalleled among the craftsmen, merchants, and chefs who were at the exclusive disposal of the court. Throughout the Middle Ages these purveyors were given special wooden placards granting them admittance to the Imperial Palace compound. Though the practice was abolished after World War II, many old shopkeepers still proudly keep their original placards as family heirlooms and as symbols of the "royal" quality of their traditional products.

Several *kunaichō-goyōtashi* shops can be found in the area around the old Imperial Palace, between Imadegawa and Oike, from Kawaramachi to Horikawa. (See Fūka and Kagoshin in the shop listings.)

Among the crafts that developed under the influence of the Heian court were the fine silk brocades for the twelve-layered *jūnihitoe* of the courtiers; painted and natural-wood folding fans (*sensu*); musical instruments like the *koto* (zither), the *biwa* (lute), the large *taiko* (drum), the *tsuzumi* (hourglass-shaped hand drum), and a variety of *fue* (flutes). Lacquerware (*shikki*) was so popular at court that it replaced pottery as the most popular type of serving vessel. One of the aspects of Kyoto cuisine, or *Kyō-ryōri*, that adds elegance to the overall sensory experience is the continued use of fine lacquerware. *Maki-e*, the technique of sprinkling gold dust on a lacquer ground, was developed during the Heian period for the exclusive benefit of the imperial court.

Religious Reflections

Shinto and Buddhism, the two major religions of Japan, have always been centered in Kyoto, and many great monuments to both are located here. The Five Great Temples of Zen (Nanzen-ji, Daitoku-ji, Kennin-ji, Tenryū-ji, and Tōfuku-ji, though others vied for the title) were located in Kyoto. So were a number of powerful shrines (Kitano-jinja, Yoshida-jinja, and Yasaka-jinja). Both shrines and temples acted as places of relative stability during times of war in the capital. Merchants and craftsmen conducted regular fairs at the major shrines and temples, which were considered a kind of central gathering place for many of the guilds, offering them protection from the shogunate in exchange for special taxes, which kept the priests in a position of power.

Craftsmen and merchants built their homes and shops in front of the gates of temples, creating townships called *monzen-machi*. They produced religious articles (*butsugu*), including Buddhist home altars (*butsudan*) that are constructed of lacquered wood with elaborate gilded carvings and chased metal fittings; and sculpture (*butsuzō*) in carved wood or cast bronze.

Hundreds of small religious objects—like incense burners (*kōro*) and incense (*kō* or *senkō*), bronze bells (*kane*) and wooden gongs (*mokugyo*), candles (*rōsoku*) and prayer beads (*juzu*)—can still be found in front of the main gates of both Nishi and Higashi Hongan-ji temples north of Kyoto Station. These two powerful temples are the headquarters of two branches of the powerful Jōdo sect of Buddhism, and worshipers from rural prefectures make frequent pilgrimages here, buying Buddhist articles made by Kyoto craftsmen to take home to their local temples.

At least one shop in almost every neighborhood makes Shinto household altars (*kamidana*) and the portable shrines (*mikoshi*) for neighborhood festivals. The smooth, natural finish of a Shinto shrine and its smaller representations epitomizes the Japanese love of simple, unadorned beauty. The fine Japanese woodwork and joinery that goes into the making of these diminutive spirit houses was handed down by the highly specialized craftsmen (*miya-daiku*) who built (and rebuild) the shrines, temples and teahouses of Japan. Today, the skills are known to only a few, and one craftsman is reportedly booked with orders for more temple repairs than he could possibly accomplish in his lifetime.

The Illustrious Influence of Tea

One of the strongest and deepest influences on the arts and crafts of Kyoto is that of the tea ceremony. When tea was first brought to Japan from China in the eighth century, it became a permanent item on the list of exotic luxuries reserved for the imperial court. They imbibed the heady beverage with formal pomp and ceremony, collecting the treasured utensils of the Chinese, and holding lavish tea parties in the pavilions of the aristocracy.

Not until the time of Murata Jukō (1422–1502) did ceremonial tea take on the spiritual aspect that gave it a central role in the development of Japanese culture. Following the teachings of Ikkyū, the legendary Zen priest, Murata developed a concept of ritual tea as a discipline for the mind and body combined with the same aesthetic values promoted by the Zen priests—simplicity, refinement, and restraint. These were qualities that the samurai sought as a counterbalance to the decadence and excesses they saw as having caused the decline of the aristocracy.

The popularity of the tea ceremony stimulated the development of crafts that could not only produce the many specialized utensils that became an aspect of central importance to the tea ceremony, but that could meet its unique aesthetic demands for *wabi*, the sensibility of rustic refinement sought after by the great tea masters of Kyoto, such as Sen no Rikyū, who designed the first *raku* ware tea bowls made by the Korean potter Chōjiro in the sixteenth century.

The tea bowl (*chawan*) was of primary importance, though bamboo tea whisks (*chasen*), tea scoops (*chashaku*), lacquered tea caddies (*chaki*), freshwater containers (*mizusashi*), waste-water containers (*kensui*), bamboo ladles (*hishaku*), iron teakettles (*kama*), flower vases (*hana-ire*), and an assortment of other objects all fall under the category of *cha-dōgu*, the necessary utensils for the tearoom.

Bamboo ware, ceramics, lacquerware (for the service of *cha-kaiseki*, the meal that accompanies a formal tea ceremony), metalwork, and textiles (both for garments worn by *chajin*, or "tea people," and for wrapping the precious utensils before they are placed in their wooden storage boxes) all became essential elements to the practice of tea.

Other skills required were the making of special charcoal (*sumi*) for heating the tea water, the preparation of aromatic woods and subtly blended incense (*o-kō*) burned before the guests arrived, and the making of tatami mats, *shōji* paper windows, and *fusuma* sliding doors—all of which evolved from the tearooms of the shogun Ashikaga Yoshimasa at Ginkaku-ji. His Silver Pavilion in the northeast of Kyoto and the tiny four-mat room called the Dōjin-sai were the settings for countless tea ceremonies, and created a standard for those that followed.

The Ashikaga also promoted a solemn form of theater called Nō drama, which conformed with the Zen principles of economy of expression and restraint admired by the samurai. Many of the masks (*nō-men*) and ornate costumes in silk damask or embroidered silk gauze made by craftsmen in the seventeenth and eighteenth centuries are still in use today.

Reflections from the Floating World

A more down-to-earth, if equally esoteric, influence on the arts and crafts of Kyoto came from the bawdy night world of the geisha quarters. The peaceful seventeenth and eighteenth centuries brought prosperity and leisure time to the merchant class, who created their own colorful world of entertainment. Considered vulgar by the upper classes, the "floating world" in *ukiyo-e* woodblock prints of the day was one of willowy courtesans arrayed in exuberantly decorated kimono, draped languidly over balconies, sighing under a midsummer moon.

The brilliantly dyed and embroidered kimono of the geisha; the elaborate hair ornaments (*kanzashi*) of lacquer, gold, silver, tortoiseshell, and glass; the tall platform *geta* of their *maiko* apprentices; the sweeping kimono sashes (*obi*); the oiled paper umbrellas (*wagasa*); and a long list of accessories, including everything from round *uchiwa* fans to long, slender tobacco pipes (*kiseru*)—all were a part of the romantic world of Gion, the main geisha quarter of Kyoto.

Kabuki, the people's theater, with its boldly patterned costumes, exotic makeup, and swashbuckling flamboyance, provided Kyoto craftsmen with ever-new challenges in pattern design and color composition.

Threatened by the economic prowess of the rising merchant class, the Tokugawa shogunate forbade them to wear the costly silk brocades that were the pride of the upper classes. But not to be easily dismissed, the merchants urged dyers to match the extravagance of woven fabrics with dyeing techniques that produced an equally sumptuous effect. Yūzen, the paste-resist technique of fabric dyeing invented by a former fan painter, was developed during this era, achieving fine-lined results that must have aggravated the floundering lawmakers beyond words.

Objects for Every Day

To the rich and powerful of every culture go the finest of its arts and crafts, but the refinement and skillfulness of even the most common household objects in Kyoto are a clue to the level of craftsmanship the society attained. A simple hand-cut, hand-polished boxwood comb (*tsuge-kushi*)—something no bride would be without in old Kyoto—is an object of delicate beauty. Buckets (*oke, taru*) with staves that have been carefully planed to fit the proper angle, then joined with tiny bamboo pegs, seem as suitable for displaying on a shelf as for carrying sushi. The same goes for handmade wooden footwear (*geta*) carved from a single block of paulownia.

The everyday necessities of life for the common people of Kyoto—the butcher knives (*hōchō*), the sewing needles (*hari*), the roof tiles (*kawara*), the workmen's coats (*hanten, happi*), the shop curtains (*noren*), the farmer's trousers (*monpe*), the chests of drawers (*tansu*), the name stamps (*hanko*), the paper lanterns (*bonbori, chōchin*)—all possess an undeniable sense of gentility not ordinarily associated with something like an ordinary pair of socks, until you've had the pleasure of being fitted for a dazzling white pair of cotton *tabi* that button neatly at the ankle.

The Traditional Local Cuisine

Western food—
Every damn plate
is round.

—Anonymous
modern *senryū* (satirical poem)

A length of split green bamboo, a three-layered ceramic serving dish the shape of a gourd, a red and black lacquered tray with the single bow of a cherry tree in full bloom painted delicately in the center in gold . . . Japanese food is never boring. Kyoto, as the old imperial capital, was also the birthplace of *kaiseki*, the formal cuisine that doesn't forget the other four senses.

Environment is the first consideration. Seated on cushions in a private tatami-mat room overlooking a meticulously groomed garden with only the sound of water trickling from the stone basin just outside to accent the silence . . . you are ready to begin.

The door slides open and a lady in kimono (sometimes jolly, more often demure) enters to hand you a hot towel to wipe your hands—a simple, civilized custom that's hard to live without, once you've been regularly spoiled.

A *kaiseki* meal is served in courses (from seven to twelve), each prepared in a different manner from seasonally appropriate ingredients. The range of flavors, from sweet to sour, from salty to plain, is subtly planned so that each succeeding flavor complements the last. Only ingredients in the peak of season are used, and accents of seasonal color—a maple leaf in autumn or a sprig of plum blossoms in spring—inevitably appear. One particularly "Kyoto" touch is that only the lightest seasoning is used. Kyoto restaurateurs believe that the natural flavor of the finest ingredients available speak for themselves.

A typical course might include appetizers (*zensai*), raw fish (*otsukuri*), a seafood and vegetable "salad" (*aemono*), one or more soups (*suimono* or *shirumono*), simmered foods (*nimono*), steamed dishes (*mushimono*), broiled or grilled foods (*yakimono*), deep-fried tidbits (*agemono*), vinegared "salad" (*sunomono*), rice (*gohan*), pickles (*tsukemono*), and perhaps a bowl of fruit for dessert. The combinations are endless and left up to the discretion of the chef, though a very formal order of dishes and ingredients appears in the case of *cha-kaiseki*, which is the meal that accompanies a tea ceremony.

Cha-kaiseki is actually a concept all its own. The word *kaiseki* in this case is written with characters that mean "a stone in the folds of a kimono" and refers to an old Zen practice of sending priests to bed with nothing but a hot stone tucked into their kimonos to keep their bellies warm. A *cha-kaiseki* meal served in "artful proportions" is intended to be just enough to do the same, while complementing the flavor of thick green tea.

The *kaiseki* served in most restaurants is of the other variety, written with characters that mean "banquet," which evolved from the saké parties at teahouses that were popular in the nineteenth century and often required the services of geisha.

Part of the magic of a *kaiseki* meal for the novice is having no idea what you are eating, much less what comes next. The possibilities are so vast that warlords and wealthy merchants of the Edo period (experts in the realm of the senses) even made a game of guessing which foods they had been presented during an evening's entertainment and drinking. A spirit of adventure is a prerequisite; the reward is a sensory experience you will not soon forget.

A *kaiseki* meal in one of Kyoto's finest *ryōtei* can be very expensive, though ¥15,000 is not thought to be exorbitant, considering the long hours involved in making such a wide variety of delicate dishes. In addition, the best of Kyoto's restaurants make it a rule never to serve a guest the same meal twice. The proprietress (often the owner's wife) takes careful note of each guest's likes and dislikes, catering to the guest's every whim and presenting a memorable meal every time.

One retired restaurant owner confessed that anything over ¥15,000 pays for the fine porcelain on which the meal is served and the treasured appointments (hanging scrolls by famous calligraphers and flower vases two centuries old) of the private room. The connoisseur of Kyoto cuisine looks forward with each visit to which priceless serving dish will appear that evening.

Much less expensive options do exist, and one marvelous alternative is the elaborate Kyoto box lunch (*Kyō-bentō*) served at many of the best places for a fraction of the cost. Usually served between 11 and 2, it ranges from ¥2,000 to ¥5,000 and provide you with an excellent sampler of the cuisine offered at each restaurant, though often (but not always) you must forego the private room and the luxury of spending a minimum of two hours over a full-course *kaiseki* meal.

Although most people think only of *kaiseki* when they hear *Kyō-ryōri*, the essential elements of an old-fashioned Kyoto-style meal were simply salted fish and pickled vegetables. Living far from the nearest sea, the people of Kyoto found it necessary to invent a thousand ways of preparing both. For a "real" Kyoto meal in the old style, Hirano-ya in Maruyama Park comes closest to the essence of traditional Kyoto cuisine with their preserved fish and boiled potato meal (*imobō*). *Kyō-tsukemono*, the pickled vegetables served with rice, are famous throughout Japan and are one of the most popular souvenirs among visitors from other districts.

Shōjin ryōri, the vegetarian food served in Buddhist temples, also developed in Kyoto from its prototype *fucha ryōri*, brought by priests from China. Both styles are still served and the best place to try them is in the temples themselves. Local specialties like *yuba* (skimmed soybean milk), *nama-fu* (a wheat gluten delicacy), and an assortment of tofu dishes are all a part of *shōjin ryōri*. These high-protein, low-calorie foods served in a variety of unusual dishes make vegetarian eating a pleasurable as well as healthy experience.

Though sushi and sukiyaki are popular in the West, many people hesitate to try the more exotic foods of Japan because of understandable misgivings about squid, fish roe, and sea urchin. Skipping a night at one of Kyoto's top *ryōtei* is like going to New York without trying the lox and bagels. I recommend swallowing it first and asking questions later. You'd be surprised how good a sea urchin can taste.

A Night in a Traditional Inn

A night in a traditional Japanese inn, or *ryokan*, is an experience not to be missed, no matter how much easier it may sound to seek refuge in one of the major hotels. A hotel is a hotel whether you are in St. Louis or St. Moritz, but a *ryokan* is a sample of traditional Japanese living at its finest.

Stone walkways lead off narrow side streets to one- or two-story tile-roofed inns in which hand-polished wooden corridors twist and turn past peaceful interior gardens to your room. Tatami mats, an alcove (*tokonoma*) in which a bamboo basket of fresh flowers was placed this morning in anticipation of your arrival, a hanging scroll (one that's been in the family for generations), a small lacquered writing box, and a closet full of thickly quilted *futon* bedding . . . a combination of small things that surround you with comfort and the sense of being a true guest. Acclaimed internationally for their warm hospitality, fine service, and excellent cuisine, the traditional inns of Kyoto offer a chance to experience first-hand the amenities once reserved for noblemen and feudal lords.

For this singular pleasure, however, there are certain minor difficulties that must first be surmounted, and this is where the real cultural adventure begins.

There's the one about the American who walked into his immaculate tatami-mat room at the *ryokan* to find the maid, who had just arrived with a fresh pot of tea, staring down at his feet in horror. After what seemed an eternity of shocked silence, the man asked himself if perhaps she had never seen foreign toes before. Then suddenly, much to his chagrin, came the stark realization that he was still wearing the toilet slippers! Stories like these have kept Japanese in stitches (and Westerners in the Holiday Inn) for years. There are a few classic intricacies to "*ryokan* life" that once unfolded could put an end to an entire school of contemporary Japanese humor. Let's give it a try:

1. *Take off your shoes and relax.* If you spend any amount of time at all in Japan, this becomes a way of life. Shoes are considered dirty and should always be left at the door. This seems reasonable enough—until you carry the principle to the matter of slippers.

2. *Slippers fall into two basic categories: corridor slippers and toilet slippers . . . and never the twain shall meet.* When you take off your shoes in the entryway to a traditional home, restaurant, or inn, you will be given a pair of slippers to walk down the wooden corridor to your room. Take them off

before you walk on tatami. Stockinged feet are preferable to bare feet in Japan, but even bare feet are better than slippers on tatami. Put your slippers on when you leave your room to shuffle down the corridor to the toilet, take them off, and step into the wooden slippers you'll find inside the restroom door. The catch is to remember to reverse the process on your way back to your room.

3. *Take a bath before you take a bath.* In other words, bathtubs in Japan are for soaking, not for washing, which is done seated on a little stool before you get in. Soap up, rinse off, and then step into the tub, which is usually torrid enough to make you think that someone has mistakenly left the hot water running. (This is a carry-over from the days when a two-story Japanese home was heated by a single charcoal hibachi and the heat you absorbed from the bath was intended to keep you warm long enough to get inside your *futon* and go to sleep before frostbite set in. Modern gas heaters are taken for granted in many homes today, but lots of old customs have yet to be replaced.)

4. *Don't let the term "communal bath" frighten you.* Though there is generally only one bath in each *ryokan*, it doesn't mean that everyone jumps in at once. There is usually one for men and one for women, or a time for women to use the bath and a time for men. Many *ryokan* call guests to the bath one family at a time so you have all the privacy you like. A few of the most expensive inns have installed private baths in some of the rooms to accommodate their more modest guests, but there is a fine custom in Japan called *hadaka no tsukiai*, or naked friendship, which refers to the great ice-breaking effect of taking a bath with a roomful of strangers. You meet the nicest people and have the opportunity of starting a new friendship with no secrets. (The public bathhouse really separates the men from the boys, so to speak, but that is another story.)

5. There really aren't any more rules to remember, but four is an unlucky number in Japan, so I've added one more suggestion to round things off. You usually pay by the person at a *ryokan*, rather than by the room. At a moderately priced inn you'll pay ¥8,000 to ¥10,000 each, but this includes breakfast and dinner. Nowadays, many of the old inns do permit guests to stay overnight without meals (*shokuji nashi*), which often brings the price down to a more palatable ¥6,000 or so per person. When in doubt ask the very helpful staff at the Kyoto Tourist Information Center (TIC; see Getting Around) to call for you. They will check prices, service charges and whether or not you can stay without meals. It is, however, true that many of the finest inns in Kyoto are noted for their excellent cuisine, and passing up a chance to sample it (served decadently in your own room) can be a definite loss when you consider that comparable meals elsewhere in town often end up costing you more.

None of this matters in the least when you wake up in the morning, snuggled inside a thick *futon*, to watch the snow fall in the garden just outside your room. In a few moments, the maid will arrive with the breakfast tray, bowing politely as she begs your pardon for disturbing an elegant night's sleep.

Machiya, the Bedrooms of Eels

Local people call the old wooden row houses of Kyoto *unagi no nedoko*, the bedrooms of eels. Casting no aspersions on the character of residents, the dubious nickname given the long, narrow dwellings (often less than thirty feet wide and up to ten times as long) is certainly a title well-earned. The *machiya*, or city houses, as they are formally called, have been the homes and work places of the townspeople of Kyoto for hundreds of years, and as such they reveal much about the nature of this city.

The *machiya* that remain intact in Kyoto today are monuments to a complicated system of cooperation and interdependence between the people of the miniature townships they formed. These neighborhoods were made up of orderly blocks of forty family units each and were called *chō* (the same character that reads *machi*). The *chō* were formed originally between members of a particular craft—weavers, dyers, lacquerers, and so on—or grew up near the gates of the city's many temples and shrines, among groups of innkeepers who housed the throngs of pilgrims that arrived to worship each year, or among candle and incense makers, for example, whose products were required there.

Each *machiya* is but one part of an overall community whole, both socially and physically. Every dwelling relates directly to the four houses that are nearest, two on either side that share its walls and two on the opposite side of the street. They form a five-family cooperative unit that is called a *goningumi*. About eight of these units make up a whole *chō*, which then relates to the nearest local shrine, whose activities it supports. The local shrine is not only a religious center, but a social gathering place at which regular festivals and ceremonies are held, bringing the whole neighborhood together several times a year.

Before the ground is broken for construction of a new house in the neighborhood, a priest from the shrine must conduct a ceremony on the site to appease the spirit of the land, who just might resent another intrusion.

These ceremonies are observed today, in the building of a five-story bank or a small private residence.

Geomancy, a determining factor in former days in deciding things such as the proper orientation of entrances, ovens, and even toilets, is still in use today in Kyoto, though not as widely practiced as in the past. Many people still consult priests or seers in choosing the most auspicious location and orientation for their new homes.

Historically, the *chō* were formed in self-defense against the constantly warring political factions that periodically left the city in ruin during the Middle Ages. Remnants of moats that were built originally by residents to defend their *chō* can still be found in some of the old neighborhoods. An even more formidable enemy of the wooden *machiya* and its inhabitants was that of fire; a thousand years of Kyoto history reads like a list of regularly scheduled conflagrations; the last major fire of the eighteenth century destroyed nearly eighty percent of the city. In fact, virtually no examples of *machiya* remain in downtown Kyoto that are more than 120 years old, since a fire that started during the struggle to restore the emperor to power swept through the matchstick wooden row houses again in 1864. Through repeated destruction and rebuilding, the bonds among the townspeople and merchants grew stronger. The communities which were formed as a result each had their own special customs, rules, and architectural features that symbolized the unity within each neighborhood.

The architectural style of a particular *chō* was determined by the requirements of the group's trade and its proximity to a shrine or temple. With harmony as the keynote, similarities within a township were demonstrated in a unified style of elements like the type of roof tiles, the depth of the eaves, and even the pattern and number of slats in the window grates. It was considered a breach of propriety to flaunt one's personal wealth by outdoing your neighbors in the adornment of a façade, so the prosperous merchant displayed his success with lavish touches to the interior: hand-carved transoms, lacquered trims, the use of elaborately decorated paper on sliding paper doors (*fusuma*), etc.

But tact and good taste were not the only considerations which determined the restrained visage of the homes of Kyoto's merchants. Strictly enforced edicts were handed down by the shogunate during the Edo period (1603–1868) forbidding any extravagant displays in the merchants' houses, inside or out, in an attempt to keep the rising merchant class in their place at the lower end of the class system. For example, no merchant was allowed to build a house over two stories high.

Nonetheless, by the middle of the Edo period, the merchants had achieved a powerful enough position financially to manifest their individual tastes, regardless of the shogunate and its ludicrous edicts.

Every *machiya* is essentially constructed on one basic unit of measure—a single tatami mat—roughly three by six feet. Rooms are measured by the number of mats they contain, which then determines the width and length of every house. This uniform system of measurement, by which not only elements within an individual house but in the neighborhood and city as a whole are determined, makes the *machiya* unique in the world of architecture.

The façade of a typical *machiya* in Kyoto (although styles differ from neighborhood to neighborhood) has certain design features that are interesting to note. Many houses have curved bamboo covers over the gutter in front. This is called an *inu-yarai*, which literally means a dog barrier, though it was used as a sort of buffer to keep all kinds of pests (even the two-legged kind) and street traffic at a distance since *machiya* were built right on the edge of the road. Some of the houses still have a *komayose*, the now decorative wooden railing that was used originally as a hitching post.

The heavy, somber façade of a typical kimono merchant's house, for example, often seems aloof at first as you approach from the street. The dark, slatted windows called *kōshi-mado* were a means of creating privacy amid the hustle and bustle of city life that went on outside just inches away. Originally, the front windows of merchant dwellings opened up to reveal the *misenoma*, or shop room.

Mushiko mado, literally "insect cage window," is another characteristic of Kyoto city houses and refers to the porthole-type windows cut out of the walls of buildings in which the second-floor façades were made of clay. Oblong or rectangular in shape, these windows have thick vertical clay bars and appear to be used for ventilation. Appearances being very important in

Machiya, exterior view

Kyoto, the *mushiko mado* were actually used as hidden vantage points from which the merchants could observe the goings-on in the neighborhood without being seen by passers-by in the streets below. Strict rules of deportment enforced by the Tokugawa shogunate during the Edo period forbade members of the lower class ever to have their heads above those of their superiors. The *mushiko mado* enabled merchants to "look down" on the snooty samurai, without being arrested for impudence.

Customers entered via the sliding door in front and stepped into the *tōri niwa*, a stone walkway that led back through the kitchen all the way to the interior of the house. When the *noren* curtain is hung in place over the entry, it is an indication that the shop is open for business. Another curtain, often a *nawa noren*, or rope curtain, separates the kitchen from the shop front. Stepping up from the *toriniwa* to the raised shop room, customers sat down on tatami to discuss business with the proprietor over a cup of green tea.

Except for the *tōri niwa*, which often had a plain dirt floor, all the rooms of the house were raised about two feet above ground level to provide adequate ventilation during Kyoto's humid summers: there is nothing worse than a moldy tatami mat. Every *machiya* in Kyoto is designed with the idea of keeping cool in the summer. Though the winters are cold, it is easier to bundle up than to survive the hot and humid months. The use of woven tatami mats as flooring material throughout is said to allow the floor to "breathe." The sliding paper doors which act as room dividers are replaced

Machiya, interior view

with reed screens during the summer to help ventilation, or can be removed completely, creating as much of a breeze as possible. The rooms of *machiya* are lined up in a row, one behind the other, parallel to the *tōri niwa*, creating the famous "eel" effect. The ancient division of the city into a tidy grid pattern determined the long, narrow subdivision of lots within each city block, as did the fact that taxes were once levied based on the amount of street frontage each dwelling had.

Unlike the more spacious *yashiki* homes of the privileged samurai, where a garden separated the entrance from the street, *machiya* gardens were always a private, limited space located deep in the interior—always a refreshing surprise. Here the master of the house could create a little piece of paradise all his own.

Guests, parting the *noren* curtain to wait in the *genkan* (a welcoming room where guests were officially greeted), waited for the invitation to literally "come up" into the house proper with the words *o-agari kudasai*.

Suddenly, the business world is left behind as you enter the quieter recesses of the house. The homes of prosperous merchants often had more than one interior garden, one of which acted as a divider between the *misenoma* and the living quarters in the back. Polished wood verandas run along the edges of these interior gardens, linking inside and out. The deep eaves make this a fine location for contemplating the harvest moon in comfort, protected from the possibility of an unexpected evening shower.

To the left of the little garden is the *zashiki*. This is the heart of the house. The *zashiki* is used as a room for entertaining guests, though the function of rooms in a *machiya* can change instantly with the addition or subtraction of the easily removable *fusuma* doors that take the place of walls. This makes for the flexible environment which was necessary in houses in which there were often only two rooms for every possible family function.

The *zashiki* is the most elegantly designed room in the house. Facing the main garden, the *okuniwa*, this room more than any other shows the influence of the tea ceremony on *machiya*. Just like the traditional tearoom, the *zashiki* has a *tokonoma*, the recessed niche of honor where a single scroll painting and one small ceramic vase are the only embellishments. They sit quietly in the shadows of which novelist Junichirō Tanizaki once wrote so fondly: "The quality we call beauty must always grow from the realities of life, and our ancestors, forced to live in dark rooms, presently came to discover the beauty in shadows, ultimately to guide shadows to beauty's end. And so it has come to be that the beauty of a Japanese room depends on a variation of shadows, heavy shadows against light shadows ... it has nothing else. Westerners are amazed at the simplicity of Japanese rooms, perceiving in them no more than ashen walls bereft of ornament. Their reaction is understandable, but it betrays a failure to comprehend the mystery of shadows." (A failure, I might add, that is shared by most modern Japanese as well.)

Beyond the gracious refinement of the *zashiki*, the most impressive room is, surprisingly, the kitchen. Built to one side of the stone-floored *tōri niwa*, the ceiling of this room stretches high above, leaving the massive curved beams that support the heavy tile roof exposed to view. Light streams down through the skylights overhead. An old well, no longer in use, sits in one corner and a large clay oven, the *kamado*, with its giant iron cauldrons, squats in the other. Near the oven is one of the very special features of the machiya, the one that has to do with "soul." No *machiya* kitchen would be without a tiny shrine to the god of fire. The roots of ancient Japanese culture are founded in a deeply spiritual, highly superstitious tradition of paying respect to the *kami*, or gods, who protect everything from ovens to rice fields. Not to be meddled with even today, the *kami* are sure to receive their daily due of flowers and votive candles, just to be safe.

In old Kyoto, there were no automatic dishwashers, no electric toasters, no microwave ovens . . . just simple two-burner stoves, and tiled sinks. Not even a refrigerator disturbed the old order, when the lady of the house went out each morning to the local market street to buy just enough food to last the day. Dry goods and housewares were kept in the long wooden cabinet called a *mizuya* that lined one wall of every kitchen. Pickling, salt preservation, and drying were the only means available to housewives in the days before the refrigerator became a standard household appliance after the Tokyo Olympics in 1964.

Behind the main garden at the back of the property of most merchants was the *kura*, or storehouse. The thick walls and heavy doors provided a place to keep the family treasures safe from fires and thieves. Many merchants used their *kura* as warehouses to store goods for sale, since the small shop room in front usually provided only enough space to display samples and conduct business.

Many of the old shops in this book were chosen not just for the fine traditional products they sell, but for the beauty of the *machiya* that house them. Although the government, both on national and local levels, has made some effort to preserve the few isolated *machiya* that have been maintained in original condition, every day they fall under the bulldozers of progress in Kyoto. Most of the shopkeepers who have maintained their old shops have done so at their own expense, and it is due largely to them that bits and pieces of old Kyoto are still around for us to enjoy.

A Few Helpful Notes

Closing Time

Punctuality is a blessing and a hindrance in Japan. Trains are unfailingly reliable. It takes something near catastrophic to stop them, and an earthquake or flood will often only result in a short delay. Shops, too, and most particularly restaurants are conscious of the clock. Though shopkeepers may stretch to accommodate a last-minute customer, restaurants follow a strict regime, and the posted closing time refers to the hour in which the shop locks its doors for the night, with all customers on the outside.

So if you wish to linger over your meal, allow yourself ample time by arriving several hours before closing. Because the cleaning up procedures are time-consuming, kitchens frequently shut down thirty to sixty minutes prior to closing. You will be asked if you have any "last order," which, depending on the establishment, may also include alcoholic beverages. If you are still seated as the evening draws to a close, your waiter or waitress will most likely whisk away your bill to tally it up. Sometimes done as early as thirty minutes before closing, this standard procedure is meant as a gentle reminder. An eye to the other clientele will suffice as a guideline to the uninitiated.

Credit Cards

Purchasing with plastic (or traveler's checks) is a relatively new concept to the Japanese, who have traditionally dealt with cash and are not adverse to carrying large sums of it. More and more shops have subscribed to credit card services, but many mama and papa shops remain steadfastly opposed to the credit system, dismissing it as unnecessary for one reason or another. If the card you carry is not listed in the shop data, it is wise to call ahead if you plan to use it. The major credit cards accepted in Japan are:

AE American Express
DC Diners Club

JCB
MC Master Card (also Diamond Credit)
MIL Million Card
NC Nihon Shimpan
UC Union Card
VISA Sumitomo Card

A Crash Course in Suffixes

Though a working grasp of a foreign language is not possible for a short stay, a quick lesson in the common suffixes that sprinkle the tourist literature of Kyoto will go a long way in helping you navigate. Helpful suffixes include the following:

SUFFIX	ENGLISH	EXAMPLE
-dōri	street	Gojō-dori
-ku	ward	Higashiyama-ku
-kawa/-gawa	river	Kamogawa

As any first-time visitor soon discovers, Kyoto abounds with temples and shrines. At times it seems there is one around every corner and down every alley. Attention to the suffixes will allow you to decipher what stands before you.

-tera/-dera	temple	Kiyomizu-dera
-ji	temple	Daitoku-ji
Jinja or *Jingu*	Shinto shrine	Yasaka Jinja

RAKU-CHŪ

Central Kyoto

As the heart of the old capital city, Raku-chū is still the busiest, most densely populated area in Kyoto. Most of the shops, both old and new, for which the city is famous are here in a broad area that runs from Kita-ōji in the north to just below Kyoto Station in the south, and from Nishi-ōji in the west to the Kamogawa river in the east. This is roughly the district which the emperor Kanmu branded with a grid pattern of streets that has existed since 794, though by the eleventh century the center of the city had shifted to the east where it remains today.

With the Imperial Palace as the axis point of both politics and commerce, the area around it was inhabited by both wealthy men of power, and merchants and craftsmen who were purveyors to the imperial household before the capital was transferred to what is now Tokyo in 1868.

Nishijin weaving and Yūzen dyeing districts are still located in the northwestern part of Raku-chū. Downtown near Kawaramachi-Shijō you'll find Pontochō, the geisha quarter; Nishiki, the city's oldest market street; and Teramachi, once a temple district and now an area of booksellers, antique dealers, and shops selling utensils for the tea ceremony.

Raku-chū—bustling, vibrant, and eclectic—with the contrast (and sometimes conflict) between old and new is the heart of Kyoto. Exploring the old shops that crowd its backstreets could keep you busy for years.

🏛 Hōkyō-ji

🏛 Shōkoku-ji

DEMACHI YANAGI

KARASUMA LINE

Nishijin

Nishijin Textile Center ■

○23

IMADEGAWA

Imadegawa-dōri

KAMO RIVER

● 1

KAMIGYŌ-KU

Ichijō-dōri

Karasuma-dōri

Imperial Palace

Ōmiya-dōri

○24

● 2

Horikawa-dōri

■ Raku Art Museum

Y.W.C.A. ■

Imperial Park

Sendō Palace

Kawaramachi-dōri

Kyoto Prefectural Office

Shimodachiuri-dōri

Palaceside Hotel ■

●3

●4

Ogawa-dōri

Nishi-no-tōin-dōri

MARUTAMACHI

Marutamachi-dōri

Teramachi-dōri

Gokomachi-dōri

Nijō Castle

Ikawa-dōri

○25

Nijō-dōri

●5

■ Hotel Fujita

Oshikōji-dōri

○26

Oe Nō Theater

27○

Kyoto City Hall

28○

Kyoto Hotel

Shinsen-en Garden

NAKAGYŌ-KU

6●

Honnō-ji

■ Nijō Jinya

Oike-dōri

OIKE

7● 8● 29○

Royal Hotel ■ 11●

Anekōji-dōri

Heian Museum

9●

10●

30● 31○

13●

Sanjō-dōri

14●

32○

12●

Rokkaku-dō 🏛

Y.M.C.A.

33○

34○

Ponto-chō

SANJŌ

Rokkaku-dōri

●15

Yanagi-no-banba-dōri

Tomi-no-kōji-dōri

Fuyachō-dōri

TAKASE RIVER

Kiyamachi-dōri

KEIHAN LINE

Takoyakushi-dōri

Shin-kyōgoku

Kongo Nō Stage

Nishikikōji-dōri

Takakura-dōri

ŌMIYA ■

Shijō-dōri

KARASUMA

SHIJŌ

1/2 mile

SHIJŌ

HANKYŪ KYOTO LINE

KAWARA-MACHI

0 — 500 m

CENTRAL KYOTO (south)

Takoyakushi-dōri

Nishikikōji-dōri

ŌMIYA HANKYŪ KYOTO LINE KARASUMA

SHIJŌ ŌMIYA
KEIFUKU LINE

Shijō-dōri SHIJŌ

Ayakōji-dōri

Bukkōji-dōri ●21

Takatsuji-dōri ☰ Bukkō-ji

Matsubara-dōri

SHIMOGYŌ-KU

Gojō-dōri

GOJŌ

22
● Aburakōji-dōri

Nishi ☰
Hongan-ji

Higashi ☰
Hongan-ji

Kikokutei
Garden

Shichijō-dōri

Tower Hotel
Kyoto Tower

Grand Hotel ■

Station
Hotel

JNR TŌKAIDŌ LINE

KYOTO

SHINKANSEN (BULLET TRAIN)

○46

Shin Miyako
Hotel

Tō-ji-dōri

MINAMI-KU

☰
Tō-ji

TŌ-JI

Kujō-dōri

Shōsei-en

Sakaimachi-dōri

16 ●

40 ○
41 ○
SHIJŌ

36 ○ 39 ○

17 37 18 38
35 ○ ○ ○ ● ○ 42 ○

KAWARAMACHI

19 ●
20 ●

GOJŌ

KAMO RIVER

TAKASE RIVER

43 ○
44 ○

45 ○ SHICHIJŌ

Hōkō-ji ☰

☷
Hōkoku
Shrine

National
Museum ■
Sanjūsangen-
☰ dō

Tourist
Information
Center (TIC)

Hachijō-dōri

JNR NARA LINE

TŌFUKU-JI TŌFUKU-
JI

Ōmiya-dōri
Horikawa-dōri
Karasuma-dōri
KARASUMA LINE
Shinmachi-dōri
Higashi-no-tōin-dōri
Takakura-dōri
Kawaramachi-dōri
Kiyamachi-dōri
KEIHAN LINE
Yamatoōji-dōri

KINTETSU KYOTO LINE

0   1/2 mile
0   500 m

43

AIZEN KŌBŌ
indigo textiles

Ōmiya Nishi-iru, Nakasuji-dōri, Kamigyō-ku
上京区中筋通大宮西入　☎ (075) 441–0355 (English spoken)
OPEN: Daily, 9 A.M.–5:30 P.M.

Down a narrow backstreet in Nishijin, the heart of the textile district in Kyoto, is Aizen Kōbō, the house of an old kimono-sash (*obi*) weaving family established over a century ago. Today they specialize in indigo dyeing, or *ai-zome*, a traditional folk technique most often found in remote areas of the Japanese countryside.

A century ago, the Utsuki family were masters of *tsuzure-ori*, the tedious fingernail weaving technique that produces the complicated relief brocade patterns seen in the finest Kyoto-style *obi*, often laced with threads of silver and gold. With the introduction of the Jacquard loom and the decline in popularity of kimono and *obi* for everyday wear, there was less call for the costly *tsuzure-ori obi*, and the Utsuki family was faced with a dilemma that has become a fact of life for traditional craftsmen all over Japan.

It was then that Shōzō Utsuki had the good fortune to become involved with members of the Mingei (Folk Art) Movement in Kyoto. Kawai Kanjirō, renowned potter and one of the leaders of the group, persuaded Shōzō to learn the old folk ways of indigo dyeing and *sashiko* embroidery, crafts that were then considered lowbrow and seemed destined to vanish. Few Japanese appreciated folk crafts in the 1920s and 1930s when the deluge of manufactured goods from the West caused them to turn their backs on crafts they saw as crude or outmoded. Kawai saw that the beauty of natural indigo dye and the quality of simple handwoven, handmade garments would one day again come into their own. Fortunately, Shōzō agreed and began to change the complex production methods of his large *obi* business to the simple folk-methods of weaving cotton and linen using only 100 percent natural dyes. Today his shop is one of the only places in Kyoto where handwoven, hand-dyed, and hand-embroidered garments of *hon-ai*, or "real" indigo, are produced.

When Shōzō Utsuki changed over from making extravagant silk *obi* to simple folk wear, the famous novelist

Junichirō Tanizaki gave the shop a new name to fit its new way of life. The *ai* in "Aizen Kōbō" is a play on words, meaning both love and indigo. *Kōbō* means workshop. Kawai Kanjirō himself did the calligraphy for the solid zelkova sign, which was carved by Tatsuaki Kuroda (later to be designated one of Japan's Living National Treasures).

The most popular garment made at Aizen Kōbō is the *samu-e*, a loose-fitting, two-piece garment worn by Zen priests and local craftsmen. Dyed with *hon-ai*, they look and feel better after five years of regular wear than they do the day you first put them on. The color fades gracefully and the durable fabric becomes softer and softer. When *sashiko* embroidery, a farmer's technique of stitching layers of cotton together to make the garment stronger, is also used, the result is a *samu-e* that is nearly indestructible.

Aizen Kōbō makes not only fine *samu-e*, but also *happi* coats (workmen's jackets), *monpe* (farmer's pants), and a newer line of Western-style clothes designed by Utsuki-san Jr.'s vivacious young wife Hisako. Skeins of natural-dyed threads are available, as are a number of accessory items at reasonable prices. The best *samu-e* woven with the finest cotton fiber and dyed with natural indigo come in all sizes (even extra-large). Although the price is higher than the machine-made variety, compare the beauty of natural indigo dye with synthetics (and divide the price by the number of years the handmade garment will last); it is still a bargain. The Utsukis say that most of the indigo-blue–colored fabrics you find today in department stores and boutiques in Japan are produced from synthetic indigo dyes. They recommends letting your nose find the *hon-ai*, which has a very pungent smell before it has been washed.

The much photographed building that houses Aizen Kōbō was built in the Meiji period. It is one of a few in the Nishijin area that have been kept in their original condition, and is considered a cultural asset.

Many of the beautiful doorway curtains (*noren*) you see hanging outside traditional Kyoto shops were made at Aizen Kōbō. Not only do they dye and weave *noren*, but it is possible to order one with your shop's name written in the hand of a noted Kyoto calligrapher. They have a limited but fine selection of antique textiles. *Ramie*, a rare linenlike fiber that becomes feather soft with use, is also woven here and is available by the meter.

In an age when the kimono is no longer a costume for everyday wear, many Nishijin looms now produce theater curtains and brocade seat covers for the man-who-has-everything's imported car. Aizen Kōbō is one of the few Nishijin weavers that has found a new medium in which to survive.

SHIOYOSHI-KEN
Kyoto confectionery

Nakadachiuri-agaru, Kuromon-dōri, Kamigyō-ku
上京区黒門通中立売上ル ☎ (075) 441–0803
OPEN: 9 A.M.–9 P.M. ■ CLOSED: Sundays, holidays

In the fall of 1587, the great feudal lord Toyotomi Hideyoshi pulled his gilded boats into port at Yodo to begin his grand procession northward to his residence at Juraku-dai, the "Palace of Gathered Pleasures," which legions of workers had built for him atop, significantly, the ruins of the old Imperial Palace. Hideyoshi ordered 4,763 loads of earth to be hauled in to construct the mound on which the walled palace stood. Its luxurious gardens were filled with plants requisitioned from the gardens of the local citizenry. The doors of its gates were of solid copper, and the pattern of its tiles brought to mind "jeweled tigers breathing in the wind, and golden dragons intoning in the clouds." Hideyoshi had outdone his own reputation as the most extravagant showman with Juraku-dai.

But the glory of Juraku-dai was destined to be short-lived. Soon after it was completed Hideyoshi left the palace and his duties as imperial regent to his adopted son to lead an invasion of China. Not ten years later he ordered the palace to be destroyed when his adopted son's allegiance came under suspicion.

Shioyoshi-ken has captured something of the legendary palace in its sweet bean cakes for posterity, dubbing them "Juraku manjū," and branding each bun with "Tenchō," the name of the era in which the palace was constructed. Each cake is wrapped in handmade paper that bears Hideyoshi's family crest, the five-pointed paulownia leaf.

Kyoto confectionery, or Kyō-gashi, are known not only for their delicate flavor and imaginative seasonal shapes and colors, but also for the poetic names contrived for each. These often allude to legendary characters, events, or places in Japanese history, or to quotations from memorable passages in Japanese literature. As sweets are an important part of the tea ceremony, recognition of the particular allusion in the name of the confection offered at a tea gathering adds to the pleasure of appreciating the theme which the host wishes to convey. The history of the tea served, the scene depicted on

the side of a lacquered tea caddy, the particular flower chosen for the arrangement in the alcove—all relate to the subject of the hanging scroll which gives the guests a hint as to their host's unstated scheme. The more obscure the relationships between the "clues," the more delighted the guest may feel for having discovered it.

It is the business of Shioyoshi-ken to indulge the fantasies and tastes of Kyoto's tea masters, a task they have spent a hundred years refining. Another of their sweets, a *higashi*, or dry sweet, has been named after the beautiful Princess Kōgō, an imperial concubine who was banished from the palace when the emperor tired of her. She lived out her days in shame at a nunnery in Arashiyama. The real key to the allusion is perhaps the tiny bit of salty Daitoku-ji *nattō* hidden in the center—the irony of love, the inevitable shock of finding a teardrop at the heart of an experience so sweet.

Apart from their *Juraku manjū* bean cakes and their *kōgō higashi* dry sweets, they also have the hard ribbon candy called *ariheitō*, made from an old Portuguese recipe, and *yōkan*, a jellied sweet bean paste wrapped in sheaths of dried bamboo leaves. In addition to these, Shioyoshi-ken has a selection of *namagashi* sweets (jellies, pastes, and doughs) whose form and flavor are designed to match the season. The owners pride themselves on using only the best available ingredients, including a specially hand-processed sugar called *wasanbon* made at a traditional refinery on Shikoku. The old-fashioned process by which cane sugar is refined produces a delicate, powdery white sugar that melts in your mouth.

Sweetness aside, the other quality for which Shioyoshi-ken is known is the beauty of their Taishō-period building. The traditional *machiya-zukuri*, or townhouse construction, of Shioyoshi-ken has the shop (with family living quarters and interior garden in the rear) on the right side and the kitchens on the left. The *mushiko-mado* windows on the second floor overlook a wrought-iron gas lantern typical of Kyoto shops that date to the Meiji or Taishō periods. The large, six-paneled *noren* curtain gives the shop's name and also lists its most famous products.

Be sure to examine the floral arrangement inside the glass case that lines the wall on the left. Camellias, peonies, plum blossoms, maple leaves, and even wisteria are fashioned out of solid candy by Takaya-san, Sr., who participates in one of Kyoto's more esoteric hobbies, *kōgei-gashi*, elaborate floral designs made from traditional confectionery.

FŪKA
wheat gluten

Sawaragi-chō-agaru, Nishi-no-tōin-dōri, Kamigyō-ku
上京区西洞院通椹木町上ル ☎ (075) 231–1584
OPEN: 9 A.M.–5 P.M. ■ CLOSED: Wednesdays

Leave it to the people of Kyoto to take a food as simple as *fu*, the wheat gluten product that once provided Zen monks in China with needed protein in their vegetarian diet, and turn it into a dainty sweet to be served with ceremonial tea or used as a decorative touch in Kyoto cuisine, a different color and shape for every season served in soups and sauces: pink cherry blossom *fu* in spring, bright purple eggplant *fu* in summer, red and yellow maple leaf *fu* in autumn, and festive New Year's *fu* for January 1. Although an accurate translation, "wheat gluten" hardly seems adequate in describing the fanciful Kyoto specialty known as *fu*.

Fūka, just west of the Imperial Palace grounds, has been making *fu* for 130 years. Kōichi Kobori, the present owner, is the sixth-generation master of a shop once designated as an official purveyor to the imperial household.

There are two main types of *fu*: *nama-fu* and regular *fu*. *Nama-fu* is the chewy variety that is made of half gluten and half *mochi* rice flour most frequently used in the making of confections. *Sasamaki-fu* is one variety of *nama-fu* filled with sweet bean paste and beautifully wrapped in bamboo leaves to be served with green tea. *Nama-fu* is also used in soups and sauces in the form of *saiku-fu*, in special shapes and colors that evoke the seasons. Regular *fu* is a spongelike substance made of pure gluten which is often used as a neutral, flavor-absorbing ingredient in soups and sauces.

Rikyū-fu, named after the tea master Sen no Rikyū, is a variety of regular *fu* that is boiled in a spicy broth and then deep-fried. It can be sliced and served cold as an appetizer with saké or beer. Sen no Rikyū was the tea master who popularized both *fu* and *nama-fu* for use in the tea ceremony in the sixteenth century. During the Edo period *fu* and *nama-fu* became so popular that an entire street in downtown Kyoto still bears the name Fuyachō-dōri, after the many *fu* shops that once lined it. Today, only a few shops that specialize in this delicacy remain in Kyoto.

The process of making *fu* is both quintessentially simple and back-breaking hard work. A plain wheat dough is made of flour and water, and then kneaded for two long hours to bring out the gluten. Next the dough is placed under water and kneaded again until it separates into its two basic elements, starch and gluten. The gluten that floats to the surface is removed and allowed to stand at room temperature until it turns spongelike, the same process that causes bread to rise. It is then boiled in plain water to set the protein.

Nama-fu is made from a combination of gluten and *mochi* rice flour that is not allowed to rise, giving it a smooth, chewy consistency suitable for forming into different shapes. *Nama-fu* is sometimes flavored with herbs or seaweed and filled with sweet bean paste, making a confection unlike any to be found in the West.

Only enough *nama-fu* is made each day at Fūka to fill the orders of the tea masters and restaurateurs who are their regular customers, so it is best to place your order a day ahead of time.

(Sometimes there is just enough left to sell over the counter, but not always.)

Recently, Kobori-san, in collaboration with a French chef, has experimented quite successfully with both kinds of *fu* in dishes that perhaps belong to the category of *nouvelle cuisine*. The culinary possibilities for this very flexible ancient food may one day lead it to an appearance on the tables of some of the finest French restaurants in the world.

Kobori-san is an easygoing man who is generally unimpressed by the fuss made over so-called *shinise*, the name given to revered old Kyoto shops. "Too many places rely on an established name and use the *Kyō* prefix on their products as if that were enough to ensure quality. My family has been making *fu* for many generations, and our shop has become famous for it. But good *fu* is now made in many places all over Japan. Saying 'Kyō-this' and 'Kyō-that' doesn't mean it's the best. I just try to make the finest product I can ... people who like *fu* can be the final judge."

IRIYAMA TŌFU

tofu

入
山
豆
腐

Aburanokōji-kado, Sawaragi-chō, Kamigyō-ku
上京区椹木町油小路角　☎(075) 241–2339

OPEN: From 10 A.M. until sold out ▪ CLOSED: Sundays

Mame de	*Made of beans*
Shikaku de	*Squarely cut*
Yawarakaku te	*And soft*

When the priest Ingen wrote this poem in 1661, he was not only praising the qualities of good tofu, but implying something about the human spirit. *Mame* means both beans and diligence, *shikaku* means honest (or square), and *yawarakai* means soft or gentle—a desirable combination, in bean curd or people.

Tofu is as much a part of the diet in Japan as cheese is in the West. High in protein and low in calories, this soybean product was first made in China over two thousand years ago. Tofu can be fried, simmered, grilled, and even eaten fresh dipped in soy sauce and covered with diced green onions. Tofu is a simple food that absorbs and enhances the flavor of soups and broths, adding vital protein to the traditional Buddhist vegetarian diet. The most frequent dishes in which it can be found in modern-day Japan are *miso* soup, *yudōfu* (a one-pot simmered dish), *oden* (a stewlike dish with tofu and other specialties simmered in broth), and *hiyayakko* (cold, fresh tofu, popular in summer).

Few shops in modern Kyoto persist in the traditional methods of making tofu, but at Iriyama Tōfu (if you rise early enough in the morning) you can watch a ninth-generation tofu-maker whose ancestors made tofu for the imperial court in the early nineteenth century. Today the shop specializes in "cotton" tofu (*momen-goshi*), a more coarsely textured variety than the "silk" tofu (*kinu-goshi*) that has become popular supermarket fare in recent years. Cotton tofu has the ring of farmhouses and home cooking that makes most fancy chefs in the pursuit of Kyoto-style elegance tend to turn up their noses, according to the unaffected Mrs. Iriyama. "We don't make pretty tofu here," she says, fanning the charcoal fire with one hand as she turns the skewered tofu with the other. An occasional charcoal cinder on the surface of Iriyama's grilled tofu (*yaki-dōfu*) just adds to the flavor.

Unlike many of the tofu shops in Japan today, Iriyama uses no chemical additives to gel their tofu, preferring the use of refined *nigari* sea brine as a coagulant for the subtle sweetness it imparts even if it is less predictable.

Two large vats of soybeans simmer over the old wood-burning cookstoves inside this 120-year-old building on the same site where Iriyama's ancestors cooked soybeans long ago. The sagging stone floors, old well, and crumbling clay ovens comfort each other in modern times when most other tofu-makers have turned to concrete and stainless steel. Mrs. Iriyama complained that a delivery truck barreling down the narrow backstreet not too long ago took out the west wall of the shop, plowing into the back of the old clay ovens in the process. It would have been easier to replace them with new gas-burning stoves, but the Iriyamas felt that the traditional stoves cooked a better-tasting batch of beans. Finding someone who still knew how to make an old cookstove was a task in itself (almost as difficult as it was to find a tofu shop like this one in an age when many Kyoto housewives buy tofu at the supermarket), but they did, and though they resemble giant anthills with a chimney, the "new" ovens crackle and shoot off sparks through the early morning hours at Iriyama Tōfu just as the old ones did.

Mr. Iriyama is somewhat of a history buff. Working here from dawn to dusk since he was a small boy, he had to give up any dreams of academia. Nonetheless, he has memorized the names of all the eras in the Edo period and can recite the history of this neighborhood back to the great Nishi-jin Fire in 1730. Not far from the Imperial Palace, the neighborhood (formerly a guild of fishmongers) was the scene of constant battles between warring military factions in their struggles for control of the capital. Iriyama-san tells of fierce samurai with flailing swords destroying wells and terrorizing the peasants two hundred years ago, as if he had been there himself. In the rafters at the back of his shop is a wooden pole nearly two meters long used by his great-great-grandfather to carry giant dangling buckets of tofu door to door on his rounds.

Cotton, or regular, tofu, deep-fried plain tofu (*o-age*), and deep-fried tofu mixed with sesame or chopped vegetables (*hiryōzu*) are available at Iriyama Tōfu year round. The grilled tofu made fresh daily during the cooler months may have a coarser texture than that sold in local supermarkets, but the aroma of fresh soybean curd and the old-fashioned, homemade flavor (not to mention the free history lesson) are well worth the wait for neighbors who bring their own containers and wait in line, sharing the latest local gossip, while Mrs. Iriyama and her husband grin and sweat and grill their delicious tofu.

IPPŌ-DŌ tea

Nijō-kita, Teramachi-dōri, Nakagyō-ku
中京区寺町通二条北 ☎ (075) 211-3421 (English spoken)
OPEN: 9 A.M.–7 P.M. ■ CLOSED: Sundays, holidays ■ CREDIT: AE, DC, JCB, MC, UC, VISA

It is Ippō-dō's fault that everything on Teramachi-dōri within two blocks is permeated with the enticing aroma of freshly roasted tea leaves. In fact, Ippō-dō has been perfuming the neighborhood for 140 years with the finest green tea from Uji, the most famous tea-producing region in Japan, just south of Kyoto.

Uji, where the round, carefully trimmed hedgerows color the hills a vivid green, has the perfect climate for growing tea. Situated on the foggy banks of the Uji River, this area with its misty air and rich soil give forth the best tea in the country—with the help of what Mr. Watanabe, the present owner of Ippō-dō, calls a secret ingredient—the addition of herring to the soil as a natural fertilizer.

Ippō-dō was once designated by the Imperial Household Agency as a purveyor to the imperial family (though such designations were officially discontinued after World War II).

Up until the twentieth century, tea was a luxury in which only the upper classes could indulge. Said to have been brought back from China by the Buddhist monk Eisai in 1191, tea gained prominence as a beverage among the samurai when Sen no Rikyū perfected the tea ceremony some four centuries later. For the next five hundred years it was drunk in its powdered form, called *matcha*. In the mid eighteenth century the process for making *sencha*, the rolled-leaf type of green tea, was developed. When a tea-processing machine was introduced in the early 1920s, the common people were finally initiated to the formerly exclusive pleasures of green tea.

There are several different types of tea (*o-cha*) available at Ippō-dō: *matcha*, the powdered tea of the tea ceremony; *gyokuro*, a sweet, fragrant leaf tea using only the finest leaves at the top of the best plants; *sencha*, a leaf tea from the same plants as *gyokuro*, but with a sharper astringency (*sencha* is the type most often served to guests in Japan today); *bancha*, a coarser green-leaf tea, the most common roasted variety; *hōjicha*, a lightly roasted blend of *bancha* and *sencha*;

Central Kyoto

57

mugicha, roasted with barley; and *Uji-shimizu*, a powder for making iced green tea. Within each type of tea there are also many varieties and grades to be sampled. Over thirty varieties of *matcha* alone are available, with indications on the price list (in Japanese) as to which tea is preferred by which tea master. Watanabe-san says that fine tea should not be stored for more than two weeks and therefore recommends buying only forty-gram containers of *matcha* at a time. Many of Mr. Watanabe's foreign customers prefer the aromatic *hōjicha* or the delicate *gyokuro*.

Each year in May, the tea leaves are handpicked in Uji, and just like the year's new wine, connoisseurs look forward to sampling the fresh *shincha*, or "new tea." The Tokugawa shogunate halted all other traffic along the Tōkaidō Highway when the convoy bearing the annual shipment of *shincha* from Uji made its way to Edo in the seventeenth and eighteenth centuries.

The fluttering black shop curtains at Ippō-dō veil a remarkably unchanged interior lined with old tea jars along the north wall. The present building was constructed after the Tenmei Fire in 1864 that destroyed a large part of the city. The original shop, called Ōmiya, was established in 1715 and was located across the street. But in 1846, a nobleman who purchased tea there exhorted the shopkeeper to carry on his fine trade with the words "*Cha hitotsu o tamotsu yō ni*," or "Promise you'll never sell anything but fine tea." From that day forward the shop took the name Ippō-dō, using Chinese characters that indicate the same.

Attentive clerks wait behind the old counter to steep a sample cup of whichever tea the customer would like to try, and then carefully measure out the requested amount. The airtight canisters with their turn-of-the-century green and orange labels in which the leaf teas are sold are a treasure in themselves. *O-cha* has all the eye-opening, mind-clearing effects of coffee, without the strain on the stomach. The fresh, astringent flavor and aroma of a cup of the finest tea from Ippō-dō may convert even the most inveterate coffee drinker to the fold of tea.

NOTE: Many of the shops along Teramachi-dōri near Ippō-dō specialize in both antique and new tea utensils. (Hōrai-dō, another tea shop on Teramachi about a block north of Shijō, offers a variety of ceramic bowls, teapots, whisks, and accessories along with a selection of fine Uji teas. See separate entry.)

YUBAHAN
yuba (soy milk "skin")

Oike-agaru, Fuyachō-dōri, Nakagyō-ku

中京区麩屋町通御池上ル ☎ (075) 221-5622

OPEN: 8 A.M.–sunset ■ CLOSED: Thursdays

One brisk autumn morning not long after I arrived in Kyoto, I came upon a sight I shall never forget: an old wooden row house whose heavily gridded front windows were open wide to the street, with its crisp linen shop curtain flapping softly in the breeze, and a scene that had to come right out of another era.

Hard at work was a man who was pulling sheets of a paperlike substance out of steaming vats to hang dripping wet in the morning air to dry. Walking from vat to vat he repeated the process, one, two, a dozen times, rhythmically, like a machine, but not like a machine, like a man performing a very old task his bones knew by heart. He stopped from time to time to stoke brick furnaces beneath the rows of vats with more sawdust (sawdust burns more evenly than firewood, though it is more expensive to use). Steam rose and spun its lazy way up through the heavy curved rafters to the skylight twenty feet overhead. I asked if he was making paper. He snorted a laugh. "No, it's yuba," he

said, knowing where that would leave me. "Yuba?" I repeated to be sure I'd heard him right. He looked at me with proud amusement, wiped his hands on his apron, and disappeared into the back. Soon he was back with a tiny dish and a cruet of soy sauce. "Yuba. Try some." I don't remember what else he told me then. All that lingers is the fragrance of wood smoke, and the memory of my first taste of yuba, the pale yellow soy milk skimmings that look an awful lot like paper—but aren't.

To make yuba, soybeans are soaked overnight, ground in a giant stone mortar, and then boiled for hours over an old clay kamado stove. Next they are placed in a cheesecloth bag and pressed in an old lever contraption weighted with huge stones that have been in the family for longer than anyone can remember. The extracted soy milk is then placed in long, flat, open vats over a sawdust-burning fire which must be constantly stoked to keep the milk at an even simmer. A thin skin forms over the steaming soy

milk which is lifted gently off in one even sheet and hung on wooden sticks suspended above to dry.

When I returned several years later, the man and his wonderful old shop hadn't changed—but I had. I'd tasted the popular Kyoto specialty a hundred times in the soups and subtle sauces of Kyoto-style cuisine. He had one surprise left for me, though—he asked his wife to fry up some *yuba*, potato-chip style, and she brought us a sample basket of the crunchy delicacy which we proceeded to devour with lust and speed.

He dusted off a spot for me to sit amid the stone grinding mortars, the giant wooden tubs, and old clay *kamado*, and went on with his work. (I was there this time for an interview, but boiling soy milk waits for no woman.) Each sheet of *yuba* takes eight to ten minutes to form; no clocks or timers are involved, just one continuous motion of lifting, hanging, moving on to the next vat, all day long. To comments on the difficulty of this kind of work Tomizo Asano, the ninth-generation *yuba* maker, volunteered one of his family's most guarded trade secrets. "Standing over these steaming trays all day is enough to make a man sweat even in the middle of winter . . . it's that extra salt," he grinned. The dashing Asano-san is always ready with quips and backhanded comments. He even wisecracked that "it's no big deal" to keep on in an age-old tradition like this. He's been making *yuba* since he was thirteen years old. "It's just what I do," he says.

Yuba can be purchased fresh (*hikiage yuba*) or dried flat (*ita yuba*) or in rolls (*kiri-komaki yuba*). The dried variety lasts a year, but the sooner it is eaten the better. Sliced and added to soups, *yuba* absorbs the flavor of any seasoning and contains the highest concentration of protein found in any natural food, making it an important part of *shōjin ryōri*, the Buddhist vegetarian cuisine. (To use dried *yuba*, you simply soak it in hot water or soup until it softens.)

Yubahan started making *yuba* in 1716, but all family records were destroyed in the huge fire in 1864 that destroyed much of the city, a result of the battles that took place at the time of the Meiji Restoration. The 120-year-old building was reconstructed not long after the fire, but apart from that fact, little is left of the shop's history besides hand-me-down tales.

Lifting yet another sheet of *yuba* onto a rack to dry, Asano-san shot me a nonchalant grin when I asked why his shop name "Yubahan" is written with Chinese characters meaning "half a wave of hot water," rather than with the usual characters for *yuba*. "Who knows," he shrugged. "There are a couple of questions I just never thought to ask the old man before he died." We can assume that this time too he was only joking.

HIIRAGI-YA
inn (ryokan)

Oike-kado, Fuyachō-dōri, Nakagyō-ku
中京区麩屋町通御池角 ☎ (075) 221-1136 (English spoken)
CHECK-IN: 3 P.M. ■ CHECK-OUT: 11 A.M. ■ RATES: ¥25,000–¥70,000 ■ CREDIT: Major cards

Somehow Hiiragi-ya still bears the ambience of an inn that caters to samurai. Something in the scale and aesthetics of each room—the black lacquered trim of an alcove, the ornate gilded detail on a painted screen—join to create an air of the luxury and privilege that belonged exclusively to the upper classes in Edo-period Japan.

Indeed, it was the samurai who were among Hiiragi-ya's most frequent guests in the mid–nineteenth century.

The inn was founded in 1861 by a man named Teijirō, a renowned metalsmith whose sword-guards (*tsuba*) were sought after by the samurai. Teijirō's father, Shōgorō, had left his hometown on the Japan Sea to establish a trading post in Kyoto. He set up a boardinghouse for his porters there (as well as for others who came to the capital in search of work). Shōgorō named the place after Hiiragi Shrine, his favorite shrine, which

Charlie Chaplin participates in a tea ceremony at Hiiragi-ya

stands on the grounds of Shimogamo Shrine, just north of the fork in the Kamogawa river. Hiiragi-ya means "House of Holly." In the endlessly complicated Japanese tradition of dual meaning and coincidental associations, Hiiragi Shrine is surrounded with holly (*hiiragi*), and Shōgorō couldn't resist the play on words, as is so often true in the names of old shops in Kyoto.

After Shōgorō's death in 1853, his son Teijirō the metalsmith was urged by his samurai friends to open an inn to accommodate the lords and their retainers from the provinces who made frequent trips to the capital. The decade that led up to the revolt that ousted the shogunate and reinstated the emperor as ruler of Japan was a time of political unrest in Kyoto. *Daimyō*, the rulers of the provinces, converged on Kyoto, prepared to fight for one side or the other. Hiiragi-ya, in those days, was undoubtedly the scene of many a midnight plotting between samurai determined to champion their cause. Like most diplomatic Kyoto families, the present proprietress refrains from saying which side her samurai guests were on—perhaps both.

At various times in the inn's 125-year history, noted politicians and ministers of state, celebrities (like Charlie Chaplin), and famous writers, such as Yukio Mishima and Yasunari Kawabata, have been guests at Hiiragi-ya. In one room you may sit at the same desk from which Mishima gazed out over the beautiful gardens with pen in hand. More extravagant in its tastes than its reserved neighbor, Tawara-ya (see the following entry), whose subdued decor calls to mind the philosophy of the tea ceremony, Hiiragi-ya has the luxurious sense of elegance associated with the old ruling class.

The exterior of Hiiragi-ya, whose long clay walls run all the way to the corner of Oike-dōri, has the old *komayose* wooden hitching post reminiscent of the days when samurai arrived in a flourish on horseback. Inside, the lobby has a few modern touches—carpeting and a souvenir corner—that go along with the owner's wish to keep up with the times. Each room also has a private bath, although family-size baths are also available with large Meiji-period stained-glass windows to enjoy.

Another unique "modern" feature at Hiiragi-ya is a push-button automatic control box which dims lights, opens and closes curtains, and calls the maid—a very exotic-looking device invented by the last generation-proprietor long before the push-button phone or the computer arrived in Japan. Hiiragi-ya, with its samurai flair and turn-of-the-century charm, is among the most beloved inns in Kyoto.

TAWARA-YA
inn (ryokan)

Anekōji-agaru, Fuyachō-dōri, Nakagyō-ku
中京区麩屋町通姉小路上ル ☎ (075) 211–5566 (English spoken)

CHECK-IN: 12 noon ■ CHECK-OUT: 11 A.M. ■ RATES: ¥38,000–¥70,000 ■ CREDIT: AE, JCB, VISA

"I would call back this world of shadows we are losing. . . . I would have the eaves deep and the walls dark. . . . I would strip away the useless decoration. . . . I do not ask that this be done everywhere, but perhaps we may be allowed at least one mansion where we can turn off the electric lights and see what it is like without them."

The nostalgia Junichirō Tanizaki felt for the loss of the sense of shadowy beauty that was once characteristic of the Japanese house is understandable when you look at how rapidly modernization has changed the face of Kyoto. Even in the so-called traditional Japanese inns, it is not unusual to find a coin-operated TV set in the *tokonoma* alcove, formerly a place of honor in a Japanese room in which only a classic hanging scroll and a simple flower arrangement would be placed.

There is a place in Kyoto where the beauty of the play of light and shadow is tended as carefully as a dying flame. Tawara-ya is such a place—so precious

that reservations are taken a year in advance for a night in Kyoto's quintessential inn.

At one time in Japanese history there were no inns in Kyoto. Emperors stayed in villas, visiting noblemen were accommodated by the imperial court, feudal lords made camp wherever they chose, pilgrims were put up at temples, craftsmen were too busy, city commoners couldn't afford it, and farmers were forbidden to travel at all. Only the merchants had reason (and permission) to roam the countryside peddling their wares. Fortunately for travelers in the twentieth century, a few of them tired of a life on the road and settled down in Kyoto, opening their homes to others like themselves who trod the long miles from country villages bearing heavy loads of rice to feed the imperial city.

Wasuke Okazaki, a textile merchant from a village called Tawara, was such a man. Nearly three hundred years ago, he sent his son to establish a post in Kyoto from which he could conduct business and provide lodging for his

own employees and eventually for others whose lot it was to be on the road.

Gradually Tawara-ya gained a reputation for excellence. Since the turn of the century the inn has been host to people of nobility and fame from all over the world. Members of the imperial family have stayed at Tawara-ya, as did Hirobumi Itō, the first prime minister of Japan. The guest book bears the names and inscriptions of Rothschilds and Rockefellers—even of Marlon Brando.

The present owner, Toshi (Okazaki) Satō, has ten generations of tradition to uphold. Glaring fluorescent bulbs, coin-operated TV sets, and refrigerators have no place of honor in the alcoves at Tawara-ya. Instead, Satō maintains a classic Japanese inn with all the traditional elements of beauty, but without the usual accompanying inconveniences: no need to share the bath, no bone-chilling mornings without proper heat, or sweltering afternoons with droning electric fans.

It is possible to lose yourself down the long, twisting corridors of Tawara-ya, where each turn reveals another intimate scenario: a folding screen adorned with a mountain scene in the Zen style of brush painting, an arrangement of wildflowers in a natural salt-glazed ceramic vase, a stone water basin into which cold, clear water drips oh so slowly from a bamboo spout. King Carl Gustav XVI of Sweden once nearly missed his officially scheduled tour of the city, having lingered so long in the morning light of Tawara-ya's splendid gardens.

Every room is different. Each is furnished simply but elegantly with fine antiques that have been in the Okazaki family for generations—lac-quered tables, brocade armrests, intricately woven basketry. Every room has a private bath done in ceramic tiles from a local kiln, and cedar bathtubs whose fragrance when heated scents the air like a mountain breeze.

With all this to speak for it, Satō-san says that the key to the success of Tawara-ya is simply the service. There are only nineteen rooms, so each guest receives fastidious personal care. Even the elderly gardener bows as you pass the stand of new bamboo where he is busily snipping off a leaf that has outlived its time.

A night at Tawara-ya is quite expensive, starting at ¥38,000 per person per night without meals. Translated into New York dollars, this doesn't amount to much more than the price of a unexciting room in a first-class hotel (sans lamplight, private gardens, and devoted service).

Saul Bellow summed up the sentiments of all the guests who've spent a peaceful night at Tawara-ya: "I found here what I had hoped to find in Japan—the human scale, tranquility, and beauty." How Tanizaki would have envied his good fortune.

SAIUN-DŌ
Japanese painting supplies

Fuyachō Higashi, Anekōji, Nakagyō-ku
中京区姉小路麩屋町東　☎(075) 221–2464 (English spoken)

OPEN: 9 A.M.–6 P.M. ■ CLOSED: 1st & 3rd Wednesdays

Saiun-dō (Painted Clouds) was named by Tomioka Tessai, one of the great masters of Japanese literati painting, and one of Saiun-dō's best turn-of-the-century customers.

In 1863, Tsukio Fujimoto, himself an accomplished Kyoto painter, succumbed to the urgings of his painter friends and opened a shop selling the special colors he had formulated for use in his own work. Preparing them in separate porcelain dishes, Fujimoto called them *gansai* (face colors), for the subtle, transparent quality that his formulas produced. Unlike the cumbersome mineral colors (*iwa-enogu*), which must be ground with a mortar and pestle and mixed with a special medium (*nikawa* hide glue) before they can be applied, Fujimoto's colors were obtained from plant pigments and were water soluble, making them ideal for the delicate washes applied to *suiboku-ga*, or ink paintings.

Saiun-dō sells all the supplies necessary for Japanese painting—brushes (over a hundred kinds), inks, paints, water containers, brush holders, even handmade papers. They have brushes for every imaginable purpose, from a six-inch-wide *hake* flat brush for temple-door-sized washes, to a one-millimeter-wide *kegaki* fine line brush for painting the hairs on a brow. There are even special *ten-tsuki* brushes for painting dots or tears. Ask to see the brush catalog, which has some notations in English as to type of bristles, and name and function of each principal type of brush. One type of brush thought to be unique to Japan is the *renpitsu*, actually five separate brushes bound together with a single handle. The *renpitsu* is used for large sweeps of color where a gradation of shades is desired with one stroke. Unlike the broad, flat *hake* brush, the combination of individually pointed brushes in the *renpitsu* is designed to produce with one stroke a clean, sharp edge of deep color that fades to a lighter overall wash.

Saiun-dō's guest book lists world-famous painters and designers from New York, Paris, and Tokyo—artists who have come to appreciate the beauty of a handmade badger-hair (*tanuki-ke*) brush for fine-detail work, or a sheep-hair (*hitsuji-ke*) brush for applying color washes.

Aside from specialized supplies for professional painters, Fujimoto-san can also provide the novice with everything needed to begin painting in the *suiboku-ga* style. *Sumi-e*, the word most commonly known among Westerners, refers to paintings which do not have color, while *suiboku-ga* includes ink paintings with light washes in color. An all-purpose *suketate* brush is capable of producing a fine line as well as a fully gradated wash; a traditional *shitajiki* felt cloth to place under paper; *sumi* ink sticks ranging in tone from blue to brown; a *suzuri* ink-grinding stone; a square *hissen* water vessel for rinsing brushes; a set of small, white porcelain bowls for mixing colors; a package of off-white *gasen-shi* paper for practicing; and a twelve- to sixteen-color set of *gansai* paints that provides the full range of traditional Japanese colors from the original secret formulas developed by Fujimoto-san's great-grandfather over a hundred years ago. Everything

necessary to start will total around ¥10,000—unless the glass display cases overpower you with temptation. There you'll find beautiful cast-metal paperweights, handmade bamboo brush cases, painted porcelain water containers, and hand-braided silk scroll tassels.

Saiun-dō's one-room shop was built in the late Edo period, and has the intimate atmosphere of the traditional Kyoto-style shop dealing in very specialized products for a limited clientele. Seated on tatami behind a low wooden desk, the Fujimotos weigh small packets of powdered mineral colors (*iwa-enogu*) and chunks of dissolving colors (*suihi*) to fill the stack of orders from the many artists of the contemporary Nihonga Japanese painting school, who prefer the thick, crystalline texture that the mineral paints provide. Fujimoto-san is knowledgeable and friendly and though he says that he barely manages in English, the number of foreign artists in his guest book attests to his ability to communicate. It gives him as much pleasure to advise beginners as to serve Japan's greatest masters.

MISOKA-AN KAWAMICHI-YA
buckwheat noodles (soba)

Sanjō-agaru, Fuyachō-dōri, Nakagyō-ku
中京区麸屋町通三条上ル ☎(075) 221–2525, 231-8507 (English spoken)

OPEN: 11 A.M.–8 P.M. ▪ CLOSED: Thursdays ▪ PRICES: ¥550–¥2,800 ▪ CREDIT: AE, MC, VISA

Though acrobatics do not qualify for a mention on the list of revered martial arts of Japan, the sight of a delivery boy on a bicycle frantically dodging taxicabs, buses, and pedestrians with a tray overflowing with steaming bowls of *soba* noodles balanced on one shoulder is proof that juggling is indeed high art in Kyoto.

The making of *soba*, or buckwheat noodles, served in a variety of delicious soups is another traditional art form too often overlooked. Found everywhere—on train station platforms, next door to movie houses, down the street or around the corner in everybody's neighborhood—*soba* can range in flavor from dishwater to delicacy. Connoisseurs in Kyoto frequent the two or three old *soba* shops that have survived several generations of discriminating customers by serving the finest handmade buckwheat noodles in homemade broth.

Kawamichi-ya is one of the best. Not far from the center of town, they serve a wide variety of noodle dishes in a shop that is as wonderful as the menu (which is available in English). It is difficult to tell whether Kawamichi-ya is in a garden or vice versa. The long, narrow Kyoto-style building has three gardens: a front garden with a beautiful plum tree that drapes its blossom-laden branches over the gateway in spring, a central courtyard garden with tables, and a lovely garden that surrounds the small, open-air room at the back, all to assure that you are surrounded by greenery in any season. Light streams in through the windows to catch the sheen of polished wood in the interior—a hanging scroll depicts a crow huddled on a snowy branch in midwinter, a flower arrangement of graceful pampas grass heralds early fall, or a tiny porcelain wind chime catches the slightest breeze on a sultry August afternoon.

The tradition of *soba* noodles in Japan dates back to the early seventeenth century, and Kawamichi-ya traces its own history to a time some three hundred years ago when they provided noodles for pilgrims climbing Mt. Hiei to pray at Enryaku-ji, the

great Tendai Buddhist temple at the top. Every year on May 16, the birthday of Emperor Kanmu, who founded the city of Kyoto, the people at Kawamichi-ya set up stalls on top of the holy mountain, serving *soba* to faithful worshippers who scale the steep slopes to attend memorial services. The emperor Kanmu apparently gave aid to the ancestors of the Kawamichi-ya family way back in the ninth century (just what he did has become obscured over the ages), but even in the twentieth century their descendants have not forgotten to thank him each year with this special service in his memory.

In the old days, Kawamichi-ya was strictly a takeout shop, as most noodle shops were. Noodles were something to be cooked (or at least eaten) at home, so Kawamichi-ya's bicycling delivery boys have been practicing their backstreet noodle-juggling routines for as long as there have been bicycles in Kyoto.

The full name of the shop is Misoka-an Kawamichi-ya. Misoka refers to a long-neglected custom of eating noodles for good luck on the last day of every month. There is still a custom of eating noodles called *toshi-koshi-soba* on the last day of the year, and every New Year's Eve at midnight, the shop is full of well-wishers slurping out the old, while listening for the temple bells to ring in the new.

The specialty at Kawamichi-ya is a one-pot noodle dish called *hōkōro*, prepared at your table in a interesting metal pot that more than one customer has coveted.

Kawamichi-ya also makes cookies out of the buckwheat flour for which they are famous. During the Meiji period when Western confectionery

(along with weapons and machinery) enjoyed a vogue all over Japan, Kawamichi-ya fell upon a great Portuguese recipe for cookies, which they later named *bōro*. Though the famed old Kyoto shop makes them in the shape of plum blossoms, the word *bōro* is thought to come from the Portuguese *bola*, meaning ball. The cookie shop, built in the late Edo period, is located around the corner from the noodle shop.

Just inside the rope curtains that separate the kitchen from the cookie shop you'll find another of the secrets to Kawamichi-ya's long success—a row of round-bellied grinning Hotei, the guardian deity of traditional Kyoto kitchens. Though only a few of the set of fifteen are on display above the old cookstove, the remainder may now be seen across the street in a niche on the wall of the new garage to which they have recently been relegated. Perhaps they'll learn to adapt to their new (if less glamorous) role of guarding delivery trucks.

TSUKIMOCHI-YA NAOMASA
Kyoto confectionery

Sanjō-agaru 8 Ken-me, Kiyamachi-dōri, Nakagyō-ku
中京区木屋町通三条上ル八軒目 ☎(075) 231-0175
OPEN: 9 A.M.–8:30 P.M. ■ CLOSED: Thursdays (or Friday, if Thursday is a holiday)

The moon may be made of green cheese in the West, but in Japan it's just a lunar bean cake. "Tsukimochi" means "moon cake," and the flavor too is extraterrestrial. Whether the shop took its name from the small baked bean cakes or vice versa is a question that the years have obscured, for when the first toasted cake was baked on this site five generations ago, neither family nor bean cake had a name. In fact, commoners in Japan were not allowed to have family names until after 1868 when the Tokugawa shogunate was ousted and the rigid feudal class system was officially denounced. People were often known by what they made. Although the family name is now Kimura, Tsukimochi-ya Naomasa, the shop's formal name, once meant Naomasa, the moon-cake baker. It is said that Naomasa invented the type of cake from which he and his shop once took their name. Rather than simply steaming his cakes like ordinary *manjū*, Naomasa decided to try placing them in a small clay oven just long enough to give them a light,

golden crust. The resulting bean cakes, known as *geppei* (or *tsukimochi*), are as tempting to the Western palate as to the Japanese. Another baked specialty of the house, *yaki-guri geppei*, has a chestnut in the center of a *koshian* filling with the same light crust. A set of five of each kind (the *hitokuchi*, or bite-sized ones, are best) makes a mouthwatering souvenir, but should be eaten within a week as no preservatives are added.

Wa-gashi, the general term for Japanese sweets, refers to a wide variety of confectionery that includes *nama-gashi* (jellies, pastes, and doughs), *han-nama-gashi* (steamed, paste-filled buns), *yaki-gashi* (lightly baked cakes, like *tsukimochi*), and *higashi* (sugary wafers). The main ingredients used in all *wa-gashi* are sweet potatoes, chestnuts, red and white beans, brown or white sugar, and rice (or wheat) flour. No animal products (butter, lard, milk) or chocolate are used, and *wa-gashi* are seldom served as dessert after a meal. They are snacks to accompany a cup of green tea when guests drop by, or with *mat-cha*, the thick powdered tea of the tea ceremony. Sweets are occasionally served before a meal—as appetizers—rather than after dinner when fruit is considered the appropriate finishing touch.

Tsukimochi-ya uses two special kinds of sugar in the making of their sweets: Okinawan brown sugar (*kurozatō*), said to be the best, and a specially processed cane sugar (*wasanbon*) from Shikoku. Their "moon cakes" have a *koshi-an* (pureed sweet bean) filling and a thin egg and flour crust.

Tsukimochi-ya also offers a selection of *nama-gashi* in a variety of colors and shapes and with poetic names that elicit spring, winter, summer, and fall. *Nama-gashi* decorate the windows at Tsukimochi-ya in turn—delicate doughy peaches, flaky white snowballs, or maple leaves tinted yellow and crimson. *Nama-gashi* can be purchased individually, and should be eaten the same day, perhaps with the cup of green tea that awaits you at your inn.

The shop, as well as the delicate

sweets presented, possesses an air of miniature perfection. Delicate sweets it fashions. Soft light from a Meiji-period glass lamp glows through the stained glass "moonscape" border on the front window that was a decorative touch added around the turn of the century by Kimura's flamboyant great-grandfather. Apart from the display of seasonal specialties, there is always a different *mame* (or "bean-sized") bonsai placed discreetly in the window. The cultivation of miniature plants in small containers is a little-known art form, but one at which Hironao Kimura, the present owner, is a respected local master. Kimura-san braved city hall for years to preserve his old shop in its original condition until official fire regulations necessitated the change from a wood-burning oven to gas. But all the intricate bamboo work and old wooden pantries belong to an era gone by. You can still sit on a low bamboo bench inside and watch through the shop curtain as the owner's mother, now in her eighties, rolls out the sweet cakes you have just ordered one by one.

Note the original *kanban* shop sign that hangs inside on the north wall. It had hung outside until World War II, when rumors that Kyoto was the next city to be bombed forced Tsukimochi-ya to bring their old treasure indoors. A small painting showing business as it was in 1804, when Geppei first started, hangs above the kitchen window—two ladies in kimono side by side making bean cakes while the baker slides another paddle-full into the glowing oven. Not much different from today, really.

NAITŌ brooms

内
藤

Sanjō-ōhashi Nishi-zume, Nakagyō-ku
中京区三条大橋西詰　☎ (075) 221-3018
OPEN: Daily, 8 A.M.–8 P.M.

Anna otoko wa hōki de haku hodo aru (That kind of man is as plentiful as broom sweepings; i.e., Men like him are a dime a dozen)

A good broom (just like a good man) is getting harder and harder to find these days, and usually costs a good deal more than a dime a dozen. But one shop in Kyoto still has the real thing. Across the Sanjō Bridge from Keihan Sanjō Station on the north side of the street, the Naitō family has been dealing in handmade brooms and brushes for over one hundred years.

The shop was built in 1869 and is typical of Kyoto merchant shops dealing in practical items for everyday use. Open to the street, their wares are displayed hanging from walls and rafters, with a raised tatami mat area in one corner at the back where the proprietress sits chatting with customers over a cup of tea, helping them choose "the right tool for the right job." Unlike many similar shopkeepers whose businesses now face a crowded modern thoroughfare, Naitō-san has never found it necessary to enclose her shop in metal-frame sliding glass doors. It remains as it always has

been—a part of the bustling activity of Sanjō-dōri just outside. Naitō-san insists that her old shop will hold its own until she herself leaves this world behind. She remembers a time when the shop sold dozens of brooms a day. Now only a shadow of the former selection hangs from hooks along its precious old walls. When her husband Rikimatsu Naitō, a fifth-generation broom maker, passed away seven years ago, no one was left to carry on the family trade, a difficult and time-consuming process that requires strong muscles and calloused hands. Now the shop sells brooms made by his former apprentices and friends, who are among the last remaining traditional broom makers in Kyoto. According to Naitō-san, when these men pass on, their trade dies with them. The advent of the vacuum cleaner and the rising popularity of carpet over tatami mats in Japan have left few people who appreciate the value of a hand-tied hemp palm *shuro-bōki* broom these days.

Soft enough to sweep tatami, *shuro-bōki* come in a variety of sizes made to fit the job (as well as the sweeper). There is a broom or brush for everything: one for cleaning your *hanko* (seal), another for ashtrays, one for the corners of desk drawers, toilet bowls, the collars of shirts, rusty iron kettles, the wooden frames of *shōji* windows, or simply for brushing the crumbs off your kitchen table. The palm fibers used in making them must be brought in from outlying prefectures where they are grown. Their soft bristles are designed especially for sweeping tatami mats, and though they are more expensive than mass-produced brooms, they last a good twenty years and are a particular favorite in Kyoto, where housewives are notoriously meticulous.

The other kind of broom featured at Naito's is the *kibi-bōki* (millet-stalk broom). These are the stiffer green brooms for sweeping hardwood floors and rugs, resembling their Western counterparts more than the soft-bristl-ed *shuro-bōki*. *Kibi-bōki* last only three to five years and are less expensive than *shuro*, but are hand-tied with colorfully dyed cord, making them quite unexpectedly an art all their own.

In the display boxes at the front of the shop there are specialty brushes for Yūzen fabric dying that are made of animal hair. There is also an assortment of wonderful body brushes made of either *shuro* or horsehair, to which many of the elderly residents of Kyoto attribute their longstanding good health.

The largest broom in the shop hangs in a dark corner at the back and is Naitō-san's most valued keepsake from days gone by. It was made by her great-great-grandfather a hundred years ago and has taken on a deep brown patina and a lot of character. Although it's been grasped by a thousand hands and swept as many floors, it still looks like new. The bristles of a handmade *shuro-bōki* never fall out; they just gradually wear down. It is unfortunate that the *shuro-bōki*, as well as Naitō-san's beautiful shop, are on the endangered species list in the world of Kyoto crafts.

FUNAHASHI-YA
rice crackers

舩はしや

Sanjō-ōhashi Nishi-zume, Nakagyō-ku
中京区三条大橋西詰　☎(075) 221–2673
OPEN: Daily, 9 A.M.–9 P.M. ■ CREDIT: JCB, VISA

When Yasuyuki Tsuji was eight years old, he could stand outside his grandfather's shop and listen to the *karankoron* of wooden *geta* across the old bridge at Sanjō. But wooden footgear is no longer in fashion, and when the giant wooden planks of the Sanjō Bridge could no longer bear the weight of modern traffic, it was replaced with reinforced concrete.

Established in 1885, Funahashi-ya still stands on its original site beside the bridge on the west bank of the Kamo River. Funahashi-ya was named after the long, wooden flatboats that plied the river for centuries, carrying loads of charcoal and cotton back and forth to Osaka in the south.

Funahashi-ya has long been a landmark for tourists returning home via the Sanjō-Keihan train on the east bank of the river. It is an inevitable last stop to pick up a souvenir of Kyoto for family and friends: a sampler of Funahashi-ya's rice crackers carefully packaged in handmade paper or wooden boxes.

Rice crackers are known as *o-kaki* in

Kyoto dialect (they are called *arare* or *senbei* in other regions). Originally, they were a midday snack for farmers working in the fields. Crisp, flavored with soy sauce or sesame or wrapped in a sheet of dried seaweed, the rice crackers at Funahashi-ya are baked fresh locally. Over fifty varieties are available, including several exotic flavors such as curry, chili pepper, and *wasabi* (the green horseradish paste for sushi). Tsuji-san's suggestion for health-conscious customers are the *daizu*, or dried soybeans—roasted, salted, battered, or plain.

Despite the gleaming rows of cracker jars that first catch one's eye at Funahashi-ya, their real specialty is a confection called *go-shiki-mame*. These "five-colored beans" have been a popular Kyoto treat for over five hundred years. With a flavor for every color (plum pink, citrus yellow, cinnamon brown, seaweed green, and the elusive "snow" white), these bite-size sweets are actually dried green peas in a naturally flavored sugar coating. Samples are available for the skeptic, and Tsuji-san guarantees their freshness since he makes them himself from the original family recipe.

The shop is open to the street in typical Kyoto style. The fact that theft has never been a problem may reflect either the ethics of traditional Japanese society in general or the vigilance of Shōki, the guardian figure whose clay likeness can be seen on the lookout for trouble in his perch above the first floor eaves. Though the kitchen has been modernized and the lighting improved, Tsuji-san has kept the fine wood, bamboo, and tile details of the interior, making Funahashi-ya an excellent example of how an old Kyoto shop can be adapted to fit modern times without giving up its traditional beauty. Notice the old wooden *kanban*, or signboard, hanging on the back wall of the shop. It once hung outdoors on Sanjō Street, until the threat of bombing during World War II prompted the owner to bring his hand-carved zelkova wood treasure indoors, as did many of the merchants in Kyoto at the time.

Funahashi-ya, like most old Kyoto shops, has living quarters upstairs and to the rear of the kitchen. The wooden-slatted *kōshi* that cover the windows on the second floor are also typically Kyoto, a means of providing privacy in a crowded city where houses and shops were built right on the street.

Early every morning, the Tsujis can be seen in front of Funahashi-ya sweeping the sidewalks and splashing them with water in another of Kyoto's traditions. Not only does the water keep the dust away from the open shop front, but it serves as a symbol of welcome to the day's first customers.

NISHIMURA
woodblock prints

Teramachi-kado, Sanjō-dōri, Nakagyō-ku
中京区三条通寺町角　☎(075) 211–2849 (English spoken)
OPEN: Daily, 1 P.M.–9 P.M.

Ukiyo-e—images of the floating world, the mundane, mortal world that slips from our hands and leaves us with only the memory of squandered fortunes and ill-spent youth. Beautiful winsome women, the light of neglected oil lamps flickering out at daybreak, the painted flowers of a priceless silk kimono lying in disarray on the floor where it was flung in a moment of careless passion—the excesses of a world that no longer exists—except in *ukiyo-e*, the woodblock prints which depict life in the entertainment quarters of Edo-period Japan.

Nishimura is the oldest shop in Kyoto dealing exclusively in antique woodblock prints. It has stood for sixty-five years on the corner of Teramachi and Sanjō (once the hub of downtown activity), silently watching the transformation that has left it and one or two of its old neighbors amid a circus of new souvenir shops and glittering *pachinko* parlors.

Nishimura-san believes in doing business in the old style. He has no random piles of prints stacked here and there on glass showcases, just one small tatami-mat room, with a single scroll hanging in the alcove, and a cup of tea and courtesy waiting for every customer. His carefully selected collection of antique *ukiyo-e* prints is tucked neatly away in lacquered boxes and old cabinet drawers waiting to be unveiled, one by one, at the customer's request.

Although this style of business was intended for the buyer who knows what to ask for, Nishimura-san is happy to bring out dozens of prints for any novice who shows a real interest in this fascinating art form. You can ask to see prints by specific artists: Hiroshige, Utamaro, Kuniyoshi, Hokusai, Sharaku, and others. Or you may ask to see those of a particular genre: *bijin-ga*, portraits of beautiful women; *yakusha-e*, portraits of kabuki actors; or *fūzoku-ga*, prints depicting the scenery or way of life in the city.

In vogue recently among collectors are the *Yokohama-e* prints done around 1860 focusing on foreigners, Western ships, and fashions in

Yokohama after the port was opened for trade by Admiral Perry in 1854. The most popular artist in this genre is Taisō Yoshitoshi.

There are several different types of prints, one developing out of another over a period of about two hundred years (ca. 1680–1850). The oldest kind are the *sumizuri-e* (Nishimura-san's personal favorite), printed simply in black ink. Next are the *tessaishiki*, or hand-colored prints in which the red *tan-e* or red and yellow *beni-e* colors were applied to the prints with a brush. *Urushi-e* refers to the kind of prints in which details are colored with a shiny black ink that gives objects like hats the look of real lacquer. *Benizuri-e* are prints in which three to six colors are printed, rather than painted, and *nishiki-e*, or "brocade" prints, are elaborately printed in six or more colors.

Nishimura-san says that the value of a *mokuhan-ga*, or woodblock print, is determined by the artist's name, the era in which it was printed, the beauty of the composition, the quality of the printing impression, and the state of preservation. He doesn't sell anything for less than ¥5,000. Prints available elsewhere for less generally tend to be in poor condition or merely copies of an original. He sells no print that cannot be identified as to age and artist, and every print is tagged with this basic information in Japanese and English, as many of his regular buyers are collectors from abroad.

His advice on the care and display of *ukiyo-e* is simply to keep them out of direct sunlight because ultraviolet rays cause color changes, particularly in the green hues. Hang your print for no more than three months out of the year, but don't store it too long without airing it for a few days in a dry place. Dry climates are better than wet for the preservation of woodblock prints, which are highly sensitive to humidity. The best *ukiyo-e* are sought after not only by art collectors, but by rodents and insects who devour them with unparalleled zeal. It's best to store them with ordinary mothballs in a pest-free location.

Nishimura-san has no plans to modernize his shop in the future, beyond making structural repairs when necessary. He tried carpeting the tatami and moving in a desk after his father retired some years ago. But, sliding out an elegant lacquered tray with a fresh cup of tea, he says, "In the end, I decided tatami was the best place to spread out my prints and chat with customers. Besides, nothing pleases me more than talking with a middle-aged lady on a trip to Kyoto from the countryside who stops in to tell me how happy she is to find my shop just as she remembered it thirty years ago on a school excursion to Kyoto."

C15

MIYAWAKI BAISEN-AN
fans

宮脇売扇庵

Tominokōji Nishi-iru, Rokkaku-dōri, Nakagyō-ku
中京区六角通富小路西入 ☎ (075) 221–0181
OPEN: 9 A.M.–5 P.M. ■ CLOSED: Periodically ■ CREDIT: AE, JCB, UC, VISA

Art has surely sounded its lowest depths when it comes to portraying a lager-beer bottle on one side of a fan, and to providing a railway timetable on the other.

—B.H. Chamberlain (1904)

Since the turn of the century, Westerners have been upbraiding the Japanese for busying themselves with modernization while age-old traditions die at their feet. Chamberlain missed out on the real tragedy; television commercials do all the advertising these days and fans are no longer needed at all. Once commonplace in Kyoto, the old round *uchiwa* fans now appear only during festivals or as wall decorations for those who delight in nostalgia.

Miyawaki has been making beautiful fans since 1823 and, fortunately for Kyoto, still believes in the reason they exist. Fans in Kyoto are important, not only as a means of fighting off the summer heat, but as eloquent accessories a lady should not be without. For the most part, the Japanese have no tradition of wearing jewelry. The earrings, brooches, pendants, bracelets, and rings that adorn beauties in the Western world are not acceptable accessories for the simple lines of the kimono. Apart from elaborate hair ornaments worn by geisha, a Japanese woman's most eloquent accessory has always been a hand-painted, delicately scented folding fan.

Although many of the arts now associated with Japan actually originated in China, the *sensu*, or folding fan, is said to have been an invention of the Japanese. (The Japanese even accused the Chinese of pirating technological secrets when they adopted the *sensu* in the fourteenth century.) Legend tells of a beautiful young woman who entered a nunnery after the unfortunate death of her warrior husband not long after their marriage. Once when the abbot of the temple fell sick, she made a fan of folded paper to ease his fever. A folding-cypress fan called a *hi-ōgi* dated 877 found inside a statue of Kannon at Tō-ji temple is considered to be the oldest in Japan. There are many references to fans belonging to members of the imperial court during the Heian period, and by the end of the period even the common people were using them. Painted wooden fans, scented sandalwood fans, lacquered fans with decorations in gold and silver, dyed silk fans, and paper fans all belong to one of Kyoto's oldest traditional crafts.

Miyawaki has fans of every description, each with its own special name: *Rikyū ōgi*, tea ceremony fans named after the famous sixteenth-century tea master Sen no Rikyū; *hi-ōgi*, or court fans; *mai-ōgi*, fans used in traditional dance; *uchiwa*, the stiff, flat fan which originated in China; *chūkei*, used in the Nō theater; and ordinary *sensu* carried by both men and women to add a touch of class (and a cooling breeze) to a formal kimono ensemble.

Every famous Japanese painter has decorated at least one fan in his time, making this one example of a Japanese craft that overlaps the world of fine art. The ceiling of Miyawaki is covered with forty-eight paintings by master artists, such as Tessai Tomioka and Takeuchi Seiho, which were commissioned by the Miyawaki family in 1903. (Look for the tiger fan by Takeuchi and the orchid and rock fan by Tessai.)

The building that houses the fan shop is a treasure among the old shops of Kyoto. The Miyawakis have maintained their hundred-year-old building, adding modern lighting and the comfort of air conditioning without marring the old elegance of its style. The *batari shōgi* bench in front folds down each day when the shop opens for business to give customers a place to rest, and folds back up each evening to become a part of the storm shutters that protect the building against the elements. The deep eaves and the dark *noren* curtains that bear the shop's name hide the gilded fans from the damaging rays of the sun. The *mushiko mado* windows, said to resemble a Japanese insect cage (hence the name), were ostensibly a means of ventilation, though this leads to the question of why such a restricted view was allotted to those on the second floor. One theory says that it was against the law for members of the lower classes to have their heads higher than their superiors, so these narrow slats provided a glimpse of royalty from above without being seen from below. The clever merchants always had their ways of getting around the most absurd of laws.

Miyawaki Baisen-an gives hope to those, like Chamberlain, who'd like to see the best elements of the past survive. There is not a lager-beer advertisement or a train schedule in the place.

YAMATO MINGEI-TEN folk art

Takoyakushi-agaru, Kawaramachi, Nakagyō-ku
中京区河原町蛸薬師上ル ☎(075) 221-2641

OPEN: 10 A.M.–8:30 P.M. ■ CLOSED: Fridays ■ CREDIT: AE, JCB, UC, VISA

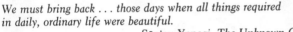

*We must bring back . . . those days when all things required
in daily, ordinary life were beautiful.*
        —Sōetsu Yanagi, *The Unknown Craftsman*

With these thoughts one of the leaders of the Mingei, or Folk Art, Movement noted the loss of appreciation for naturally made, simple objects—brooms and baskets, bowls, buckets, and ladles—that were once commonplace in Japan. Yanagi, a philosopher and critic, Kawai Kanjirō, Hamada Shōji, Bernard Leach, and a handful of others in the 1920s attempted to save what was left of Japan's unpretentious country craftsmen by calling attention to their plight in a rapidly industrializing society which at the time was infatuated with the West.

The founders of the Mingei Movement were not interested in the individual artist-craftsmen who produced a limited number of precious objects that were more decorative than functional in purpose. These "art pieces" were affected and self-conscious, they believed, lacking the rustic beauty of unsigned works produced in rural villages across Japan.

The members of the movement set about collecting the everyday objects they so much admired, making trips as far away as Korea and Okinawa to remote areas as yet unaffected by modernization. The objects they gathered are now kept in the Tokyo Folkcraft Museum in Komaba which Yanagi and his friends founded in 1936. They hoped to preserve a wide selection of fine folk crafts for future craftsmen to use as inspiration long after their tiny villages had joined the ranks of concrete and stucco.

But the craftsmen themselves were in need of help that no museum could offer. As the population turned its back on folk crafts as crude and old-fashioned, the livelihood of the country craftsmen declined until many were forced to seek other employment, to use synthetic materials and mass production techniques, or starve.

Shortly after World War II, a man named Yaei Hayashi, at the suggestion

Kurodani, lacquered bowls from Wajima, baskets from Miyajima, blown glass from Okinawa, Nanbu teakettles from Iwate—all are made with traditional techniques and materials and tagged with the name of the area from which they came. In keeping with Yanagi's views that *mingei* objects should also be affordable, the prices at Yamato Mingei are reasonable, especially when considering the value of handmade objects in modern times.

The main shop faces Kawaramachi-dōri and sells a wide variety of smaller items; the branch shop on the alley south of Maruzen has larger objects—furniture from Tottori and hand-hewn stone basins and lanterns from the Kita-Shirakawa district in northeastern Kyoto. The branch shop also holds exhibitions which feature the works of different craftsmen or from different crafts villages each month, including occasional exhibitions of folk crafts from around the world.

of friends in the Mingei Movement, came to the aid of the folk craftsmen of Japan by opening a shop in the middle of Kyoto that sold nothing but folk crafts from all over Japan. Almost forty years later Yamato Mingei Ten on Kawaramachi-dōri (next to Maruzen Bookstore) still sells the finest in folk crafts gathered from village craftsmen from Hokkaido to Okinawa.

The highly refined crafts produced in Kyoto itself have never been considered "folk," but many of the villages in the surrounding area (still within Kyoto Prefecture), such as Kurodani where paper is made, number among the finest of the crafts villages in Japan.

The selection is always changing and every month different crafts from different areas are featured among the stacks of ceramics, glassware, lacquerware, basketry, and textiles in their impressive stock. Handmade Japanese paper (*te-suki washi*) from Echizen or

KINMATA
inn (ryokan), restaurant

407 Shijō-agaru, Gokomachi, Nakagyō-ku
中京区御幸町四条上ル407　☎ (075) 221-1039 (English spoken)

CHECK-IN: 4 P.M. ■ CHECK-OUT: 10 A.M. ■ RATES: ¥6,000 (room only), ¥8,500 (w/breakfast), from ¥15,000 (w/2 meals) (reservations required) ■ RESTAURANT OPEN: 11:30 A.M.–2 P.M. (last seating), 5:30 P.M.–7 P.M. (last seating) (reservations required at least one day in advance) ■ PRICES: Mini-*kaiseki* lunch from ¥6,000, *kaiseki* dinner from ¥10,000

No gambling.
No prostitution.
No mahjong.
No credit.
No noisy parties. . . .

So begins the long list of house rules that have hung in the hallway at Kinmata since the nineteenth century. No arbitrary mandate from the innkeeper, these were the rules of the day for all Japanese inns by order of the Tokugawa shogunate, whose rigid reign prescribed the daily life of citizens down to the finest detail for over two hundred years.

Seven generations later, Ukai-san, the young innkeeper at Kinmata, has admittedly relaxed some of the old rules, but the order for peace and quiet is still strictly enforced. Located in the very heart of the downtown area, the interior recesses of the inn are surprisingly removed from the noise of the city.

In 1801, the year Kinmata opened for business, their most frequent guests were traveling salesmen bring-ing herbal medicines to Kyoto from Ōmi and Shiga near Lake Biwa to the east of the former capital. A few old medicine peddler *kanban*, or signboards, are kept in the entryway as mementos of the inn's first customers.

The meals at the family-run Kinmata are planned and prepared by the innkeeper himself, who worked for a time at a fishmonger's shop in the Nishiki street market just half a block away. Nishikikōji is where the most famous of Kyoto's restaurateurs shop for the ingredients of their elegant *kaiseki* cuisine. This proximity gives the young Ukai-san an inside lead on the finest of the day's catch, and the seafood meals prepared at Kinmata have become as popular as the unchanged traditional beauty of the inn itself.

Ukai-san has kept the original furnishings and decor of this old-style *ryokan*, despite the trend toward modern trappings among other Japanese inns. Fine lacquered lanterns and mirrored dressing stands, curved cedar handrails, and two bamboo-fenced interior gardens contribute to the atmosphere of traditional Japanese hospitality. Kinmata has only nine rooms in all and welcomes anyone who appreciates the intimate at-

mosphere and gracious amenities of an old-style Japanese inn.

Kinmata does have modern air conditioning, and one room has private bath facilities. The large communal bath (*o-furo*) downstairs was recently redone in solid *hinoki* cypress wood with its own tiny window-box garden, offering the classical Japanese "soak" that is said to relieve all the tension and stress a medicine peddler—or a modern traveler—can accumulate in a hectic day.

JŪSAN-YA combs

Otabi-chō, Shinkyōgoku Higashi-iru, Shijō-dōri, Shimogyō-ku

下京区四条通新京極東入御旅町　☎(075) 221-2008 (English spoken)

OPEN: Daily, 10 A.M.–9 P.M. ■ CREDIT: DC, JCB, MIC, VISA

A simple comb can be a work of art, when you consider that the man who sits on the floor before his workbench day after day filing each tooth by hand has lived in a world full of plastic since his birth. Pocket combs are disposable items in a plastic world, and who takes the time or trouble to fuss with a hand-made wooden comb that could easily be lost and just as easily replaced with celluloid for a fraction of the price?

Michikazu Takeuchi does—and has for sixty years. He is a fifth-generation maker of boxwood combs (*tsuge-kushi*). He says it takes over forty years to make a proper comb, giving thirty years of credit to the boxwood tree itself. After the tree is felled, another ten years are required for the drying process. The wood is cut into wedges and fumigated with smoke from its own sawdust to ensure that each comb will be durable and strong. After this process is completed, each wedge is planed by hand and ready to be sawed into teeth. Takeuchi-san uses only old-fashioned Japanese planes, saws, and files. One item you might expect to find in his toolbox is a ruler for measuring and marking the location of each tiny tooth. He doesn't have one; a steady hand and practiced eye are the only instruments he uses to space them. This process requires concentration. Takeuchi-san used to do all the work in his shop on Shijō Street, but now does all the exacting parts at his home in Yamashina, a quiet suburb east of Kyoto. He opened the present shop in 1930 at a time when the neighborhood still kept a slower pace. Before then the shop was located to the southwest, where his great-great-grandfather opened it in 1868.

The fine finishing process is what makes the boxwood combs worth the few extra yen they cost. Each tooth is polished with sharkskin, then with dried *tokusa* (a hollow reed with a coarse texture), and finally buffed to a golden sheen with a soft deerskin cloth. No one can convince Takeuchi-san that sandpaper and an electric buffer produce a finer finish than techniques like these that have been used in Japan since the tenth century.

The simplest boxwood combs Takeuchi-san makes bear only his family crest engraved on the side, but there are several more decorative styles carved with plum blossom, bamboo, and other traditional designs. Takeuchi-san also sells *kanzashi*, the ornamental hairpins worn with formal kimono. Especially beautiful are the long, slender hair ornaments in the shape of a gingko leaf which come in both boxwood and cherry. Apart from the natural-finish *kanzashi*, Jūsan-ya has a selection of lacquered combs done by Takeuchi-san himself, unusual in Kyoto where most craftsmen specialize in only one technique.

In the old days every bride received an elaborate set of boxwood combs as a necessary part of her trousseau. They were used to dress the exotic hairstyles called *marumage* worn by married women up until World War II. Today only geisha and kabuki actors require comb sets like these, but Jūsan-ya has a full display of them in a glass case at the back of the shop.

Aside from the appreciation he has for the traditional methods of making combs for everyday use, there is another reason why Takeuchi-san maintains a craft that most people consider outdated. It has been his family's responsibility for generations to make the set of ninety-one combs that is offered in a special ceremony every twenty years to the goddess Amaterasu at Ise Shrine, the center of Shintoism in Japan. At this time, the main buildings at Ise Shrine and all the treasures contained therein are destroyed in a ritual fire of purification. Fortunately, there are twenty years between fires, because that is how long it takes the Takeuchis to make the exquisite set. How does it feel to devote two decades to the making of a perfect set of combs that you know are destined for destruction? "It's wonderful," says Takeuchi-san. "The greatest honor of my life."

At Jūsan-ya, plain boxwood hair combs start at ¥1,200, depending on the fineness of the teeth. One small comb in the display case, seemingly no different from all the rest, has a price tag of ¥40,000. When asked why it was so expensive and if it was made of something special, Takeuchi-san replied, with half a smile, "Special? Yes, it's made of love. That's the last comb my late father ever made."

TAKASEBUNE
tempura

188 Sendō-chō, Shijō-sagaru, Shimogyō-ku
下京区四条下ル船頭町188　☎(075) 351–4032

OPEN: 11 A.M.–10 P.M. ▪ CLOSED: Mondays ▪ PRICES: ¥500–¥3,000

Today the Kamo River runs calmly through the middle of Kyoto like a reliable old friend, but in its youth the river definitely had a mean streak. In the old days it stormed through town, drowning citizens and destroying homes and shops with a vengeance, always unexpected, always devastating. Floods followed by plagues, droughts followed by famines—the Kamogawa river was incorrigible. But the city always forgave it, like a helpless parent does an intractable child, until one day in the early seventeenth century when a wealthy merchant named Suminokura Ryōi decided to teach the spoiled child a lesson. Ryōi ran a shipping trade to ports in Southeast Asia (a daring venture in its day) and wasn't about to let one ruffian river stand in his way. With permission from the shogun, he dug a canal that drained the river of its wild juices and enabled his boatmen to carry their loads to Fushimi and on to the port city of Osaka in the south without further harassment.

The Takasegawa river runs along the western edge of the Kamo River all the way to Fushimi, where it joins the Yodo River six miles to the south. Until the late nineteenth century, boatmen plied their long flatboats up and down the canal carrying firewood, charcoal, rice, salt, and prisoners off to exile. The area between Nijō and Gojō on the canal is known as Kiyamachi, a name derived from the many charcoal and firewood merchants whose shops provided a somber backdrop for the old canal. At present the canal is the heartline of a glittery entertainment district filled with restaurants, bars, and hostess clubs.

When modern transportation came to Kyoto in the form of streetcars and trains around the turn of the century, the backbreaking job of boatmen on the Takasegawa Canal became obsolete. The system of carrying merchandise downstream was not such an arduous task, but the boatmen had to drag the heavy barges back up the river using poles and ropes which were manipulated from the banks of the canal.

When Shōtarō Okajima opened his restaurant on the west bank of the canal thirty years ago, he named it Takasebune after the flatboats his father once pulled up that same river. Takasebune is a small family place that has become famous for its *tempura teishoku*, a table d'hôte tempura dinner which includes a generous bowl of *miso* soup, rice, and pickles, along with a basket of crisply fried tempura shrimp, fish, and vegetables. The amazing thing about Takasebune's tempura meal is that it is delicious and inexpensive at the same time. Served only at lunch time, it costs only ¥500, and there is no place in Kyoto that serves a better tempura meal for twice the price.

Takasebune actually specializes in a variety of fine fish dishes with a new menu penned each night by Okajima-san himself. He is a handsome gentleman with a full head of snow-white hair and an endearing gruffness that adds flair to the way he fries his fish. He and his soft-spoken son will seat you at the counter where you can watch all the activity (though private tatami rooms are available upstairs

and in the back). The fish they serve comes from Torizane, a bit farther north in Kiyamachi, the best fish market in Kyoto, according to the Okajimas. They should know. Before they opened the restaurant, they were fishmongers themselves in a small shop on the same site which was run by the grandfather after he retired from his job as a Takasegawa boatman (an old photograph of him and his boat hangs just inside the entrance). They decided to offer the local people a decent midday meal of tempura at a reasonable price. That's the spirit of Takasebune; even the deluxe full-course dinners served in the evening are not geared to earn them a fortune. Apart from the counter, there are two rooms upstairs that seat up to twelve people, and two small rooms downstairs in the back of the tiny restaurant.

The shop is on an alley east of Hankyū Department Store and can be identified by the boat oar that leans against the side of the building out front (prompting foreign residents to nickname the place "The Oar").

Notice the short curtain that hangs above the counter. It says, "Came down the river through Kyoto on a boat, just me and the cows." The haiku poet Akamatsu Ryūshi wrote the message—a pun about the owner, Shōtarō Okajima, having been born in the year of the cow. Somehow it sets the mood of the whole place.

NOTE: A replica of one of the original boats that plied the old river can be seen moored near the head of the canal where Kiyamachi meets Nijō-dōri.

MURAKAMI-JŪ
pickles

⊕村上重本店

Shijō-sagaru, Nishi-Kiyamachi-dōri, Shimogyō-ku
下京区西木屋町四条下ル ☎(075) 351–1737

OPEN: 9 A.M.– 7 P.M. ■ CLOSED: 1st & 3rd Wednesdays Jan.–Sept.

"Feed not autumn eggplant to your daughter-in-law."

Don't spoil your son's blushing bride with needless luxury . . . a spiteful old saying which (unlike the eggplant itself) is hardly worth preserving, except perhaps as a reminder of what was wrong with "the good old days."

The best locally grown vegetables picked at the height of the season have always been considered a delightful extravagance, especially in the form of Murakami's *tsukemono*, or pickles. Pickled eggplant is only one of over twenty varieties of *tsukemono* found at this 150-year-old shop. But pickles are not the only fine Kyoto tradition preserved here. Parting the dark-brown shop curtain which bears the cross-and-circle crest of Murakami-jū (the cross is also the character for the number ten, or *jū* in Japanese), you enter a spacious shop front with rough-hewn stone floors and two giant wooden pickle barrels brimming with the day's selection of fresh *tsukemono*. A set of small ceramic crocks on the counter contains samples from which

to choose—*senmai-zuke* in winter (paper-thin slices of white radish seasoned with red pepper and lightly sweetened with kelp), *nanohana-zuke* in spring (flowers from the rapeseed plant lightly pickled in rice vinegar), or *narazuke* in summer (a variety of vegetables salt-pickled and soaked in saké lees).

As basic to the Japanese diet as antipasto to the Italians, *tsukemono* was originally the primary source of nutrition in less prosperous times when a bowl of rice and a few pickled vegetables made up the entire meal for most Kyoto townsfolk.

The most often served pickle is called *takuan*, the crisp, round, deep-yellow slices that accompany the simplest meals in any family-style Japanese restaurant. *Takuan* is said to be a good digestive and the tale goes that no matter how much raw fish or how many bowls of white rice you eat, a few slices of *takuan* will pull you through. The origin of the name may have come from the sixteenth-century priest Takuan who devised this

method of pickling. On the contrary, some say the priest never touched a pickling barrel in his life, and that the name simply comes from the strange resemblance Takuan's tombstone bore to an ordinary pickling stone.

Though the making of *tsukemono* used to be a chore every housewife took for granted, *daikon* drying on rooftops is a sight only seen these days in the country. The process is not complicated, however, with *tsukemono* falling into two basic categories: *furu-zuke*, pickles fermented for a time in a rice-bran mash with salt, which can be kept longer, and *asa-zuke*, pickled in dry rice bran and salt, which must be eaten within a few days. Plain salt pickling (*shio-zuke*) and vinegar-pickling (*su-zuke*) are two other, simpler methods, but the rice bran gives the pickles a subtle depth of flavor the other methods lack. The advantage of *asa-zuke* is that no preservatives are added, though once they are opened, they only last two or three days. Murakami-jū has not succumbed to using artificial colors to entice supermarket housewives who tend to be attracted to the most eye-catching fluorescent pink *tsukemono* and who pay no attention to expiration dates on packages (forcing major food suppliers to load their products with preservatives). Hundreds of regular customers at Murakami-jū make the brief side trip necessary daily to buy *tsuke-mono* they know are made fresh on the premises, with the color, flavor, and fragrance of vegetables straight from the garden. Unlike the sharp tang of Western pickles, *tsukemono* retain the crisp, natural taste of the vegetable itself.

Apart from their regular customers, Murakami-jū draws visitors to Kyoto from all over Japan, who make a special stop on their sightseeing tours to buy a package of the famous Kyoto-style *tsukemono*. On a busy day, especially during one of the two gift-giving seasons (*o-chūgen* and *o-seibo*, in midsummer and midwinter), you may have to wait to be served. But the thoughtful cup of tea that appears and the exquisite floral spray that fills a giant ceramic urn in the center of the room help to pass the time painlessly. Mrs. Shigeko Murakami, the proprietress, is a noted *ikebana* artist in Kyoto. Some people drop by just to see her latest creation. Her son Tōru Murakami is now in charge of the shop. He is young, handsome, gentlemanly, believes in old-fashioned Kyoto hospitality and service, and spends much of his time coaching his youngest clerks in the proper way to sell a Kyoto pickle—graciously, honestly, and with style.

MORITA WAGAMI
handmade paper

森
田
和
紙

Bukkō-ji-agaru, Higashi-no-tōin-dōri, Shimogyō-ku
下京区東洞院通佛光寺上ル ☎ (075) 341–0123
OPEN: 9:30 A.M.–5:30 P.M. ■ CLOSED: 1st day of each month, Sundays, holidays

Writing is easy; all you do is sit staring at a blank sheet of paper
until the drops of blood form on your forehead.

—Gene Fowler

Blank sheets of paper have been frightening artists and writers for a very long time. The Chinese were the first to suffer the silent taunting of the empty page: they've been writing poetry on paper longer than the West has been numbering years. The Japanese had paper in production for over five hundred years before the Moors opened the first paper mill in Spain in the twelfth century. By the end of the Edo period in 1868, the Japanese had figured out a way to use it for everything: lanterns, doors, windows, fans, candy wrappers, love letters, government orders, umbrellas, and even raincoats. The Tokugawas wrote their daily edicts on it, and it was no doubt a simple paper plot that finally brought the shogunate down. Paper has been absorbing mankind's mistakes and schemes, ideas and feelings, images and dreams, for centuries. And nowhere more beautifully than in Japan.

Morita Wagami has a cure for nervous writers and artists everywhere—paper so peerless it's encouraging. They deal exclusively in handmade paper (*washi*), with a catalog of over eight hundred kinds from papermaking villages all over Japan.

Although there are regional variations, the three main materials used in Japanese papermaking are *kōzo*, *mitsumata*, and *ganpi*. *Kōzo*, or mulberry, is the heartiest, most common variety; *mitsumata*, a cultivated flowering shrub, produces a more delicate paper; and *ganpi*, stripped from plants in the wild, gives the highest quality and smoothest finish of the three.

Particular regions in Japan have become famous for the production of special kinds of paper. Eastern Fukui to the northeast of Kyoto is known for the finest white *hōsho*, used as official stationery by the imperial court during the Edo period. Kurodani, a small village within three hours of Kyoto to the northwest, produces a rustic paper with a quality Morita-san calls *"majime-sa"*—honesty or earnestness. Everyone in the village is related, and a local wedding often stops production until the festivities are over.

Morita Wagami has *washi* for formal Japanese *shodō* calligraphy, contemporary Nihonga painting, and *hanga* printmaking. They even have paper to accommodate the current trend among Japanese painters toward large-scale works: a single sheet five by five-and-a-half meters can run over ¥50,000. Though many calligraphers use the less expensive Chinese papers for practice (sometimes five hundred tries are needed to produce a single character suitable for mounting), Morita-san stresses that Japan produces the very best and most durable handmade paper in the world today, essential for professional artists who cannot afford to risk using paper that may yellow or crumble. He suggests that paper be stored for a year after purchase; like a fine burgundy, it will improve with age if kept in a dry place.

Morita's has a gift shop beside their paper warehouse where browsers will find a variety of paper products—from stationery, postcards, and notebooks to round *uchiwa* fans and miniature folding screens (*byōbu*). The catalog on the counter contains the full range of undecorated papers offered. The back rooms will take an hour to browse through, so take off your shoes and step up to two whole rooms of single-sheet paper in large, slatted drawers. These rooms hold the largest selection of decorated *chiyogami* paper in Kyoto. *Chiyogami*, or "long life," paper was originally used by the aristocracy to wrap gifts of congratulations. One less-than-certifiable tale has it that the name comes from Princess Chiyohime, whose obsession for brightly printed paper has apparently made a niche for her in Japanese folklore. It is certain, however, that *chiyogami* was one of many luxuries reserved for the nobility of feudal Japan.

During the eighteenth and nineteenth centuries, *chiyogami* was considered a precious gift or souvenir by people returning to their homes in the countryside from a trip to Kyoto or Edo (now Tokyo). It is interesting to compare *Kyō-chiyogami* (Kyoto style), with its reserved patterns and subdued colors, with the flamboyant designs and colors of *Edo-chiyogami*. The contrast between the restrained tastes of the people of the ancient capital and the riotous preferences of the townsfolk of Edo is apparent in matters as simple as package wrapping.

KUNGYOKU-DŌ
incense

Nishi Hongan-ji-mon-mae, Horikawa-dōri, Shimogyō-ku
下京区堀川通西本願寺門前　☎ (075) 371–0162 (English spoken)
OPEN: 9 A.M.–7 P.M. ■ CLOSED: 1st & 3rd Sundays

Life goes up in smoke: fleeting—gone before you know it, it rises, fades, and disappears. For those practicing Zen meditation, incense (*o-kō*) is a way to mark the passage of time, without the necessity of dividing it into minutes and seconds; the dying stick of incense defines an interval of silence. The composure of meditation, the moments that are "so quiet you can hear the powdered ash of incense fall ...," so the saying goes. Brought from China to Japan in the sixth century, it is still an important part of Buddhist ritual today.

As incense appeals to the senses, it also possesses age-old associations with the pursuit of pleasure. The wide range of scents developed over the centuries throughout the world appeal to the vulnerable human psyche with everything from the excitement of an aphrodisiac to the quieting effects of a midnight snowfall.

The enjoyment of incense in Japan has evolved into a refined and subtle art. Long before the tea ceremony came into practice, the nobles of the imperial court in Kyoto played a "parlor game" called *kō-awase*. It was a guessing game in which participants tried to name different scents lit one by one by the host. The rare imported aromatic woods and spices that were used in these games were expensive and difficult to obtain in the days of Genji, and it was not until much later in the Muromachi period that the game became formalized into a ritual called *kōdō* (the Way of Incense). Although *kōdō* is still practiced by a small group of followers, its popularity has declined steadily since the end of the Edo period.

Kungyoku-dō has dealt in fine woods, herbs, and spices for four hundred years. The owner, Yoshio Ōno, handles only the finest ingredients imported from Asia and the South Seas (including Java, Sumatra, and India), as none of the raw materials are indigenous to Japan. Ōno-san explains that incense used for personal enjoyment today can be divided into those derived from aromatic woods, those derived from herbs and spices, and

those derived from flowers. Perhaps the most intriguing of these types are the aromatic woods. Sandalwood (*byakudan*), aloeswood (*jinkō*), and resinated aloeswood (*kyara*) are the three main kinds. Sold in chips or granules, some of these woods are taken from root sections, some from green wood, and some from pieces found buried for a thousand years. The older the piece, the more earthy and subtle (and expensive) the fragrance.

Unlike *senkō*, the stick form of incense, *wari-byakudan* or *wari-jinkō* (the wood-chip varieties) must be burned in small charcoal-incense burners (there is now a new electric model). Fine blends of incense in stick form are available, though many of them are more pungent and insistent than the natural woods that are a bit more troublesome to burn. A lighted piece of charcoal (*sumi*) is placed in the center of a mound of ash in a ceramic or metal *kōro* burner. Over this a small glasslike square is placed to keep the incense from touching the charcoal directly. It is then covered with ash, leaving just a small opening in which to place the incense. This method affords the longest-lasting, most delicate aroma, according to Ōno-san. His shop also offers a special house blend in pellet form called *kun-kō*. The recipe is a well-kept family secret.

Rather than worry about the dozens of exotic names by which the various blends are known, he recommends "letting your nose be the guide."

Located beside the east gate of Nishi-honganji, Kungyoku-dō is a part of the *monzen-chō*, or temple-gate town, that has provided worshipers with religious articles for centuries. Wandering the backstreets in this neighborhood you will find dozens of old shops selling carved Buddhist statuary, small household altars, prayer beads, candles, brocade banners, and altar pieces: all the finery a rural priest or pilgrim might ever need to pursue the path to the True Pure Land of the Jōdo Shinshū sect. Ōno-san also carries a wide selection of temple incense and *rōsoku* candles, along with the aromatic woods that are intended for more down-to-earth purposes. (The *rōsoku*, noted for its unique tapered shape, is made of plant products only, as the use of tallow is contrary to the Buddhist prohibition against killing animals. They are hand-dipped around a wound paper wick, are colored bright red or white, and burn with a tall, pulsating flame.)

Just like Japanese cuisine, *o-kō* is always a subtle and complex sensual experience. The verb *kagu*, to smell, is not used in referring to the world of incense. The Japanese prefer to use *kiku*, to hear—perhaps in an effort to describe an experience that appeals as much to a sixth sense as it does to any of the other five.

KYŌ-YA SUDARE
reed and bamboo blinds

Ogawa Higashi-iru, Imadegawa-dōri, Kamigyō-ku

上京区今出川通小川東入

☎(075) 441-7790

OPEN: 8 A.M.–7 P.M. ▪ CLOSED: Sundays (in winter)

Just inside the doorway of this old wood-frame shop sits Kyō-ya's sixty-year-old wooden *sudare* weaving machine, thumping away day in and day out (right next to it in back is the new metal one they bought a few years ago but never use . . . it "just doesn't have the right feel to it," apparently). The *yoshi* reeds are gathered from fields near Lake Biwa by the owner's eighty-four-year-old father, who believes it's best to select and strip them himself, while most makers find it easier to use imported materials. Kyō-ya's custom-made *sudare* (blinds) are sought after by some of Japan's most prominent tea masters as being the finest in the land. To the untrained eye, the difference may be insignificant, but tea ceremony aficionados insist that the quality of Kyō-ya's *sudare* makes them well worth the higher price.

KOMACHI HOUSE
antique kimono

Ichijō-agaru, Inokuma-dōri, Kamigyō-ku

上京区猪熊通一条上ル

☎(075) 451-6838

OPEN: 9 A.M.–5 P.M. ▪ CLOSED: Sundays, holidays

Located just southeast of the Nishijin Textile Center, Komachi House sells old kimono of every color, quality, vintage, and condition. This is a shop for people who either know what they are looking for or don't mind whether the kimono they buy is thirty or one hundred years old, as long as they like its design. Stacked somewhat at random on the floor in a large tatami mat room, you'll find row after row of kimono, *haori*, *happi*, and *obi* to browse through freely. Komachi-san is much more patient than many of the battle-hardened antique kimono dealers downtown. His prices are often more reasonable than what you'll find at the local flea markets, and the quality is reliable by comparison.

IKAWA TATEGU-TEN
paper-covered doors

Karasuma Higashi-iru, Ebisugawa-dōri, Nakagyō-ku

中京区夷川通烏丸東入

☎(075) 231-2646

OPEN: 9 A.M.–6 P.M. ▪ CLOSED: Mondays

One aspect of the Japanese house is the versatility of the space within. In the winter months heavy sliding paper doors called *fusuma* divide the space into smaller rooms that can be easily heated. In the summer the *fusuma* are removed and replaced by beautiful sliding reed doors called *yoshi-shōji* which allow for ventilation through the humid Kyoto summers. Ikawa sells both (and the lighter wood-framed translucent paper doors called *shōji*). They specialize in refurbishing old *fusuma* and *shōji*, which they gather from the many old homes that are now facing the bulldozers. Ask to see their catalog of interesting *fusuma* door pulls called *hikite* in a wide range of styles from inexpensive brass fittings to elaborate designs edged in silver and gold.

SEIKA-DŌ metalwork, pewter

Nijō-sagaru, Teramachi-dōri, Nakagyō-ku

中京区寺町通二条下ル

☎ (075) 231–3661 (English spoken)

OPEN: 10 A.M.–7 P.M. ■ CLOSED: Sundays, holidays ■ CREDIT: AE, MC, UC, VISA

Teapots and tea utensils in pewter and other metals done by noted local craftsmen. Yamanaka-san has provided not only an outlet for the sale of traditional objects, but a showplace in recent years for a fine collection of one-of-a-kind works by both aspiring young craftsmen and old masters. Yamanaka-san is one of the kindest shopkeepers in Kyoto and will introduce you to the little-known art of Japanese pewterware in English.

C26

OWARI-YA
buckwheat noodles (soba)

Nijō-sagaru, Kurumaya-chō, Nakagyō-ku

中京区車屋町二条下ル

☎ (075) 231–3446

OPEN: 11 A.M.–7 P.M. ■ CLOSED: Wednesdays ■ PRICES: ¥400–¥1,400

One of the oldest buckwheat noodle (*soba*) shops in Kyoto, Owari-ya is located in a neighborhood worth wandering, for northeast of Karasuma-Oike is a section of town that is not included on most of the tourist maps, but is full of interesting old shops of all kinds (an ancient Chinese medicine shop specializing in eye remedies is just a few doors north on the opposite side of the street). The old two-story building with its creaking stairways, tables wedged into nooks and crannies, and private rooms that overlook a tiny garden is worth the small price of a bowl of their delicious homestyle *soba*.

C28

ŌIWA kushikatsu kebabs

Nijō-sagaru, Kiyamachi-dōri, Nakagyō-ku

中京区木屋町通二条下ル

☎ (075) 231–7667 (English spoken)

OPEN: 5 P.M.–10 P.M., Sundays and holidays 4 P.M.–10 P.M. ■ CLOSED: Wednesdays ■ PRICES: ¥120–¥300 per skewer ■ CREDIT: JCB

An old *kura* treasure house at the head of the Takasegawa Canal on Kiyamachi near the Fujita Hotel, serving *kushikatsu*, skewered meats and vegetables which have been breaded and deep-fried. The folk-style interior has a long counter where you can order one delicacy at a time or *omakase*, a full course of thirty different skewers that will not leave you bankrupt (or hungry). If you prefer, you can take a booth in the new room in the back where you will be seated around a low table on tatami. For many people, the word *kushikatsu* brings to mind a boys' night out spent munching greasy snacks over a mug of beer, but at Ōiwa the cook was once a chef in a French restaurant in Tokyo and his skewers are *magnifique*. (Have a look at the old-style flatboat moored in the canal in front of Ōiwa; it's the same kind in which goods were ferried to Osaka in the south for hundreds of years.)

C29

KYŪKYO-DŌ
incense, stationery, brushes

Anekōji-kado, Teramachi-dōri, Nakagyō-ku

中京区寺町通姉小路角

☎ (075) 231-0510 (English spoken)

OPEN: 10 A.M.–6 P.M. ■ CLOSED: Sundays

This spacious shop opened originally in 1774 as an herbal medicine shop. It now specializes in incense, brushes, and ink sticks, with a large selection of handmade paper and tea ceremony utensils. A great shop to browse around in. Try a small bag of *wari-byakudan*, chips of sandalwood incense for use in a charcoal brazier. Some people toss a pinch into their fireplaces to add a subtle aroma to the whole room. Electric braziers made of porcelain eliminate the fuss of lighting

small, round pieces of charcoal each time you wish to burn some. The stick variety (*senkō*), though easier to use, is more pungent and used mainly for religious purposes. Unlike the overpowering, heavily perfumed stick incense from India, Japanese aromatic wood incense, *byakudan* (sandalwood) or *jinkō* (aloeswood), adds just a subtle aura to a special occasion. A complete line of paintbrushes for *sumi-e* (ink painting) is made by Kyūkyo-dō's own craftsmen.

C30

FUNDŌ-YA footwear (tabi)

Sakaimachi-kado, Sanjō-dōri, Nakagyō-ku

中京区三条通堺町角

☎ (075) 221-2389

OPEN: 9:30 A.M.–7:30 P.M. ■ CLOSED: Sundays, holidays

Tabi, the white, split-toed socks worn with thonged Japanese footwear, are custom-made to fit your foot here, where many of Kyoto's kabuki actors and tea masters order the dozens of pairs of *tabi* they need to perform (only immaculately white *tabi* are formally acceptable). Colored fabrics are used to make *tabi* for casual or work wear. Ready-made *tabi* are also available in standard Japanese sizes (meaning small).

C31

DAIMONJI-YA inn (ryokan)

Kawaramachi Nishi-iru, Sanjō-dōri, Nakagyō-ku

中京区三条通河原町西入

☎ (075) 221-0603/5 (English spoken)

CHECK-IN: 3 P.M. ■ CHECK-OUT: 10 A.M. ■ RATES: ¥23,000–¥50,000 (w/2 meals) ■ CREDIT: AE, DC ■ RESTAURANT OPEN: 11:30 A.M.–1 P.M. (last seating), 5 P.M.–7 P.M. (last

seating) ■ PRICES: Mini-*kaiseki* lunch ¥5,000–
¥7,000, *kaiseki* dinner ¥10,000–¥20,000

Hidden down a very narrow path that
leads off the bustling Sanjō Arcade in
midtown. Even people who have
spent their whole lives in Kyoto are surprised to hear that there is a first-class
inn tucked in between the boutiques
and confectionery shops along Sanjō.
Not as famous as some of the other old
inns, Daimonji-ya has the understated
beauty of a quintessentially Kyoto
establishment. Natural wood interiors
with each room overlooking its own
tsubo niwa, or "garden the size of an
urn"—a quiet haven right in the
center of town. Many of Daimonji-ya's
guests belong to the literary world (Eiji
Yoshikawa, the author of *Musashi*,
used to stay here whenever he was in
town). Of special note is the cuisine—
the chef was trained at Tsujitome, a
caterer farther east on Sanjō that is
famous for serving the best *kaiseki*
meals in Kyoto, as well as for training
the city's finest chefs.

C32

SURUGA-YA tea, sweets

Kawaramachi Nishi-iru, Sanjō-dōri,
Nakagyō-ku

中京区三条通河原町西入

☎ (075) 221-1447

OPEN: Daily, 10 A.M.–9 P.M. ■ CREDIT: JCB,
MC, UC, VISA

A hundred-year-old branch of the
original Suruga-ya in Fushimi, which
has been in the confectionery business
for over five hundred years. Their
specialty is *yōkan*, a sweet bean-paste
jelly, which is usually molded into
long, rectangular blocks to be sliced
when ordered. Suruga-ya also offers an
exquisite array of *nama-gashi* sweets in
shapes and colors to complement the

season. Sit upstairs at the counter at
the front of the shop and ask for *o-usu
to o-kashi*, and a bowl of tea-ceremony
tea and a sweet will be placed before
you. An excellent place to sample the
delights of the tea ceremony in an
unexpected location, Suruga-ya is
located just off Kawaramachi-dōri on
the south side of the Sanjō Arcade.

C33

RAKUMI
happi, purses, accessories

Shōchiku-za-mae, Rokkaku-agaru, Shin-
kyōgoku-dōri, Nakagyō-ku

中京区新京極通六角上ル松竹座前

☎ (075) 231-2924 (English spoken)

OPEN: 11 A.M.–9 P.M. ■ CLOSED: Wednesdays
■ CREDIT: AE, DC, JCB, MC, UC, VISA

Right on Shin-kyōgoku Mall opposite
the Shōchiku-za Movie Theater a
block south of the Sanjō Arcade. A
wide selection of traditional accessories—oiled paper umbrellas,
Nishijin brocade handbags, Yūzen-
dyed *furoshiki* (wrapping cloths), hair
ornaments, kimono, cotton summer
yukata robes, and *happi* coats—in one
of the few buildings on the mall that is
folk-style, complete with a unique
piece of furniture called a *hako-kaidan*,
an old-fashioned portable staircase
that has drawers and compartments

for storage. (Their printed cotton T-shirts are a popular souvenir and of better quality than those available elsewhere.)

C34

TAKUMI kimono accessories

Sanjō-sagaru, Kawaramachi-dōri, Nakagyō-ku

中京区河原町通三条下ル

☎ (075) 221–2278 (English spoken)

OPEN: Daily, 10:30 A.M.–9 P.M. ■ CREDIT: DC, JCB, MC, UC, VISA

An old shop fronting Kawaramachi that belonged to a family of carpenters who built many of the old restaurants in the Kiyamachi district. During World War II, with no men left in the family to carry on the carpentry trade, the lady of the house was persuaded to go into the dyed-goods business, and today Takumi is one of the best places in Kyoto to buy kimono accessories (*komono*) such as Yūzen-dyed *obi-age*, the silk scarves that are tucked into the top edge of *obi* sashes. Nishijin woven handbags and accessories, Tango *chirimen* (the crinkled silk crepe woven in the Tango district on the Japan Sea coast), and hand-embroidered silk collars for kimono are also available. The stacks of colorful

furoshiki (squares of cloth used to wrap and carry gifts to friends) on display in the front window in both synthetics and silk make Takumi the best *furoshiki* shop in Kyoto.

C35

TACHIKICHI ceramics

Tominokōji-kado, Shijō-dōri, Shimogyō-ku

下京区四条通富小路角

☎ (075) 211–3141

OPEN: 10 A.M.–7 P.M. ■ CLOSED: Wednesdays ■ CREDIT: AE, DC, JCB, MC, UC, VISA

Since 1752, Tachikichi has been selling fine *Kyō-yaki*, or Kyoto ceramics, noted particularly for a delicate blue or multicolored overglaze enamel decoration, often edged in gold. Their present shop is a modern though elegantly designed four-story building (on Shijō-dōri about a seven-minute walk west of Kawaramachi) that has become Kyoto's exclusive emporium for fine ceramics. Traditional wares for serving *kaiseki*, tea sets, vases, tea bowls, and everyday dishwares in a wide range of prices are all here. Offerings include everything from an inexpensive set of five beer glasses delicately etched in bamboo, plum, and pine-branch motifs to a costly, but incomparable, Kiyomizu-ware tea bowl stamped with the master's seal in its own signed wooden box. You can also arrange to have items shipped safely anywhere in the world.

C36

ARITSUGU
cutlery, kitchenware

Gokomachi Nishi-iru, Nishikikōji-dōri, Nakagyō-ku

中京区錦小路通御幸町西入

☎(075) 221–1091 (English spoken)

OPEN: 9 A.M.–5:30 P.M. ■ CLOSED: Sundays, holidays

In business for four hundred years, Aritsugu deals in fine hand-wrought cutlery and traditional kitchenwares of all kinds, from sushi knives to vegetable peelers, all handmade. Everything you need to prepare a formal meal in the Kyoto-style tradition is here—strainers, ladles, confectionery molds, bamboo steamers, wooden buckets, copper teapots, large soup pots, tempura pots, and radish graters. Aritsugu was originally located a few blocks south of Shijō-dōri, but moved to Nishiki five years ago to join the lively market street unanimously lauded as the "kitchen of Kyoto."

HŌRAI-DŌ tea, tea utensils

Shijō-agaru, Teramachi-dōri, Nakagyō-ku

中京区寺町通四条上ル

☎(075) 221–1215

OPEN: 9:30 A.M.–8:50 P.M. ■ CLOSED: 2nd, 12th & 22nd of every month ■ CREDIT: AE, MC, VISA

An old tea shop just half a block north of Shijō on Teramachi amid a jungle of shiny new clothing boutiques that have popped up in recent years. Not only do they have fine Uji teas, both in leaf (*sencha*) and powder (*matcha*), which you can order by the gram, but they also offer a selection of utensils used in the tea ceremony—tea bowls, whisks, bamboo spoons, ladle rests, and tea caddies—at reasonable prices. The friendly family shop has all the charm of traditional Kyoto and refuses to give in to the downtown trend toward modernization. (A price list is now available in English.)

TAGOTO Kyoto "box lunch"

34 Ōtabi-chō, Teramachi Higashi-iru, Shijō-dōri, Shimogyō-ku

下京区四条通寺町東入御旅町34

☎(075) 221–1811

OPEN: Daily, 11:30 A.M.–8:30 P.M. ■ PRICES: From ¥2,300 ■ CREDIT: AE, DC, JCB, MC, MIL, UC, VISA

On Shijō Street west of Kawaramachi in a very narrow passageway just down from the Kyoto Central Hotel. Blink twice and you'll miss the entrance to this old shop established in 1880—a tiny corridor that leads through a narrow garden (complete with pond and carp) to the doorway. Ask for a room upstairs and store your shoes in the wooden lockers at the bottom of the stairway before you go up. There are private tatami rooms with alcove, flower arrangement, and painting to greet you—teahouse-style right in the middle of the city. Try their beautiful *Koetsu-mizusashi-bentō*, served in double-decker round lacquered boxes named after a famous sixteenth-century artist. This Kyoto cuisine sampler will introduce you to the delicacies of the ancient capital without overburdening out-of-town tastebuds.

TSUJIKURA lanterns, umbrellas

Shijō-agaru, Kawaramachi-dōri, Nakagyō-ku

中京区河原町通四条上ル

☎(075) 221–4396

OPEN: 11 A.M.–9 P.M. ■ CLOSED: Tuesday

Umbrellas of all kinds, both traditional Japanese ones (*wagasa*) and Western-style, are the specialty at Tsujikura, though they also have a fine collection of handmade paper lanterns (*chōchin*) in a small room in back that shouldn't be missed. Round traditional *bonbori* lanterns in contemporary shapes, as well as festival lanterns with *mon* crest designs painted in black on a white background, are available.

garden, to a tatami room that overlooks the river. During the summer, when all the restaurants and teahouses along this stretch of the Kamo River build platforms for their customers to enjoy a meal cooled by the river breezes, you can sit out over the river and relax in the knowledge that the people on the platform next door have paid ten times the fare at Fujino-ya for the same simple pleasure. A full-course tempura dinner is amazingly inexpensive for Pontochō, which is famous for its costly restaurants and geisha parties. The food here is simple and delicious and the old Kyoto atmosphere is unretouched.

FUJINO-YA
tempura, kushikatsu kebabs

Shijō-agaru, Pontochō, Nakagyō-ku
中京区先斗町四条上ル
☎ (075) 221-2446
OPEN: 5 P.M.–10 P.M. ■ CLOSED: Mondays
■ PRICES: ¥500–¥1,600

Enter this one-hundred-year-old teahouse and walk all the way down the dark corridor to the back, past the kitchen and the pocketsized interior

YAMATOMI
teppin-age, oden stew

Shijō-agaru, Pontochō, Nakagyō-ku
中京区先斗町四条上ル
☎ (075) 221-3268
OPEN: 12 noon–12 midnight ■ CLOSED:
Tuesdays ■ PRICES: ¥300–¥2,500, English
menu available

Located about halfway up from Shijō on Pontochō before you reach the park. On a cold winter evening, try Yamatomi's *oden*, a potpourri of vegetables, eggs, tofu, and other delicacies simmered in a tasty broth. You can order an assortment (*moriawase*) or a piece at a time, choosing from the steaming vats on the counter. If you are interested in a complete dining experience, order *teppin-age*, a fry-it-yourself tempura meal which arrives with a cast-iron kettle of hot oil. Place the skewered, batter-dipped pieces of shrimp, vegetables, and meat in the kettle one by one yourself—with soup and rice, a real delight. Because of the popularity of Yamatomi, they decided a couple of years ago to expand and modernize, so some of their old teahouse charm has gone. It is still a lively eatery though (and the food and prices have not suffered much in the transition).

C42

NIJŪSAN-YA combs

85 Shin-chō, Kawaramachi Higashi-iru, Shijō-dōri, Shimogyō-ku
下京区四条通河原町東入真町85
☎ (075) 221-2371
OPEN: 10 A.M.–8:30 P.M. ■ CLOSED: 3rd Wednesday

Boxwood hair combs (*tsuge-kushi*), both as hair ornaments and pocket combs, have been sold here since 1820. The shop itself is a work of art with a flower arrangement by a local *ikebana* master always on display in the front window. Their combs are now made in Osaka, since their last Kyoto craftsmen retired recently. Nijūsan-ya also has a number of barrettes and hair clasps for modern hairstyles as well as the traditional hair ornaments worn by geisha.

GOJŌ-RAKUEN AND THE BARGAIN INNS

The Takasegawa river runs through this now quiet neighborhood like a theme— *one whose tune has definitely changed. The canal is lined on either side with old brothels, in all the turn-of-the-century sense of the word. No barkers hawk their "wares" beneath spasmodic neon tombstones as they do further north on Kiyamachi-dōri. Dimly provocative doorways frame the old "mama-sans" who sit silently beside their gurgling fishtanks, waiting for the few patrons who prefer anachronism to rhinestones. Though such areas in other countries could expect their share of shady characters and crime, the police box on the corner is seldom troubled with more of a problem than putting the occasional drunk into a cab to send him home. There is even a kindergarten amid it all. In days gone by, it was known as the Gojō-Rakuen, the Fifth Street "pleasure park." Today it has become better known for its inexpensive inns than for the few remaining "teahouses" that dot the canal. Many of these inns are registered with the Japanese Inn Group, an organization that encourages tourists to "experience the real Japan" by taking a room in an inexpensive, family-run ryokan, or inn. Popular with young travelers, the inns offer some of the lowest rates in town; they are clean, comfortable, within walking distance of downtown, and are a very good place to meet other travelers and find out what's going on. Three of the most hospitable and charming are listed below (C43–C45).*

C43

RIVERSIDE TAKASE inn

Shōshinji-chō, Kaminoguchi-agaru, Kiyamachi-dōri, Shimogyō-ku
下京区木屋町通上之口上ル聖真子町
☎ (075) 351-7920

CHECK-IN: 3 P.M. ■ CHECK-OUT: 10 A.M. ■
RATES: From ¥3,000, double from ¥5,000 ■
CREDIT: AE

The owners of this annex to Kyōka Ryokan (near Kyoto Station) are teachers of flower arrangement and tea ceremony, so appointments for lessons can be made easily here. The annex overlooks the Takasegawa river and is just half a block from the largest public bathhouse in the neighborhood (sauna included).

C44

HIRAIWA inn (ryokan)

314 Hayao-chō, Kaminoguchi-agaru, Ninomiyachō-dōri, Shimogyō-ku
下京区二ノ宮町通上之口上ル早尾町314
☎ (075) 351–6748
CHECK-IN: 3 P.M. ■ CHECK-OUT: 10 A.M. ■
RATES: From ¥3,000 ■ CREDIT: AE

The largest and most popular of the inns in this neighborhood, Hiraiwa is the place to go to meet people, find out what's happening, where to eat and drink—even how to get a job—on a shoestring in Kyoto. This has become a mecca for young (and not so young) travelers seeking an inexpensive and interesting stay in the city. The owners welcome foreign guests, and at Hiraiwa you can experience both the funky, old ambience of the Gojō-Rakuen district and meet people from Amsterdam or Arkansas—all in one eclectic place. (The newer Hiraiwa annex is fine for connoisseurs of stucco and whitewash.)

C45

RYOKAN YUHARA inn

188 Kagiya-chō, Shōmen-agaru, Kiyamachi-dōri, Shimogyō-ku
下京区木屋町通正面上ル鍵屋町188

☎ (075) 371–9583
CHECK-IN: 3 P.M. ■ CHECK-OUT: 10 A.M. ■
RATES: From ¥3,000

A small, inexpensive inn that overlooks the Takasegawa river and is within a fifteen-minute walk of Kyoto Station. Especially delightful in midspring when the cherry blossoms along the canal are in full bloom. The proprietress is gracious and friendly, and, though a short jaunt to the public bath is required for a real soak, showers are available.

C46

HIRATA clay dolls, folk toys

89 Tō-ji, Higashimonzen-chō, Minami-ku
南区東寺東門前町89
☎ (075) 681–5896
OPEN: Daily, 8 A.M.–8 P.M. ■ CLOSED: Periodically

A block north of Tō-ji temple, this little shop is not one of the usual guidebook selections, even for Japanese. Once a saké shop, later selling ceramic bonsai planters (some of which they still have), Hirata now specializes in folk toys from all over Japan, which the owner has been collecting for over thirty years. Mr. Hirata's *Miharu ningyō*, delicately painted dolls of papier-mâché from Fukushima Prefecture, are exquisite and difficult to obtain. He also has *Saga-men*, the paper masks from the Saga area (there is only one elderly craftsman who still makes them), wooden toys, and clay figures from hundreds of villages all over Japan. An expert on Japanese folk toys, he recently published an authoritative book on the subject.

RAKU-TŌ

Eastern Kyoto

Raku-tō is a district of elegance and distinction. Kiyomizu Temple, the grande dame of Kyoto temples, has drawn pilgrims to Raku-tō since the Heian period. The cobbled paths that lead up to it are lined with ceramics shops. The area was once the main pottery district in Kyoto, producing the delicately painted Kiyomizu ware. The sixty-seven-ton bronze bell of Chion-in of the popular Jōdo sect of Buddhism has tolled the arrival of every New Year in Kyoto since the seventh century, and the Silver Pavilion, where the shogun Ashikaga Yoshimasa held his elegant tea ceremonies four hundred years ago, still stands as a symbol of the height of culture attained in Raku-tō so long ago.

Raku-tō has always been the home of temples, great and small, and Zen became the influential force in Japanese society that it remains today here at Nanzen-ji in the center of Raku-tō. Black-robed monks with begging bowls in hand can still be heard chanting for alms in the neighborhoods around the gates.

The Philosopher's Walk, the lovely path that follows an old canal from the foot of Ginkaku-ji southward, with its cherry blossoms in spring and maple leaves in fall, is as popular today with young lovers as it once was with great thinkers.

Kyoto's most famous geisha quarter, Gion, is in Raku-tō. Here the streets are lined with old "teahouses" out of which the sound of shamisen music still floats on warm summer nights.

If you have but one day free to spend in Kyoto on your own, walk the paths at the foot of Higashiyama (whether it be philosophy or femininity that strikes your fancy).

EASTERN KYOTO

Hakusason-sō ■

to Ginkaku-ji

Kyoto University

Yoshida Shrine

SAKYŌ-KU

Shōgo-in

SHIRAKAWA RIVER

Shirakawa-dōri

Kawabata-dōri

KAMO RIVER

Higashiōji-dōri

Marutamachi-dōri

Hotel Sunflower ■

12

Heian Shrine

Okazaki

○11

Okazaki Park

Eikan-dō

Nijō-dōri

Museum of Modern Art ■

Museum of Art ○

Okazaki Zoo ○

1

Niōmon-dōri

Nanzen-ji

Sanjō-dōri

2 ○

HIGASHIYAMA SANJŌ

○ 13

KEAGE

Awataguchi

KEIHAN KEISHIN LINE

Gion

14 ○

Miyako Hotel

Hanami-kōji-dōri

SANJŌ

○15

●3

○16

Shōren-in

17

Furumonzen-dōri

○ 21

Chion-in

18

●4   ○20

19

Yasaka Shrine 22

27 ~30

SHIJŌ

○25

Maruyama Park

5

Shijō-dōri

26

6●

BIWAKO CANAL

○23

○24

Minami-za

7●

HIGASHIYAMA-KU

KUJŌYAMA

●31

○32

○33

○34 Kōdai-ji

●8

Kenni-ji

Ryozen Kannon

Yasaka-dōri

●9

Yasaka Pagoda

10● Ninenzaka

35

Rokuharamitsu-ji

36○

Kiyomizuzaka

37 Sannenzaka

Kiyomizu Temple

to Gojō

Gojōzaka

38○

Gojō-dōri

○39

Tōjiki Kaikan

to Yamashina

1/2 mile

500 m

120

Keihan Line

Yamatoōji-dōri

OKUTAN
tofu cooking

86–30 Fukuchi-chō, Nanzen-ji, Sakyō-ku
左京区南禅寺福地町86-30　☎(075) 771-8709
OPEN: 10:30 A.M.–6 P.M. (seating until 5:30) ■ CLOSED: Thursdays ■ PRICES: ¥2,500

Making a holy pilgrimage to a revered Kyoto temple has been a praiseworthy endeavor in Japan for hundreds of years. Travel was difficult (especially after the shogunate outlawed the use of the wheel to help keep an eye on things). For a hardworking agrarian populace, time was more than money; it was life. Taking time off from toil in the Middle Ages in Japan (almost as difficult as it is today) required an iron-clad excuse, but who could doubt the sincerity of a religious man? Undertaking a holy pilgrimage was a chance to see the world, and still is—a fact you'll notice when busloads of faithful travelers from the countryside unload before the gates of Nanzen-ji, one of Kyoto's most popular religious attractions. In the Middle Ages, people would undertake a pilgrimage to one thousand temples and shrines in a circuit, often under the patronage of a particular deity. People marked the completion of each step in such a circuit by affixing stickers imprinted with their names (*senja fuda*) to the gateway of each temple or shrine they visited.

Entering the main gate at Nanzen-ji you can count the hundreds of *senja fuda* whose namesakes have long since ended their pilgrimages through life. Aside from the joy of traveling, many people undertook such pilgrimages to pray for sick relatives or for success in special endeavors. The higher up on the gateway a sticker was placed, the more likely it was to come to the attention of the gods. During the Edo period, pilgrims used long, retractable walking sticks to reach the heights of spiritual achievement, as it were.

During the eighteenth century, when such excursions were at their height of popularity, the constant influx of pilgrims prompted the opening of dozens of inns and teahouses along the roads that lead to temple gates. *Monzen-jaya*, the name by which these rest stops were known, provided simple, nourishing meals (vegetarian style, in keeping with the teachings of Zen).

Near the gates of Kiyomizu-dera, Yasaka Jinja, and Nanzen-ji, there are still a few old *monzen-jaya* which serve the finest "temple-gate" fare. Okutan,

inside the north gate at Nanzen-ji, hasn't changed much in three hundred years. For twelve generations this small teahouse has served *yudōfu*, an old Zen recipe for fresh tofu simmered in a big ceramic pot over charcoal, with soy sauce for dipping, and an array of vegetable dishes on the side. At Okutan, the side dishes include vegetable tempura (*yasai tempura*) and *tōfu dengaku* (skewers of grilled tofu covered with sweet *miso* sauce).

Okutan is located inside the white-washed walls of a sub-temple of Nanzen-ji called Chōshō-in, and shares the lush garden and pond that slopes between them. Rustic cedar-shingled tatami rooms open onto a stone walkway overlooking the garden, which seems to be at its best in every season: cherry blossoms in spring, brilliant greenery in summer, red maple leaves in fall, and the possibility of snowfall in winter.

Though every season is beautiful, perhaps winter is the best—with or without the snowflakes. *Yudōfu* was meant to warm chilled bones on a frosty afternoon in January when each breath hangs a split second in the air—hot tofu, the heat from a charcoal hibachi, surrounded by a natural setting of trees as old as the nearby hills. In warmer weather the menu features *karashi-dōfu*, a spicy tofu dish, and *hiya-yakko*, chilled tofu sprinkled with green onions and ginger.

Just outside the entrance to Okutan you can see the great Sanmon Gate of Nanzen-ji, the gateless gate of Zen—leading ever inward, locking no one out. A notorious sixteenth-century thief named Ishikawa Goemon (a kind of Oriental Robin Hood) once hid from the wrath of the warlord Toyotomi Hideyoshi here on the

veranda atop the great Sanmon. Knowing he was close to a violent end, he surveyed the rooftops of Nanzen-ji and the slopes of the Higashiyama Mountains all around him and composed this poem:

——Splendid . . . splendid!
——The view from here
——Is worth more than
——A thousand pieces of gold!

Quite a recommendation for a man who spent his life in pursuit of gold coins. He met his fate (like a pot of simmered tofu, and much less pleasantly) on the banks of the Kamogawa river, where Hideyoshi had him and his son boiled in oil.

Below Kiyomizu-dera, where Ninenzaka meets Sannenzaka, there is a more recent branch of Okutan housed in the former villa of a wealthy merchant. You'll be seated in sunny rooms on tatami mats and offered the same *yudōfu* menu as you gaze over a luxurious landscape garden—less rustic, but just as much a pleasure to view as the temple gardens at the main restaurant at Nanzen-ji.

KAGOSHIN
bamboo

7, 4-chōme, Ōhashi-higashi, Sanjō-dōri, Higashiyama-ku
東山区三条通大橋通大橋東 4 丁目 7　☎ (075) 771–0209, 751–0701

OPEN: 9 A.M.–6 P.M. ■ CLOSED: Sundays, holidays

The proudest day of Shintarō Morita's life was the day in 1920 when he climbed into the imperial roadster (see photo in History) that would carry him to the old palace to receive a special award from the emperor for his role in the introduction of bamboo ware to the West. Since 1862, he had been making some of the finest bamboo basketry in Japan and had drawn the attention of buyers in the West to an art form previously overlooked abroad. His old bamboo shop still clings to the same spot on the north side of Sanjō-dōri where it first opened for business, though it is engulfed today in modern buildings, midtown traffic, and the noise of the Keihan train as it rumbles past on its way to Yamashina.

During the Edo period, Sanjō-dōri was the last stretch of the Old Tōkaidō Highway, which connected Kyoto with Edo (now Tokyo), three hundred miles to the east. There were once many bamboo shops here beside the highway since it was a direct route for transporting bamboo from the lush forests of Shiga. Much of the bamboo

supply in Shiga has been depleted over the years and only a few of the old bamboo shops in this area remain.

Now Morita-san's grandson must go to Mukō-machi in the southwest of Kyoto, where a good supply of bamboo, though dwindling, is still available. Of the 118 varieties of bamboo in Japan, over fifty special types are used in the fine basketry done at Kagoshin, and some rare varieties are brought from rural areas such as Hokuriku, Wakayama, and Shimane. With an island climate just right for growing bamboo, the Japanese have explored every possible use for the flexible material, from water pipes to umbrella ribbings. One old account lists over fourteen hundred uses in all. Basil Hall Chamberlain in 1904 remarked that "so extensive is the part played by bamboo in Japanese domestic economy that the question is rather, what does it not do?"

Times have changed, however, and aluminum and plastic now perform most of the everyday jobs bamboo once handled so gracefully. Today

Eastern Kyoto

Kagoshin offers fine bamboo baskets primarily for tea-ceremony utensils and flower arrangement, as well as a variety of ornamental *sode-gaki* garden fence "sleeves."

One of the most interesting types of bamboo used in basket weaving is called *susu-dake*, bamboo taken from the soot-darkened ceilings of old Japanese farmhouses. The rich, natural patina *susu-dake* acquires is highly prized when woven in fine basketry, and the limited supply makes it quite expensive. It can be distinguished from artificially stained bamboo by the alternating dark and light areas on each strand, which are the result of the bamboo having been lashed to the roof beams with hemp cord.

Basketry is not the simple craft it may appear to be. Freshly cut bamboo must be dried for two years before it can be worked, as the ever-present stacks of drying stalks out front (some several meters long) attest to. Each individual stalk must then be evaluated for shape and quality. A single stone in the path of a sprouting bamboo shoot is enough to create a permanent groove that renders the stalk useless for ordinary basketry, though some tea-ceremony enthusiasts do look for vases with unusual twists and gnarls. For basket weaving, each stalk must be split and shaved to the appropriate width and thickness to suit the particular design. No two stalks of bamboo are identical, and the most difficult part of bamboo craftsmanship, according to Mr. Morita, is that each piece has an irrepressible character of its own that must be dealt with individually.

Apart from the baskets you see in the shop, special designs can be made to order. In fact, most of the baskets Morita makes are special orders for tea masters and department stores, but much of what you see in the front of the shop can be purchased directly. Many of his regular customers just describe the shape and size of the basket they want, and he tries to match the design with the most suitable type of bamboo for the shape. At no time of the year will you find Mr. Morita dozing. There are always new baskets from the more than one hundred designs he makes in various stages of completion in his workshop, which opens right onto the busy street.

When asked if he hadn't considered remodeling the hundred-year-old shop front to save himself from the street noise and air pollution, he replied, "How could I change this place? My customers like the old atmosphere here and would certainly complain if I did—and besides, that room upstairs is where my grandfather made a bamboo chair for the emperor on his coronation day! How could I possibly destroy a room like that?"

NAKANISHI TOKU SHŌTEN antique dolls

E3

中西徳商店

359 Moto-chō, Yamatoōji Higashi-iru, Furumonzen-dōri, Higashiyama-ku
東山区古門前通大和大路東入元町359　☎(075) 561-7309
OPEN: 10 A.M.–6 P.M. ■ CLOSED: Periodically ■ CREDIT: AE, VISA

A half smile, the faultless restraint, the delicate features, the irreproachable whiteness: like a Nō mask, the face of a Japanese doll silently reveals the soul of an ancient ambiguous land. They are windows to the past, and the image they pose is a half-forgotten ideal of beauty. They demonstrate in three dimensions how people lived, what they wore, what was important to them, what they felt and did not say. The Japanese doll recounts a thousand years of history without the complication or inadequacy of language.

Kyoto is the place where the finest of Japanese dolls originated, and Nakanishi's Fine Arts specializes in antique Kyoto dolls (*Kyō-ningyō*) of all kinds.

In Japanese, *ningyō*, the word that describes these figures, has a long history with its roots in the spirit world. Records from the Heian period show that figures called *hitogata* (another reading of the same Chinese characters) were used to draw evil spirits and illness away from afflicted human beings. Throwing the con-

taminated figure into a nearby stream was believed to rid the person of his misfortune. Paper figures used for the same purpose can still be found at shrines in Japan today. Another kind of *ningyō* was placed near the head of a newborn baby to act as a surrogate, absorbing misdirected mayhem and giving the new arrival a starting chance. These figures were enshrined in a place of honor, and offerings were made to them, particularly on March 3, the day of an ancient purification ceremony which is known today as Hina Matsuri (Doll Festival).

Over the centuries, the figures became more and more elaborate, and by the mid–Edo period the festival was one of the major celebrations of the year. *Hina ningyō* are displayed in pairs, dressed as a nobleman and his lady, attended by servants and surrounded by an assortment of miniature household furnishings (if your household happened to be regal, that is). Tiny flowering trees adorned the shelves as symbols of the season and of the imperial court.

The delicate domestic festival became a special day of celebration for girls—a day on which they learned what it meant to be a woman in Japan. The qualities *hina ningyō* portrayed were those of refinement and elegance, contentment, and restraint: exactly what Japanese society had in mind for its future wives and mothers.

The old custom has evolved into a display of wealth and status in recent years, with a top-of-the-line set of dolls costing well over a million yen. Still the celebration of Hina Matsuri and the eloquence of the earlier *hina ningyō* have much to teach the modern observer about the customs and background of old Japan.

So do Mr. and Mrs. Nakanishi. Mr. Nakanishi was once a fan maker by trade. Now the few fan makers that remain in business are faced with increased material costs, the necessity of higher wages for their employees, and the low retail price of fans. Fifteen years ago, Mr. Nakanishi decided to turn his long-time hobby of collecting antique Japanese dolls into a full-time business, and today his shop on Furumonzen Street is one of the only shops in Kyoto that deals exclusively in antique Japanese dolls. Though there are many antique dealers in the neighboring Shinmonzen district who handle dolls as a side interest, the Nakanishis have by far the largest selection and the finest quality available. Collectors of fine dolls come from all over Japan to buy dolls at their little shop. Some of the dolls they sell are museum quality with prices to match, but they also carry less rare, though equally lovely, old dolls available for as little as ¥5,000.

The most popular kind of doll they sell is still the *hina ningyō*. But with the recent "shogun boom," the *musha ningyō*, or samurai dolls, are especially hard to keep in stock, with many of the finest examples going to collectors in New York and Paris. In addition to these, the Nakanishis carry a wide variety of other antique Japanese dolls, many of which are rare even in Japan, including dolls made of clay. Most of the festival dolls, like the *hina* and *musha ningyō*, are made with wooden or composition base heads that have been painted with white *gofun*, a powdered seashell paste (often mistaken for ivory or porcelain). Their elaborate brocade costumes are made of specially woven fabrics with patterns reduced to fit the miniature proportions of the dolls.

Mr. Nakanishi carves Buddhist statues from wood in his spare time, a hobby he took up a few years ago "to keep my mind alert." He feels that the wooden Buddhas he carves are a natural outgrowth of his interest in antique dolls. . . . After all, Buddha too had a human form.

SHIRAUME
inn (ryokan), restaurant

Shirakawa-hotori, Gion-shinbashi, Higashiyama-ku
東山区祇園新橋白川畔　☎(075) 561-1459

CHECK-IN: 4 P.M. ■ CHECK-OUT: 10 A.M. ■ RATES: From ¥12,000 (w/2 meals) ■ CREDIT: JCB ■
RESTAURANT OPEN: 4 P.M.–9 P.M. (last order, 7)

Kani kaku ni
Gion wa koishi
neru toki mo
makura no shita o
mizu no nagaruru.

No matter what they say,
I love Gion.
Even in my sleep
I hear the sound of water
Flowing beneath my pillow.
　　　—Yoshii Osamu (1886–1960)

Gion . . . stone bridge over the old Shirakawa Canal, willows weeping like jilted lovers, their long, wispy limbs draped sadly over the shallow water . . . Gion. When Yoshii wrote the verse that is now engraved in stone beside the river, he must have been much in love with this floating world.

Ukiyo-e, pictures of the "floating world," allude to a world of passion that dissolves in the morning light: seductive, unpredictable, exotic. Shiraume Ryokan, the White Plum Inn,

hugs the south bank of the old canal in the heart of Gion. The only way to reach the entrance is to cross a narrow footbridge over the stream. There you part the *noren* curtain with the plum-blossom crest, and step into the courtyard garden where a maid in kimono will greet you with "*Oideyasu*," a word of welcome in the gentle Kyoto dialect so often heard in Gion.

Shiraume was once a famous "teahouse" called Dairyū, the Big Willow, that was turned into an inn shortly after the war. Dairyū was the popular haunt of novelists and poets during the Meiji period who spent their nights lingering over cups of hot saké, languishing in the melancholy night breeze with their favorite geisha in attendance. Yoshii Osamu was one of those men.

An *o-chaya*, or "teahouse," has little to do with tea, though most geisha districts started out as rest stops near shrines or temples where pretty girls served tea to weary pilgrims looking for salvation of a more temporal nature. In Kyoto, an *o-chaya* is a house in which geisha parties are held. The proprietress, often a former geisha herself, arranges for geisha to meet guests who have made reservations for an evening of drinking, eating, and entertainment. Elaborate meals are prepared by special caterers. The geisha usually live in an *okiya*, a geisha house, which supplies them with room and board, a wardrobe of costly kimono, and an allowance. The word *ryōtei* refers simply to a first-class traditional restaurant to which geisha are often called to entertain guests.

The geisha world is complicated and has an air of mystery and intrigue, but these days it bears little resemblance to times past when impoverished farm girls were sold by their desperate parents into a life of servitude and prostitution. The word geisha means "artiste," and in their heyday in the late Edo period the geisha were not prostitutes at all, but licensed professional entertainers who prided themselves on their artistry in music and dance. Although sexual favors are by no means unheard of among geisha, it is strictly a matter of personal choice.

Strolling down the cobblestone path

beside the Shirakawa river in the evening, you are likely to pass a young *maiko*, an apprentice geisha, on her way to a nearby *o-chaya* to entertain guests. Dressed in an elaborate, multilayered kimono, her gold embroidered *obi* sash trailing behind, she'll clip-clop past on her high *pokkuri geta*, face painted white and hair fastened primly with lacquered combs. She probably won't look your way—often a bit pouty, tired of cameras and flashbulbs before she turns twenty.

Shiraume is in the northern sector of Gion, an area called Shinbashi. (Just around the corner from Shiraume is a street famous for the unchanged ambience of rows of old *o-chaya*, still in use today for geisha parties as they were a hundred years ago.) As a former *o-chaya*, each room at Shiraume is different, some large enough to accommodate a party of ten, some just right for two. The room to ask for is downstairs at the end of the corridor with its *shōji* doors that open onto a small garden with a stone lantern and a thick stand of bamboo.

Shiraume serves full-course *kaiseki* meals, *nabemono* (one-pot stews), sukiyaki, and tempura. As in most *ryokan*, the price of accommodation is charged per person including breakfast and dinner, but Shiraume also offers a room for two with Western breakfast at a lower price for foreign guests. Either way, "the sound of water flowing beneath your pillow" is free. Unlike most Kyoto inns which close at 10 or 11 P.M., Shiraume has no curfew. How could a former Gion teahouse close its doors to those who love the night?

HIRATA
blinds

平
田

Shijō-agaru, Yamatoōji-dōri, Higashiyama-ku
東山区大和大路通四条上ル　☎(075) 561–1776
OPEN: 9:30 A.M.–6:30 P.M. ■ CLOSED: Sundays, holidays

Just after sunset Gion begins to stir with Kyoto's own special brand of night life—geisha on their way to parties, kitchen maids hurrying back to their inns with last-minute purchases for dinner, businessmen on expense accounts gathering a second wind for a night of serious drinking at their favorite club. *Sudare* blinds flapping gently in the breeze on the windows of "teahouses" that line the old stone canal in Gion are a symbol of the geisha world they half conceal.

Sudare hide the private evenings inside the teahouses from the curious eyes of passersby, adding to the sense of intimacy and mystery in Gion. Particularly in the Shinbashi district, one of the few historic preservation districts in Kyoto, the *sudare* has become an essential element in the design of the façades of its buildings.

A block south of Shinbashi on Nawate-dōri is the shop that makes many of the famous *sudare* of Gion. Hirata has been supplying bamboo and reed blinds for two hundred years, but Yoshio Hirata, its present proprietor and a seventh-generation screen-maker, had no chance to learn his trade from his father. Hirata-san was only twelve years old when World War II broke out and his father was drafted. Kyoto lost many of its finest craftsmen to the war and Yoshio's father was one of them. The day before the surrender was declared, their shop building was torn down in the interests of the war effort, without the head of the household present to defend it. Hirata-san learned his trade after the war from other craftsmen who (unlike his father) returned home safely.

Before the war *sudare* blinds were a necessary part of everyday life in Kyoto, where summers were hot and humid, and the plague of mosquitoes was a constant problem. *Sudare* allowed the paper *shōji* windows to be removed in summertime for ventilation and still shade the rooms from the heat of the sun. They also afforded a bit of privacy along crowded streets.

With the introduction of the aluminum sash window and metal screen

after the war, *sudare* became a luxury item used primarily for decorative purposes.

There are several different kinds of *sudare* classified according to use and materials. The heavier outdoor type are called *hi-yoke sudare*. They come in a variety of materials including *take* (bamboo), *yoshi* (a hollow, jointed yellowish reed), *gama* (a solid beige reed without joints), and *hagi* (the dark brown branches of a shrub).

Sudare for interior use in tearooms and as room dividers during the summer months are called *zashiki sudare*, the kind with a fabric border in brocade or linen. The reeds of *zashiki sudare* are usually of bamboo, though more finely split than those for exterior use. Often when the material used is jointed, like bamboo, the joints are laid out to create a pattern on the finished blind—the more intricate, the more costly.

A third type of blind is called a *misu*, the very finest variety formerly used to hide the emperor from the eyes of the public. Now they are used mainly in temples or shrines. As with many of the accouterments of court life, the making of *misu* was regulated by protocol, which determined every detail—the number of reeds in each, the type of patterns their joints formed, and the kind of brocade used to border them.

Hirata will make blinds to fit any space by special order, although at busy times you can expect to wait a month or more. If you simply wish to choose your own trim from fabric samples in his catalog, a standard-size order can be filled in a couple of days since he makes each blind himself here at the back of his shop on a machine that can be seen from the counter. An average *sudare* is about a yard and a half long by a little over a yard wide.

Other products sold at Hirata's include *nawa-noren*, the hand-twisted hemp-rope curtains often seen in the doorways of kitchens or the entrances to restaurants in Kyoto, and *tsuitate*, the single-panel standing screens that are placed inside entrances for decoration or to screen the recesses of a house from view.

NAKAMURA-RŌ
restaurant

中村楼

Yasaka-jinja-uchi, Gion, Higashiyama-ku
東山区祇園八坂神社内　☎(075) 561-0016〜8

OPEN: 11:30 A.M.–7:30 P.M. (last order, 6) ■ CLOSED: Last Thursday ■ PRICES: Lunch from ¥2,500, dinner (*kaiseki*) from ¥15,000

Standing on the bridge at Shijō I see a light: Is it Yasaka
Shrine . . . or can it be the lanterns of Niken-jaya?

—Anonymous

Nobody remembers how long people have been stopping for a cup of tea and a bite of tofu beside the stone *torii* gate at Yasaka Shrine in Gion. But by the end of the sixteenth century, the pair of teahouses known as Niken-jaya were famous. Only one has survived the four hundred years since then—Nakamura-rō, said to be the oldest restaurant in Japan. Rather than tearing down the tiny one-room hut that made them famous, the twelfth-generation owner of what is now a luxurious restaurant and inn guards the humble teahouse as the precious family heirloom it is.

Sliding open the *shōji* paper doors in midwinter, you become a part of a world that no longer exists. A worn stone floor, a wood-burning clay stove with a sputtering kettle of water on for tea, the rough-hewn stone tofu basins, the old charcoal grill for heating the skewers of tofu, a stone well so deep you cannot see the bottom, with a lid so heavy that no one lifts it anymore, and a pair of imperturbable ladies in kimono who seem to be a part of the same comfortable time warp.

In summertime, the doors disappear completely, opening onto the graveled walkway to the shrine, looking much as it did in an old Edo-period woodblock print, with pilgrims and foreigners and itinerant priests gathered round waiting the *tōfu dengaku* (skewers of tofu covered with *miso* sauce) to be placed on the low benches before them. Foreign visitors are nothing new to the popular teahouse. Foreign customers stopped in centuries ago to listen to the *shamisen* players strum to the rhythm of the chopping knives of beautiful lady cutters, who sliced the tofu to precise dimensions. A bowl of *o-usu*, the powdered tea of the tea ceremony, and a platter of *tōfu dengaku* still make a fine afternoon snack, no matter which century you belong to.

Late in the nineteenth century an inn and formal restaurant were added on to accommodate the number of *daimyō* (feudal lords) who flocked to Kyoto, which had become the focal point of a struggle to overthrow the shogunate and reinstate the emperor as ruler of Japan. Tales of clandestine meetings by plotters on both sides held in the banquet rooms and parlors of Nakamura-rō are legendary, easy to imagine as you walk down the long, narrow corridors that lead up and down stairways to the inner recesses of the inn. One royally appointed room at the back of the inn, now famous for its screen paintings by Ogata Kōrin, was once the temporary residence of Arisugawa-no-miya, brother of the emperor Meiji.

All the rooms (some of which are guest rooms, some for private dinners, and others for large banquets) overlook a magnificent central garden that always has flowers in season, with cherry trees in springtime, followed by azaleas, hydrangeas, maple trees, chrysanthemums, and camellias. The inn is a popular retreat for poets and writers, who have been making annual pilgrimages to Nakamura-rō for decades.

Noted primarily in recent years as a *ryōtei* (a first-class restaurant), Nakamura-rō serves both private dinners and large banquets with *kaiseki*-style meals. It is not unusual to see geisha from neighboring Gion arriving to entertain a group of guests with an evening of *shamisen* music and dance.

Nakamura-rō is owned by Masamitsu Tsuji, one of whose relatives owns Tsujitome, the most famous *kaiseki* caterer in Kyoto. Shigemitsu Tsuji, Masamitsu's late father, was the author of an authoritative volume on tofu cuisine. The cuisine at Nakamura-rō is strictly Kyoto style. Mr. Tsuji believes that the natural flavor of the ingredients is the secret to fine cooking, and uses much less seasoning (salt, sugar, soy sauce, or spices) than chefs in other regions of Japan. (Kyoto cooking is said to be the mildest in the country.)

Apart from the full-course *kaiseki* dinners offered at Nakamura-rō, both the teahouse and the main restaurant serve a reasonably priced *bentō* box lunch between 11 A.M. and 3 P.M. every day for a sampling of the type of cuisine offered.

In Kyoto today, the younger generation often sets about modernizing the venerable old antiques left them by their parents, whether they be houses or restaurants. When the elder Mr. Tsuji passed away three years ago, the mourners who attended the funeral, many of them old customers, implored the young son not to change a thing in the cherished old inn. Tsuji Jr., much to their delight, promised that he would be only too happy to oblige.

MINOKŌ
cha-kaiseki cuisine 美濃幸

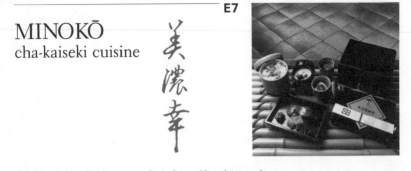

480 Kiyoi-chō, Shimogawara-dōri, Gion, Higashiyama-ku
東山区祇園下河原通清井町480 ☎ (075) 561-0328

OPEN: 11:30 A.M.–11 P.M. (last order, 8:30) ■ CLOSED: Usually 2nd & 4th Wednesdays ■ PRICES: *Bentō* lunch from ¥2,500, *cha-kaiseki* from ¥10,000 ■ CREDIT: DC, JCB, MC, MIL, VISA

Just below the stone *torii* gate, the south and main entrance to Yasaka Shrine, there is a quiet neighborhood of innkeepers and restaurateurs that forms the eastern fringe of Gion, the old pleasure quarter of Kyoto. A stroll down the narrow cobblestone path called Ishibe-kōji in this area with its high rock walls and impressive old villas leads one to believe he or she has entered an exclusive residential district belonging to the privileged few. Many of these fine structures were indeed the villas of wealthy Kyoto merchants, but after World War II, when many families lost their fortunes, most of the residences were turned into inns or "teahouses" (*o-chaya*), which now cater to the same class of people that once inhabited them. The area, like Gion, now only comes alive at night. While retaining the dignity of former days, the teahouses and inns of Shimogawara now have the added hint of intrigue that surrounds the world of the geisha of Gion, who are frequently called here to entertain.

Just before you get to the narrow alley that leads to Ishibe-kōji, you'll find one of these former villas, a *ryōtei* called Minokō, that has combined these two worlds and added a third dimension of its own—that of *cha-kaiseki*, the elegant multi-course meal served at formal gatherings for ceremonial tea. *Cha-kaiseki* differs from ordinary *kaiseki* not only in the characters that form the name, but in both purpose and style. In *cha-kaiseki*, the *cha* means tea, the *kai* means pocket or fold, and the *seki* means stone, referring to the heated stones which Zen priests placed inside the folds of their garments to warm their bellies against the chill of unheated temples in winter. The meal served with the tea ceremony is intended to be "just enough to keep you warm," a reference to the discipline and restraint sought as one of the primary goals of the practice of Tea. *Cha-kaiseki*, when combined with the tea ceremony, is a highly formal affair. At Minokō you have the chance to experience the same meal in the relaxed atmosphere of a private room.

Eastern Kyoto

139

Ordinary *kaiseki* (though by no means "ordinary" at all) is written with characters that mean banquet seat and refer to the series of snacks that accompany a bottle of saké at drinking parties in a much less formal mode. This type of *kaiseki* is also available for groups who visit Minokō for events like *bōnenkai*, the let-your-hair-down year-end parties that are intended to help weary office workers "forget the old year."

At Minokō, *cha-kaiseki* is served with a bowl of thick green tea to stimulate the appetite in a setting with all the natural beauty and simple elegance of a formal tearoom but without the accompanying ceremony and its complicated etiquette and procedures.

At lunch time Minokō serves an informal box lunch called *chabako-bentō*, after the lacquered container in which it is served. They resemble the kind of boxes that are used to carry tea utensils to outdoor tea gatherings. Luncheon guests are served in a spacious tatami room overlooking a tea garden with stone lanterns and the sound of trickling water from a stream. The occasional turtle ambling from one rock to the next in this peaceful garden adds to the sense of rustic beauty so admired by aficionados of the tea ceremony.

In the evening, by reservation only, guests are seated in private tearooms with a view of the same lovely garden and are served in the height of *cha-kaiseki* style. One course after another of carefully arranged seasonal delicacies arrive on square porcelain trays, bamboo platters, and lacquered bowls chosen to compliment the mood of the season. So careful is the owner, Kazuo Yoshida, about the seasonal appropriateness of items on each evening's menu that he mentioned that eggs, for example, are never served at Minokō during the hot summer months. "A difficult time for the chickens," as he put it.

I arrived at Minokō early one morning to find the maids busy sweeping some sort of mucky, black substance that looked like something someone had tracked in from the garden. I was told that these were tea leaves left over from last night, and that the maids sweep the hardwood floors with it every morning, which brings the surface to a deep, glossy sheen. They wouldn't think of using anything else.

BUNNOSUKE-JAYA
amazake (a sweet beverage)

文の助茶屋

Kōdaiji-mon-mae, Higashiyama-ku
東山区高台寺門前　☎(075) 551-1376

OPEN: 10 A.M.–6 P.M. ■ CLOSED: Wednesdays ■ PRICES: ¥300–¥500

Etsuzō Yamada, at age 77, carries on today with an entrepreneur's gusto the family business of selling *amazake* (reportedly the favorite drink of Buddhist nuns) left him by his theatrical father, the noted *rakugo* artist whose stage name was Katsura Bunnosuke. *Rakugo* is the Japanese art of storytelling—funny, often bawdy storytelling. One look at the riot of knickknacks and memorabilia that hangs from every inch of ceiling and crowds every shelf is all you need to grasp the essence of the tradition.

The popularity of *rakugo* began to decline when the trend for sophistication and urbanity took hold of Japan around the turn of the century. Rickshaws went out with the advent of roadsters, and *rakugo* went out with talking pictures. By the end of the Meiji period, Bunnosuke had had enough of empty theaters and decided to spend an early retirement refurbishing a rundown *amazake* shop that seemed to be fighting the same battle as he was for survival in a rapidly modernizing Japan.

There were once scores of *amazake* shops in this area about midway between Yasaka Shrine and Kiyomizu-dera temple. *Amazake* is a sweet drink that is made from saké lees. Though it has the aroma of the real thing, it contains no alcohol and is said to have been the invention of Buddhist nuns. Kōdai-ji, a nunnery just across the road from Bunnosuke-jaya, may be the reason this one *amazake* shop still exists at all.

Kōdai-ji is not open to the public. Although its gardens are said to be exquisite, the sad story of the temple's birth is enough to squelch dreams of sightseeing. After the death of the great military leader Toyotomi Hideyoshi, his widow vowed in grief to escape the cruel world by entering a nunnery. Perhaps in remorse for his own role in overthrowing Hideyoshi, Tokugawa Ieyasu, his successor, presented the distraught widow with Kōdai-ji in 1606, where she lived out her life in the cloistered halls of the nunnery. He even ordered the Sō-mon Gate of Hideyoshi's Fushimi Castle to be moved here to comfort her. Not ten years later Ieyasu would wipe out every last member of the Toyotomi line.

Just to the north of the teahouse is a garden designed by the famous tea master and landscape architect Kobori Enshū. In it he used stones from Hideyoshi's Momoyama Castle that was destroyed by Ieyasu in 1620. The *karesansui* dry rock garden can be seen from the grounds of the teahouse (where you might even catch sight of the garden's proprietor practicing his golf swing).

At the back of Bunnosuke-jaya is a small shrine to Daikoku-ten, the god of wealth (and one of the seven gods of good luck so popular in Japan). Daikoku-ten was Hideyoshi's patron saint, and his widow is said to have brought the jolly deity with her to this site from Osaka Castle.

From the low benches under the awning outdoors where *amazake* or *matcha* (the thick tea of the tea ceremony) is served, there is a full view of one of the most bizarre collections of art and trivia in Japan. First, find the photo of old Bunnosuke and his wife (the present owner's parents)

taken in the Meiji period, for a glimpse at the flamboyant character behind this whole affair, for this eclectic spot seems more like an event than a tea shop. Opposite the kitchen, adorning the illustrious wall above the storage room door no less, is a woodblock print which Yamada-san swears is a masterpiece by Hokusai himself. And in the mishmash of old clocks, *tansu* chests, wooden tobacco boxes, kites, and souvenir folk dolls collected on one of Yamada's many train trips around the countryside, there are even several interesting samples of Japanese folk erotica tucked away that he'd be simply delighted to show you.

At 77, Yamada-san has not lost his teasing rogue's grin as he places a foot-long, cannon-barrel-sized lingam in the hands of an unsuspecting young lady sipping her sweet drink on his porch. "Well, what do you think?" he beams, anticipating with glee the giggled response.

Yamada-san spends much of his time in the back room with his TV set and his beloved photo albums full of Tamasaburo, one of his favorite kabuki actors and friends. It takes a good deal of cajoling to persuade him to come out and tell stories. But when the gaunt old fellow in his somber, striped kimono finally begrudgingly sits down on the *zabuton* cushion on the tatami mats out front, adjusts his tobacco box, lights a long-stemmed *kiseru* pipe, and begins, you'd swear that *rakugo* was something in the blood.

IKKYŪ-AN
Chinese-style temple food

Kōdai-ji Minami-monzen, Higashiyama-ku
東山区高台寺南門前   ☎(075) 561–1901

OPEN: 12 noon–8 P.M. (seating until 6:30) ■ CLOSED: Tuesdays ■ PRICES: From ¥3,000 ■ CREDIT:
JCB, MC, VISA

---

*Ten years in the brothels—hard to wear out desire; I force
myself to live in empty hills, a dark ravine. Those pleasant
places—countless miles of clouds shut them from me now.
Tall pines—harsh in my ears, wind above the roof.*

—Ikkyū Sōjun (1394–1481)

Legends about the "mad Zen monk," as Ikkyū Sōjun, the famous fifteenth-century priest, came to be known, can probably only hope to come close to depicting the riotous life of one of Kyoto's most colorful monastics. The son of an emperor and one of his concubines, Ikkyū was to embarrass the haughty temple priests in whose charge he was placed at the age of five by his remarkable ability to answer all their "unsolvable" Zen riddles. By the age of twelve he astounded his teachers by writing poetry in the sophisticated Chinese literary style he had come to the temple to study. At sixteen, he set out to find the enlightenment the temple fathers failed to show him. He found enlightenment one day when the cry of a crow broke through his evening meditation on a boat in Lake Biwa.

From there he struck out again on his own, this time to the saké shops and bordellos of Sakai, carousing and vocally challenging the piety of the pompous Kyoto abbots. He wound up as abbot of Daitoku-ji, and ironically became one of the temple's most revered abbots.

He never lost that edge of "madness," however, as can be seen in a series of poems written at the age of seventy-three about the blind singer Mōri, with whom he had fallen in love. In spite of a long Buddhist tradition of celibacy, Ikkyū apparently continued to explore the spiritual possibilities of eroticism all the way to his grave. He died (happily, no doubt) fourteen years later.

Ikkyū-an, a quiet vegetarian restaurant at the foot of the Higashiyama Mountains, chose this endearing

character as its mascot, and the waitress who comes to greet you at the door even wears the white robes of a priest in Ikkyū's time. Ikkyū-an serves *fucha ryōri*, an eight-course Chinese-style Zen meal, in a beautiful building that was once a part of Kōdai-ji temple, beside whose south gate it stands. The full course includes *goma dōfu* (sesame tofu), vegetables in a delicate sweet sauce, *nasu dengaku* (eggplant with *miso* sauce), vegetable tempura, a variety of greens in vinegar or broth, soup, and rice for ¥3,000. There is no need for a menu as Ikkyū-an specializes only in this one particular type of meal. More expensive versions of the same meal can be ordered, the difference being the number and variety of courses served.

Fucha ryōri, unlike the Japanese-style Zen meal called *shōjin ryōri*, features thicker Chinese-style sauces, is often served from large platters rather than in small, separate bowls, and occasionally permits the use of pork as a soup base.

The amazing thing about Zen cuisine in Kyoto is the endless variety of flavors and textures in vegetarian cooking that have been explored in the Buddhist Orient. Dishes like *fu* (a wheat gluten dumpling), *yuba* (skimmings from soy milk), and tofu—however plain they may sound—offer a remarkable range of textures (in addition to the protein they provide) and are intended to absorb the flavor of sauces and soups, solving the problem of monotony in a strictly vegetarian diet.

Apart from the cuisine, Ikkyū-an itself is something of a sensory treat. The bell-shaped windows in the southeast room on the second floor overlook the old Yasaka Pagoda on one side and the lush greenery of the Higashiyama Mountains on the other. Each small tatami room has a *tokonoma* alcove with a scroll painting, a flower arrangement, and an image of Daikoku-ten, the god of wealth and happiness, the guardian spirit of Ikkyū-an. Notice the beautifully carved transoms (*ranma*) above the sliding doors that separate the rooms.

The fourth-generation owner, Masakazu Koyama, does all the cooking himself, a custom started by his great-grandfather in 1915 when he opened Ikkyū-an, the first *fucha ryōri* restaurant in Kyoto.

Ikkyū-an serves only guests who have made reservations to insure that every dish is fresh and nothing is left over, in the spirit of Zen. One parting word from Ikkyū himself:

——Who is the true transmitter of Rinzai's line?

——These elegant ones with their pretty boys attending?

——One bowl of muddy wine, three thousand poems.

——I laugh at Zen monks who don't know their Zen.

KASAGI-YA
sweets and tea

かさぎ屋

349 Masuya-chō, Kōdai-ji, Higashiyama-ku
東山区高台寺桝屋町349　☎ (075) 561-9562

OPEN: 11 A.M.–6 P.M. (7 P.M. June–Sept.) ■ CLOSED: 2nd, 4th & 5th Tuesdays ■ PRICES: From ¥500

Amatō no sudōri dekinai Ninenzaka
(The sweet-lover's downfall, Ninenzaka)
　　　　—by the poet Tenmin, on the wall at Kasagi-ya

Copper kettle sputtering over the hibachi coals . . . the proprietor, kimono sleeves tucked into his *obi* sash, whisks a bowl of *o-usu*, thick green tea, to a froth with elegance and ease. Carrying it gracefully across the tiny room with its sagging stone floor, he turns the bowl counterclockwise so that the *shōmen*, or "face," is directed toward his guest and places it on the table with a full bow, just as the host might at a formal tea ceremony. Although Kasagi-ya is not a formal tearoom, the graciousness and hospitality that is the essence of tea is carried on here— quietly, lovingly, and in the spirit of humility that Sen no Rikyū sought to evoke in his *wabi-cha*, the aesthetic of unaffected refinement in *sadō*, the Way of Tea.

When asked about which school of tea he attended, Hirozō Hayakawa seemed hesitant to reply. "Well, Omotesenke (the so-called aristocratic Way of Tea), but I stopped all that years ago. What I do here isn't really formal tea ceremony at all. I just serve tea and sweets the way I think is best," he said as he walked over to light another chip of natural sandalwood in an incense burner in the corner.

His wife supervises the kitchen in back, where she and her daughter make fresh *o-hagi* every morning. *O-hagi* is a very homey Japanese sweet made with a sticky rice center and a coating of sweet red azuki beans (or vice versa). *O-hagi* was originally served during the celebration of the Autumn Equinox. The name comes from a willowy bush clover that flowers only in the fall. At Kasagi-ya, Mrs. Hayakawa makes the *o-hagi* fresh while you wait and serves them still warm, a rare treat in Kyoto today. They are sweet (but not overwhelmingly), a complement to the astringent flavor of *o-usu*. (One ninety-four-year-old *o-hagi* addict in Kyoto says they're the best she's ever had.)

Kasagi-ya is located at the foot of the steps that lead up the hill to Kiyomizu Temple. The one-room shop seats just ten people and has been serving refreshments to visitors to the famous temple since 1914.

The sloping, stone-paved lanes that lead up to Kiyomizu Temple have been worn smooth over the centuries by the constant flow of pilgrims to the great temple dedicated to Kannon, the goddess of mercy. A little over a decade ago, this neighborhood was designated a historic preservation district. It is dotted with ceramic shops, antique shops, and inns (some old, some new) that make this area a mecca for tourists.

One of the most noted turn-of-the-century customers at Kasagi-ya was a Taishō-period painter named Takehisa Yumeji (1884–1934), whose female portraits are said to be the melancholy image of the frail woman he lived with in the old house next door to Kasagi-ya. A victim of tuberculosis, she died young, leaving Takehisa haunted with the memory of her

fragile beauty. Their famous love affair was doomed from the start by the young woman's domineering father and a disease that was then in epidemic proportions across Japan. One of Takehisa's rare landscape scenes hangs on the wall to the left of the entrance.

Aside from *o-usu* and *o-hagi*, Kasagi-ya serves other sweets and beverages to complement the season, such as *o-shiruko*, a smooth sweet bean soup, and *zenzai*, sweet whole red beans in a lighter broth, both popular in winter. Summer treats include *kōri-mizore*, shaved ice with sweet syrup on top, and *kōri-uji*, shaved ice with green tea syrup on top.

The interior of Kasagi-ya, with its antique lamp shades, its old wooden tobacco boxes, the wicker stools, and the *senja-fuda* stickers bearing the names of former visitors (some famous actors and artists), is one of the only places in this area that has not been tampered with. While other shops have completely remodeled to accommodate the throngs who flock here to soak up the atmosphere of "old Kyoto," Kasagi-ya quietly holds what its shinier neighbors lack: the genuine warmth and hospitality that can't be recaptured with a new coat of paint.

ROKUSEI NISHIMISE
Kyoto "box lunch"

71 Nishitennō-chō, Okazaki, Sakyō-ku

左京区岡崎西天王町71

☎ (075) 751-6171 (English spoken)

OPEN: 11 A.M.–8 P.M. ■ CLOSED: Mondays ■ PRICES: ¥2,420–¥12,000 ■ CREDIT: DC, JCB, VISA

Rokusei began as an exclusive *shidashi kaiseki* catering service at the turn of the century but expanded about fifteen years ago to its present site on the west side of Heian Shrine overlooking the canal. The building is modern, with polished marble floors and contemporary Japanese interior design. For lunch they serve a *te-oke-bentō* in handmade wooden buckets— a great sampler of Kyoto-style cuisine at reasonable prices. Rokusei is extremely popular with both local residents and out-of-town visitors.

KANŌSHŌJU-AN
tea and sweets

Tetsugaku-no-michi-iriguchi, 2–1 Nyakuōji-chō, Sakyō-ku

左京区若王子町2-1哲学の道入口

☎ (075) 751-1077

OPEN: 9 A.M.–4:30 P.M.; tea ceremony, 10 A.M.–3:30 P.M. ■ CLOSED: Wednesdays

A recent addition to the scenic Philosopher's Walk beside the old canal that runs from the foot of Ginkaku-ji southward toward Nanzen-ji. This traditional-style teahouse beneath the maple trees is a branch of an old sweet shop in Shiga Prefecture and can be reached by crossing a narrow private bridge over the canal. You can buy individual soft bean paste

(*nama-gashi*, or fresh sweets) to take out—or try one with ceremonial tea prepared for you in a traditional tatami-matted tearoom. For this you must say, "*O-cha no o-temae o haiken shitai no desu ga.*" You will then be led to a waiting room where you'll be served an "appetizer," and finally led to a room in the back that looks out on a lovely garden. Here you can watch while tea is prepared for you in a quiet, intimate atmosphere that allows you to enjoy the experience without the formality of attending a private ceremony.

MINOKICHI Kyoto cuisine

Sanjō-agaru, Dōbutsuen-mae-dōri, Sakyō-ku

左京区動物園前通三条上ル

☎ (075) 771-4185 (English spoken)

OPEN: Daily, 11:30 A.M.–9 P.M. (last order) ■ PRICES: ¥2,500–¥16,000 ■ CREDIT: AE, DC, JCB, MC, MIL, UC, VISA

Established in 1735, Minokichi is one of the largest and most popular restaurants in Kyoto. They advertise Kyoto-style cuisine (*Kyō-ryōri*) but their impressive menu also includes *shabu-shabu*, sukiyaki, sushi, and tempura as well as *kaiseki*. *Kyō-ryōri* connoisseurs who prefer the exclusive atmosphere of the more expensive restaurants criticize Minokichi as being a place for tourists, but the large, beautiful garden here is surrounded by buildings that accommodate both large groups and private parties and the interiors are tastefully done in folk-art style, with many fine ceramic pieces and woodblock prints on display. Menu in English. Call for reservations in the evening.

TAZAWA KOBIJUTSU-TEN antiques

Sanjō-sagaru Nishi-gawa, Higashiōji-dōri, Higashiyama-ku

東山区東大路通三条下ル西側

☎ (075) 561–3009 (English spoken)

OPEN: Daily, 11 A.M.–6:30 P.M.

On Higashi-ōji just north of Shin-monzen, the popular antique district for tourists, Tazawa is one of several interesting antique shops. The Tazawa family are noted experts in Meiji-period Japanese glassware though they have recently become known abroad for their fine selection of Japanese dolls. Tazawa-san speaks English and is very knowledgeable about Kyoto dolls, so this is a rare chance for doll collectors to learn about a subject on which little information is available outside Japan.

NAKAMURA CHINGIRE-TEN textiles

Sanjō Minami-iru, Nawate-dōri, Higashiyama-ku

東山区縄手通三条南入

☎ (075) 561-4726

OPEN: Daily, 9 A.M.–8 P.M. ■ CREDIT: AE, DC, JCB, MC, UC, VISA

Just south of Sanjō Station in the antique district that runs parallel with the river below Sanjō. In business for over a hundred years, the Nakamuras sell antique textiles, including hand-painted silks and stenciled cottons from all over Japan. Handbags, coin purses, neckties, and other accessories made from antique fabrics are also available, as well as an assortment of antique woven bamboo baskets for flower arrangement.

YAMAZOE TENKŌ-DŌ scroll paintings

Sanjō-sagaru, Yamatoōji-dōri, Higashiyama-ku

東山区大和大路通三条下ル

☎ (075) 561–3064 (English spoken)

OPEN: 10 A.M.–6 P.M. ■ CLOSED: Sundays

On Nawate-dōri, dealing in fine scroll paintings. Mr. Yamazoe's shop first opened its doors in the Meiji period and its customers have always been students and scholars from universities both in Japan and abroad. Inexpensive, unmounted paintings are displayed in wooden boxes right on the street. Some of his scrolls hang on a display rack inside, but the finer pieces are stored in individual wooden boxes on shelves in the back of the shop. Mr. Yamazoe will unroll one for the serious shopper to examine. He will provide a written description in English if you should decide to purchase one.

KONJAKU NISHIMURA antique textiles

381 Moto-chō, Yamatoōji Higashi-iru, Furumonzen-dōri, Higashiyama-ku

東山区古門前通大和大路東入元町381

☎ (075) 561–1312 (English spoken)

OPEN: 10 A.M.–6:30 P.M. ■ CLOSED: Wednesdays

A one-hundred-year-old shop (not far from Nakamura Chingire-ten) also specializing in old textiles. Everything from swatches of handwoven four-teenth-century indigo-dyed cottons to elaborately embroidered *obi* sashes and Yūzen-dyed kimono is on display. Also offers a variety of small purses, neckties, and belts made by local seamstresses from antique fabrics.

E18

FUJII KEI SHŌTEN dolls

Shinbashi, Nawate-dōri, Higashiyama-ku
東山区縄手通新橋
☎ (075) 561–7863 (English spoken)
OPEN: 10 A.M.–8 P.M. ■ CLOSED: Tuesdays ■ CREDIT: AE, DC, MC, UC, VISA

In a beautiful old shop front on Nawate-dōri just below Shinbashi, Fujii Kei sells Japanese dolls, both antique and new; *netsuke*, the carved baubles used on tobacco pouches; and a small assortment of fine *kanzashi* hair ornaments. The dolls they offer include *hina ningyō*, the festival dolls for Girl's Day, and *musha ningyō*, the samurai dolls displayed on Boy's Day. The doll on display in the front window changes with the season and is often a priceless piece from the Fujii's own collection.

E19

KAPPA NAWATE
robata-yaki grill

Sueyoshi-chō, Higashi-kita-kado, Nawate-agaru 2 Suji-me, Shijō-dōri, Higashiyama-ku

東山区四条通縄手上2筋目末吉町東北角
☎ (075) 531–4048
OPEN: Daily, 6 P.M.–2 A.M. ■ CLOSED: 2 days a month ■ PRICES: From ¥250

A lively *robata-yaki* grill in which you sit elbow to elbow around a crowded counter and order dishes like grilled seafood, sashimi, and *oden* (vegetables and other foods simmered in broth) from a large selection (menu available in English). Inexpensive if you order carefully. Lots of fun and a chance to experience the raucous Osaka-style workingman's hangout in a Kyoto shop that has long experience in serving foreigners because of its prime location in Gion.

E20

YAGENBORI
Kyoto cuisine

Sueyoshi-chō Kiritōshi-kado, Gion, Higashiyama-ku
東山区祇園末吉町切通し角
☎ (075) 551–3331/3421
OPEN: Daily, 12 noon–2 P.M., 4 P.M.–11 P.M. ■ PRICES: *Bentō* lunch from ¥2,500, dinner from ¥5,000

Yagenbori is right in the heart of the Shinbashi district where old "teahouses" line the Shirakawa Canal in Gion. They serve Kyoto cuisine (*Kyō-*

ryōri), which can be ordered *ippin* style (a la carte) or in full-course meals. They have a long counter where you can watch the cooks at work, tatami booths along the edges, and private rooms upstairs. It is decorated in a folk-art style with dark woods and beautiful ceramics. The food is excellent and prices are not unreasonable for the authentic Kyoto atmosphere and the delicacy with which each dish is prepared.

IWANAMI inn (ryokan)

Higashiōji Nishi-iru, Shinmonzen-dōri, Higashiyama-ku

東山区新門前通東大路西入

☎ (075) 561-7135

CHECK-IN: 12 noon ■ CHECK-OUT: 11 A.M. ■ RATES: ¥7,000 (w/breakfast)

Iwanami is a precious old inn right on Shinmonzen-dōri amid all the antique shops and has been the carefully kept secret of the many wise foreign travelers who have been patronizing it for years. The traditional rooms overlook a small interior garden (some of them even have balconies over the Shirakawa Canal that runs behind the inn). Their prices are reasonable, but do not include dinner (a system preferred by many foreigners who like to choose their own restaurants—most Kyoto inns have not made this modern concession to the West and add the cost of two meals to the price of a room). Because Iwanami is often booked a month or more in advance, it is important to write ahead for reservations. The innkeeper does not advertise and hopes to keep the word-of-mouth reputation for excellence her inn has quietly earned.

HIRANO-YA restaurant

Chion-in Minami-mon-mae, Maruyama Kōen-uchi, Higashiyama-ku

東山区円山公園内知恩院南門前

☎ (075) 561-1603/4

OPEN: Daily, 10:30 A.M.–8 P.M. ■ PRICES: From ¥2,000

Just inside the north gate of Maruyama Park near Chion-in is the hundred-year-old Hirano-ya serving *imobō*, a dish that literally comes from the roots of Kyoto cuisine. A bowl of delicious *ebi-imo* (an unusual variety of shrimp-shaped potatoes imported originally by Buddhist priests from China) and *bōdara* (a kind of preserved fish from the Japan Sea) are served with soup, rice, and the ever-present Kyoto pickles. Delicious and inexpensive, though not the standard tourist fare, this is a chance to sample "real" Kyoto-style cuisine. In a city located a two-day walk from the nearest sea, the people of Kyoto invented a seemingly endless variety of ways to serve dried and salted fish. Though it may sound unappealing at first, most people are pleasantly surprised. The restaurant has dozens of small rooms along a narrow stone walkway from which you can watch a score of kimono-clad ladies as they scurry to and fro with

their trays of *imobō*. Peek at the old-style kitchen, and don't miss the restrooms—complete with large stone basins into which water trickles down from a bamboo spout. Hirano-ya is both visually and gastronomically a place from out of the past.

E23

MATSUNO eel restaurant

Minamiza-higashi 4-ken-me, Shijō-dōri, Higashiyama-ku

東山区四条南座東4軒目

☎ (075) 561–2786

OPEN: 11:30 A.M.–9 P.M. (last order, 8:30) ■ CLOSED: Tuesdays ■ PRICES: From ¥1,500 ■ CREDIT: Major cards

The sign in English says MRS. MATSU-NO'S KITCHEN and describes the special-ty of the house as BROILED EEL. Mrs. Matsuno's *unagi* (eel), grilled in a delicious sauce and served at rea-sonable prices, has made this a favorite haunt of theatergoers for over a century. Just four doors east of the Minami-za Kabuki Theater, the folk-style restaurant retains all of its original "theater-door" atmosphere. Try a simple bowl of *unagi donburi* (grilled eel over rice) or splurge on the full-course *unagi teishoku* to sample the range of possibilities this exotic Kyoto-style cuisine has to offer.

E24

GION TANAKA-YA
footwear (geta)

Yamato-chō, Shijō-sagaru, Yamatoōji-dōri, Higashiyama-ku

東山区大和大路通四条下ル大和町1

☎ (075) 561–1993 (English spoken)

OPEN: 9 A.M.–8:30 P.M. ■ CLOSED: Wednes-days ■ CREDIT: AE, DC, JCB, MC, MIL

Geta are wooden clogs for casual wear whose clip-clop sound once provided city music with natural percussion. Worn these days most often by cooks (some pairs even raise the wearer five inches off a soggy kitchen floor) and summer festival-goers, *geta* were every-day footwear in Japan until World War II. Tanaka-ya has extra-large sizes to fit the foreigner, although a proper fit in Japanese footwear is said to leave at least three-quarters of an inch of heel hanging off the back for better balance. *Geta* come in men's and ladies' styles, the men's usually with black thongs and the women's with a variety of colors on either black-lacquered or natural-wood–finished bases. Whereas the average sushi maker goes through a pair of *geta* every month, a good pair, with or-dinary use, will last years. *Zōri* are for more formal occasions and are made of specially coated leather, grass mat-ting over cork bases, or even ostrich leather for the really stylish wearer. Again, a "proper" fit seems too narrow and short for the Western foot. *Zōri* are the accepted footwear for formal Japanese occasions—weddings, tea ceremonies, and other formal affairs—and can be worn indoors on carpeted floors, where the coarser *geta* cannot.

E25

KAGIZEN YOSHIFUSA
Kyoto confectionery

264 Gion-machi Kitagawa, Higashiyama-ku

東山区祇園町北側264

☎ (075) 561–1818, 525–1818

OPEN: 9 A.M.–6 P.M. ■ CLOSED: Mondays

Kagizen is one of the few remaining places on Shijō in Gion that have taken great pains to preserve the traditional beauty of their old shop while upholding a reputation as one of the best *o-kashi-ya*, or Japanese sweet shops, in Kyoto. Most sweet shops in town sell only takeout sweets in gift-wrapped boxes, but at Kagizen there is also a room upstairs where you may order *o-usu*, the thick tea-ceremony tea, and *nama-gashi*, or fresh sweets, to eat on the premises. Notice the fine cabinetry by the late Kuroda Tatsuaki, formerly designated a Living National Treasure, and the ceramic pieces by the famous potter Kawai Kanjiro.

MONJU lacquerware

Hanamikōji Higashi-iru Minami-gawa, Shijō-dōri, Higashiyama-ku
東山区四条通花見小路東入南側
☎ (075) 525–1617

OPEN: 10 A.M.–7:30 P.M. ■ CLOSED: Thursdays ■ CREDIT: AE, DC, JCB, UC, VISA

Lacquered trays, bowls, boxes, incense containers, and chopsticks that come with their own carrying cases. Unlike the quasi-lacquerware you'll find elsewhere in town, Monju sells nothing but the real thing. (Recently, some makers have been coating plastic bases with lacquer.) The wide price range you'll notice at Monju in bowls, for example, is not the difference between plastic and wood. The lower-priced bowls are made of a wood-chip composition base, rather than turned, solid wood. The composition-base pieces are actually much better suited for daily use. Most Japanese use expensive lacquerware only once a year at New Year's. Beautiful pairs of lacquered chopsticks in hand-finished wooden carrying cases make wonderful gifts for ardent sushi fans.

KASAGEN Japanese umbrellas

284 Gion-machi Kitagawa, Higashiyama-ku
東山区祇園町北側284
☎ (075) 561–2832

OPEN: Daily, 9:30 A.M.–9 P.M.

Selling handmade oiled-paper umbrellas since 1861. There are three basic varieties: *bangasa*, the large, bamboo-handled rain umbrellas used at inns and traditional restaurants, often with names written on the rim in Chinese characters; *janome*, the delicate lady's umbrella usually decorated with printed geometric or floral designs; and *higasa*, the hand-painted, un-oiled paper parasols. This is the oldest umbrella shop in Kyoto. Souvenir shops along the Shin-kyōgoku arcade downtown sell cheaper versions, but the paper is of poor quality, as is the workmanship, and they never last a single season. (Don't hesitate to use Kasagen's umbrellas in the rain. Dry them by hanging them up [opened] indoors overnight—not in the sun, which would fade the lovely colors—and they will last years.) In the old days when Raku-tō was still an uncrowded suburb, the craftsmen at Kasagen used to set their umbrellas out to dry in a field below Yasaka Shrine, but with no fields left nearby, they have moved their workshop to Gifu, where most of the *wagasa* in Japan are made today.

E28

KAZURASEI hair ornaments

285 Gion-machi Kitagawa, Shijō-dōri, Higashiyama-ku
東山区四条通祇園町北側285
☎ (075) 561–0672

OPEN: 10 A.M.–7 P.M. ■ CLOSED: 1st & 3rd Wednesdays ■ CREDIT: AE, DC, MC, MIL, UC

The north side of Shijō-dōri has many shops that cater to the geisha in Gion: one that started out as a hairdresser's shop for actors and dancers in 1865 now makes and sells exquisite hair ornaments (*kanzashi*) in lacquer, natural woods, or tortoiseshell. This is Kazurasei, where you'll find a wide selection of lacquered combs in every shape and size, some inlaid with mother-of-pearl and sprinkled with gold dust in a technique called *maki-e*, which dates to the eighth century. Don't miss the elaborate human-hair wigs dressed in Edo-period geisha styles. Miniature wigs on display stands for collectors are also available, styled by traditional dollmakers, each with tiny *kanzashi* of their own. Try a bottle of the shop's camellia-oil shampoo used in Gion to give the long hair of geisha a lacquer-like sheen.

E29

MIURA SHŌMEI lanterns

284 Gion-machi Kitagawa, Higashiyama-ku
東山区祇園町北側284
☎ (075) 561–2816

OPEN: 9:30 A.M.–8 P.M. ■ CLOSED: Sundays ■ CREDIT: DC, JCB, UC, VISA

Specializes in handcrafted paper lanterns—traditional and contemporary Japanese lighting fixtures of all kinds. The shop itself has been remodeled, but all products are handmade by individual craftsmen exclusively for Miura Shōmei. Hanging paper *akari* lanterns designed by Isamu Noguchi are available here, as are bronze-cast *tōrō* garden lanterns, bamboo and unfinished wooden wall lamps, *andon* floor lamps with classical cone-shaped paper shades, and bamboo table lamps.

E30

IZUJŪ sushi

292-1 Gion-machi Kitagawa, Higashiyama-ku
東山区祇園町北側292-1
☎ (075) 561–0019

OPEN: 11 A.M.–9 P.M. ■ CLOSED: Periodically ■ PRICES: ¥450–¥1,700

Established in 1892, this small sushi shop is right on the corner of Shijō and Higashi-ōji in Gion. They feature *sabazushi*, specially prepared mackerel from the Japan Sea, a traditional Kyoto favorite from a time in which only preserved fish could survive the long journey from the coast. They also offer the standard seasonal selection of sushi in a very old-style shop which has dozens of antique, ornate Imari bowls and platters on shelves overhead to enjoy while you dine (sushi to go is also available). Look for the double diamond pattern in dark wood on the white wall out front.

E31

TAKOCHŌ oden stew

Higashi-kita-kado, Donguri-bashi Higashi-zume, Kawabata-dōri, Higashiyama-ku
東山区川端通団栗橋東詰東北角
☎ (075) 525-0170

OPEN: 6 P.M.–10 P.M. ■ CLOSED: Mondays ■ PRICES: ¥500 ■ CREDIT: JCB

Only fifteen seats at the counter of this hundred-year-old *oden* shop, the best in Kyoto. Steaming vats of broth behind the counter are filled with a variety of simmering treats, like cabbage rolls and tofu, from which to choose. Order piece by piece or *moriawase* (an assortment) and dip each piece into a spicy Chinese mustard—a great combination with saké, particularly in the winter. On the narrow street that runs beside the Kamo River south of the Minamiza Kabuki Theater. Its white and black walls and Meiji-style wrought-iron lantern out front make it an easy landmark on the corner by the first bridge south of Shijō-dōri. Popular with both foreign residents and Japanese; call before you go to reserve a seat at the counter.

E32

GION UMEMURA inn

3-chōme, Hakata-chō, Yamatoōji Shijō-sagaru, Higashiyama-ku

東山区大和大路四条下ル博多町３丁目
☎ (075) 525-0156 (English spoken)

CHECK-IN: 4 P.M. ■ CHECK-OUT: 10 A.M. ■ RATES: ¥5,500 (w/2 meals), ¥4,000 (w/o meals)

A Meiji-period inn owned by former *sumō* wrestler Sawanomitsu from Hokkaido. Twenty years ago the mountain of a man and his tiny Kyoto wife opened this inn, whose evening meal features *chanko-nabe* (the hodgepodge stew guaranteed to satisfy a hungry *sumō* wrestler). Constructed in 1908, the inn has the Euro-Japanese flair of its period and is very reasonably priced (for its location in the middle of Gion). Popular with young people, *sumō* fans, and big eaters, Umemura is also just two doors south of one of the oldest *sentō*, or public baths, in Gion (rumored to be the bathing place of some of Gion's apprentice geisha, called *maiko*).

E33

KINNABE

one-pot cooking, inn (ryokan)

Hakata-chō, Yamatoōji Shijō-sagaru, Higashiyama-ku
東山区大和大路四条下ル博多町
☎ (075) 531-4188

RESTAURANT OPEN: 5 P.M.–8 P.M. ■ PRICES: From ¥5,000 ■ CHECK-IN: 2 P.M. ■ CHECKOUT: 11 A.M. ■ RATES: From ¥13,000 (w/2 meals) ■ CREDIT: JCB, VISA

A hundred-year-old inn with a beautiful traditional entry courtyard and an antique *maneki-neko* cat welcoming guests. Kinnabe does not advertise as an inn, and most of its overnight guests have been introduced by former guests. They are open for dinner and specialize in *shabu-shabu* and *mizu-taki* served in a unique style called *kaminabe*. A bamboo strainer lined with special handmade paper is filled with beef or chicken and lowered into a pot of simmering broth in this unusual Kyoto-style meal. No English is spoken, so the proprietress asks that foreign dinner guests who do not speak Japanese be accompanied by someone who does. The atmosphere and cuisine are authentic—not the typical tourist fare—and Kinnabe is located on Yamato-ōji south of Shijō, right in the heart of very traditional Gion. Don't expect any of the usual concessions or Western conveniences provided in restaurants which cater to the tourist trade.

Sannenzaka Kyō-no-Yado
KIYOMIZU SANSŌ
inn

3-341 Kiyomizu, Higashiyama-ku
東山区清水3-341
☎ (075) 561-6109, 551-3152

CHECK-IN: 4 P.M. ■ CHECK-OUT: 10 A.M. ■ RATES: ¥4,800 (w/2 meals) ■ CLOSED: Periodically

This tiny, well-preserved inn is tucked away on Sannenzaka, the slope that leads to Kiyomizu Temple through a popular historic district lined with old shops and restaurants. The very reasonable rates include two fine meals in an atmosphere that is pure Kyoto. With only six rooms available, reservations are an absolute necessity.

E34

RAKUSHŌ tea and sweets

Washio-chō, Kōdai-ji Kitamon-mae-dōri, Higashiyama-ku
東山区高台寺北門前通鷲尾町
☎ (075) 561-6892

OPEN: Daily, 9:30 A.M.–6 P.M. ■ PRICES: ¥300–¥500

This shop, with its beautiful gardens and prizewinning *koi*, serves green tea, coffee, and a variety of local sweets. A former villa just south of Maruyama Park, it is a refreshing spot to pause in your travels, at a table overlooking the pond.

E36

MATSUDA
antique Imari porcelain

3-338 Kiyomizu, Higashiyama-ku
東山区清水3-338
☎ (075) 541-4009

OPEN: 10 A.M.–6 P.M. ■ CLOSED: Periodically

One of several antique shops on Ninenzaka near Kiyomizu Temple. Specializes in Imari ware, the blue-on-white (*some-tsuke*) porcelain from Kyushu that became popular in Europe in the nineteenth century. Rather than the costly museum-quality Imari sold in shops on Shinmonzen or Teramachi streets, Matsuda's pieces are generally less ornate and more reasonably priced. Mr. Matsuda tries to maintain traditional business ways rather than cater to tourists and writes his prices in Japanese the way it used to be done everywhere in Kyoto.

He gets frustrated at times with foreigners who argue over the prices he quotes them verbally. They are already lower than many of the other shops—so take his word for it.

E37

HYŌTAN-YA gourd flasks

Sannenzaka, Kiyomizu, Higashiyama-ku
東山区清水三年坂
☎ (075) 561-8188

OPEN: Daily, sunrise–sunset

A sixth-generation craftsman of the unusual art of making *hyōtan*, or gourd flasks, once used to carry saké to picnics. A small hole is drilled near the top of the gourd and a tiny long-handled scoop is used to remove the contents. It is then soaked in water, dried in the sun, and left to hang for five years in a room upstairs above the shop before the surface is laboriously hand-polished. *Hyōtan* are said to improve the flavor of saké, but be sure to pour hot *bancha* tea into a new gourd and let it sit for twenty-four hours before using it. This removes the pungent odor the gourds have before they have been used. Though *hyōtan* appear to be fragile, they have been known to "bounce back" more than once when dropped by an inebriated picnicker. Prices vary according to size, color, weight, and shape (unusually shaped gourds are popular as flower containers for the tea ceremony and some are extremely expensive).

E38

ASAHI·DŌ ceramics

1–280 Kiyomizu, Higashiyama-ku
東山区清水1–280
☎ (075) 531-2181 (English spoken)

OPEN: Daily, 8:30 A.M.–6 P.M. ■ CREDIT: Major cards

Until recently, Asahi-dō, which was established in the Meiji period, was housed in a fine old building, but the volume of business they do as the leading local dealer in Kiyomizu ware persuaded them to expand to the big modern building they now possess. The widest selection of Kiyomizu ceramics in Kyoto can be seen here, all produced by local potteries in a wide range of prices. Kiyomizu ware is noted for its delicate blue painting on a white background, as well as for its multicolored overglaze enamels often edged in gold. Before World War II, Asahi-dō was a purveyor to the imperial household.

E39

RAKUSHI·EN ceramics

4-chōme, Gojō-bashi Higashi, Higashiyama-ku
東山区五条橋東4丁目
☎ (075) 541-1161

OPEN: 9 A.M.–6 P.M. ■ CLOSED: Wednesdays ■ CREDIT: AE, DC, JCB, UC

Located on Gojō-zaka, which has been famous for pottery in Kyoto for hundreds of years. Offers a select variety of pieces from small kilns all over Japan. The owner shows a limited selection of work by individual potters, rather than the mass-produced variety from large potteries—Oribe by Kōji Nagae, Kiyomizu ware by Rishō Katō, Chinese-style celadons by Kei Tsukamoto, a Living National Treasure. Note the paper-thin translucent porcelain Kiyomizu teacups at Rakushi-en. The owner says one way to judge the quality of a fine porcelain bowl is to pick it up (carefully!)—the best is always lighter than it appears to be.

RAKU-HOKU

Northern Kyoto

Raku-hoku is almost as much "country" as Kyoto has left. Until recent years it was an area famous for its vegetables and rice fields, but those days are largely a part of the past.

Raku-hoku boasts two old and famous shrines that existed before the city was founded in the eighth century—Shimogamo and Kamigamo shrines. The latter is a pleasant place for a stroll to catch a glimpse of what remains of rural Kyoto.

Daitoku-ji, the oldest Zen temple in Kyoto, just above Kita-ōji (the approximate southern boundary of Raku-hoku), has dozens of sub-temples and gardens to visit, and is known among gourmets for the fine Zen vegetarian fare (shōjin-ryōri) available both on the premises and outside its eastern gate.

Far to the north, nestled beside rivers in the mountain passes that lead to the Japan Sea, are several small villages that can be reached within a few minutes by bus or train. These are popular among visitors and city dwellers alike who wish to escape for a day. Kibune for lunch in the summer on a table built right over a clear mountain stream . . . Kurama for a stroll through an old post town whose old shops and houses still retain the sense of a rest stop for weary travelers . . . Ōhara for a classic mountain village with small temples (see Day Trips).

Raku-hoku, though it has recently become a popular suburban area for merchants who have grown weary of sardine life in the crowded city, still has the air of country living, though the famous symphonic croaking of frogs in its rice fields has now been reduced to the realm of a sonata.

SAGENTA
sōmen noodles

左源太

76 Kibune-chō Kurama, Sakyō-ku
左京区鞍馬貴船町76　☎ (075) 741–2244, 741–2146 (Ugenta)

OPEN: 10 A.M.–10 P.M. (seating until 8) ▪ CLOSED: Periodically in winter ▪ PRICES: From ¥5,000,
kaiseki from ¥6,000 (reservations required for large groups) ▪ CREDIT: JCB

Deep in the Kitayama Mountains north of Kamigamo Shrine is a village called Kibune, where old inns and restaurants hug the banks of a stream beneath tall cedar and maple trees that have been enticing escapees from city life for generations.

According to legend, Kibune got its name over two thousand years ago when Tamayori-hime (the mother of Jinmu Tennō, the first emperor of Japan) took a boat up the Kamogawa river on a yellow (*ki*) boat (*fune*, often *bune* when combined), and when she arrived at the river's source, she ordered that a shrine be constructed there. Kibune is now written with different Chinese characters, so the origin of the name is obscure. At any rate, a shrine has existed in Kibune since before the Heian period, and it is here that the god of water dwells.

A thousand years ago, before the river was tamed with a network of canals, floods and droughts were a constant threat to the people in the valley below. The townspeople went to Kibune, then considered the source of the unreliable river, to pray to the water god for mercy. In times of flood a white horse was offered at Kibune Shrine; in times of drought, a black one. (In those days the northern mountains were mysterious places inhabited by goblins called *tengu*, with long noses and supernatural fighting skills.)

Kibune Shrine and the water god are still revered by the people of Kyoto, who celebrate a rain festival on March 3, a shrine festival on June 1, and a water festival on July 7 as they have for centuries.

But the main attraction in Kibune today is the many beautiful inns along the roadside that serve meals all summer long on tables built right out over the river, giving Kyotoites a place to escape the torturous humidity of July and August.

Kibune is at least five degrees cooler than Kyoto, which is enough to draw hundreds of hot city dwellers here each summer ·(and enough to keep them away in winter, so this is also an ideal hideaway to spend a snowy New Year's soaking in the steamy *iwa-buro*,

or rock baths, at one of Kibune's inns). Most inns feature *botan nabe*, or wild boar·stew, in the winter months and seasonal *kaiseki* meals year round. Though summer is by far the most popular season in Kibune, the maple trees in fall and cherry trees in spring are worth the short thirty-minute train ride from Keifuku Demachi Yanagi Station to Kibune-guchi. Walk across the bridge and through the orange *torii* gate that leads left from the train station and up the road that follows the stream.

Sagenta, the last shop on the river side at the north end of the narrow road, serves a summer treat called *nagashi sōmen*, or "flowing noodles," which is exactly what they are. Thin white noodles float down into a boat-shaped trough through a bamboo pipe which carries them in a stream of ice-cold water from the kitchen in the main building above. Seated outside on a platform over the cool river (close enough to reach down and splash), you overlook a fern grotto on one side of the stream and the stone walls and thatched roof of Sagenta covered with bright green moss on the other. Enjoy your *nagashi sōmen* surrounded by nature—not the artificial, planned variety found in the temple gardens of the city below, but the overgrown, shady, breezy kind that reassures you that the whole island is not "landscaped."

Sagenta and *nagashi sōmen* are primarily a summer treat, but there are over a dozen other fine places to eat in Kibune, depending on your taste and budget. Some can be quite expensive, offering elaborate full-course *kaiseki* meals and deluxe overnight accommodations.

Ugenta, the partner of Sagenta, is located farther down on the opposite side of the road, and has comparatively new accommodations popular with large group tours.

Hiroya and Fujiya are the two most prominent first-class inns and restaurants. Any time of year (except during the peak season in mid-August), lunches can be had at any of the restaurants on the river for under ¥5,000. Dinners, however, can be quite expensive.

Tochigiku, an inn at the southern end of this stretch of the river, is a friendly place to stay overnight any time of the year or just to stop by for lunch or dinner. Tochigiku is just next door to Beniya, and is actually an offshoot of the older, more expensive inn, but the hospitality, the cozy accommodations, and the originality of their talented young chef make this an annual place of pilgrimage for many of Kyoto's younger generation, to whom the prestige of staying in one of the more famous local inns doesn't mean as much as comfort, economy, and a fine meal.

NARITA pickles

35 Yamamoto-chō, Kamigamo, Kita-ku
北区上賀茂山本町35　☎ (075) 721–1567
OPEN: 10 A.M.–7 P.M. ■ CLOSED: Wednesdays

---

*The twilight dim, the gentle breeze
By Nara-no-Ogawa stream
The splash of worshipers who wash
Before the shrine, all seem
A perfect summer's dream.*
—Iyetaka Fujiwara, *Hyakunin Isshu*
(Single Poems by 100 Poets), 1237

Kamigamo Shrine, through which the legendary stream still flows, was founded by the Kamo clan in the early sixth century and is located in a strategic position in the north of Kyoto beside the Kamogawa river that afforded protection against possible invasions from provincial clans beyond the northern mountains. During the Heian period the court awarded the shrine priests with many estates, and a line of head priests who were descendants of the imperial family was established to ensure strong permanent ties.

By the seventeenth century, the area around the shrine had come to be known as a *shaké-machi*, literally a "shrine family township," with 275 houses in the area belonging to the families of the shrine priests. Today

the area along the old canal that carries the gentle breeze down from Nara-no-Ogawa, the little stream beside the shrine referred to in the poem, has been declared a historic district, and the walled *shaké-machi* houses that line it still retain much of the rural atmosphere that Kamigamo Shrine has kept for centuries.

Michiyasu Narita's pickle shop, a part of the *shaké-machi* that runs along either side of the canal, originally belonged to one of the *shaké* families. The Naritas have done more than just maintain the impressive two-hundred-year-old structure. They have restored it to its former glory and then some. The stone and clay walls that surround Narita are typical of the *shaké* houses in this area, as are the sweeping tile roofs and whitewashed walls of the main building. A stone path leads through the gateway across a graveled courtyard and past a large stone water basin at the edge of the garden beneath the bamboo and pine trees. Step over the threshold onto the black slate–tiled floors, and have a look at the rare Edo-period chest-on-wheels, in the waiting area on the left, and the large Meiji-period kitchen cabinet. In the raised tatami room on the right are a part of the fine collection of *mingei* (folk art) furniture owned by the Narita's, a different set of which is always on display.

The rough-hewn rafters that support the massive tile rooftop are masterpieces of construction themselves. Fitted together with complicated Japanese joinery entirely without nails, the exposed beams have been blackened over the long years from the soot that rose from the open hearth below. On the outskirts of the city now, the Kamigamo area was once considered "country." Many houses here share methods of construction used in traditional farmhouses.

It is their pickled *suguki* (a turniplike vegetable), or *suguki-zuke*, that made the Narita family famous in Kyoto. In 1780, the family started raising *suguki* and pickling them to serve the priests of Kamigamo Shrine. Then in 1804, they started selling pickles to restaurants all around Kyoto. About fifteen years ago, the Kamigamo *shaké-*

machi was recognized as a historic district, and it was then that the Naritas opened a shop to sell their pickles to those who had begun to flock to this picturesque area on the weekends.

The *suguki* are salt pickled in a process that is similar to that of making sauerkraut. It begins with the late fall harvest and takes about a week for each batch. After being peeled, salted, and left to set overnight, the *suguki* are then washed, salted again, and placed in giant wooden barrels over which lids are tightly pressed down with long leverlike poles that are weighted with stones (a method still followed at Narita, while most other makers have switched to modern machinery). Narita-san believes that the old ways produce the best-tasting pickles, and his many devoted customers agree. Restaurant owners and housewives as well as tourists take the extra time required to get to this out-of-the-way location to be able to serve Narita pickles at their tables. No preservatives are used at Narita, making this one of the few pickle shops in Kyoto that hasn't succumbed to the modern trend toward chemical food additives.

If you wander into the neighborhood on the west side of the Kamo River to the south of Kamigamo Shrine, you may come across someone pulling a heavy cart full of vegetables grown in this area. Each vegetable peddler has her own route to follow. The house that is the last stop on the vegetable lady's route inevitably ends up with whatever she has left over for free. Ordinarily this works to one's advantage, but even the most inventive Kyoto housewife would have trouble dealing with a whole box of leftover burdock root, I would think.

AZEKURA
buckwheat noodles (soba)

30 Okamoto-chō, Kamigamo, Kita-ku
北区上賀茂岡本町30　☎(075) 701–0161

OPEN: 9 A.M.–5 P.M. ■ CLOSED: Mondays ■ PRICES: From ¥500

Not far from Kamigamo Shrine on an old road which leads to Midoroga-ike Pond there is a three-hundred-year-old saké warehouse (*kura*) that was saved from the jaws of progress by a very thoughtful kimono merchant named Mikio Ichida just twenty years ago. More amazing than the salvation of this old saké warehouse itself is that it used to be over twenty-five miles to the southeast of Kyoto in Nara, where the Kintetsu train station is now located. Mr. Ichida had the huge structure disassembled piece by piece, brought to Kyoto, and rebuilt on the estate of a former samurai family called Okamoto, one of the oldest *shaké* families of Kamigamo Shrine. It took nearly a year to complete the move; every beam and crosspost was fitted together as it had been originally (the complicated joinery does not have a single nail).

With only a few modifications made to the interior, the 1,500-square-yard *kura* now serves homemade *soba* noodles in the main room, which has been decorated in Japanese folk style,

and hosts exhibitions from time to time in the spacious tatami room upstairs. Whether you take a stool at a low wooden table or sit on tatami or beside the open hearth, lunch at Azekura any time of the year is a comfortable country-style experience. You can watch the cook roll out the buckwheat dough and slice it into noodles by hand at a booth beside the kitchen door. The windows on the west side overlook a rustic garden complete with churning waterwheel.

After lunch you can stroll through the grounds to see the teahouse amid a grove of bamboo at the back of the estate or visit the folk museum across the courtyard, which has a large collection of hand tools, old brewery equipment, and folk furnishings to peruse.

Since Mr. Ichida is famous in the textile world, there is also a dyeing and weaving exhibition hall on the grounds in which exhibits are held periodically throughout the year. The name Azekura is written with characters that express the owner's appreciation of fine textiles—A, love; *ze*, dye-

ing; *kura*, storehouse. Though many of the textile exhibitions are by invitation only, you can peek inside the Hida House, another building on the grounds that is a reconstruction of a country house from the Hida-Takayama district, and watch the group of weavers at work on their hand looms.

The building itself is a marvel of Japanese joinery as you will note by looking up at the massive rough-hewn posts and rafters, and the cypress cross beams which support the heavy tile roof high above. This giant *kura* was originally a brewery and storehouse for a saké establishment called Kiku-ya that was built during the early Edo period in Nara. This type of construction is no longer common because of the scarcity of timber of this size.

Between Kamigamo Shrine and Azekura there is another, smaller shrine called Ōta Shrine. Except for a few weeks in mid-May when the irises are in bloom in the pond beside it, this is a quiet place to experience what Shintoism means to a Japanese community. Surrounded by towering cypresses some twenty meters high, Ōta Shrine has the sense of being in the midst of nature that is characteristic of Shinto shrines. Even atop office buildings in midtown, you'll find that shrines which house the company's protective divinity are seldom without a backdrop of greenery.

Shrines are also used as meeting places, each with a festival that brings the neighborhood together at least once a year. Shrines are often dedicated to a particular Shinto deity, such as the god of fire, thunder, or harvest. Dedicated to Ame-no-uzume-no-mikoto, the god of good harvest, Ōta Shrine has been in the hands

of the priests and parishioners of Kamigamo Shrine since the twelfth century, and the love of generations of parishioners is evident each year in late spring when hundreds of carefully tended purple and yellow irises make their annual appearance just as they have for centuries. The exact origin of Ōta Shrine is unrecorded, but over the centuries people have come here to pray not only for a good harvest but for protection against illness, good luck in marriage, and even for a successful career on the stage. (As with most Shinto shrines, Ōta has a long list of talented deities that can be implored to help out in almost any difficult human situation.)

By far the most frequent visitors to Ōta Shrine are the children. The last and perhaps most important function of the guardian spirit of a neighborhood shrine is to provide the children with a safe and beautiful place to play. The woods make splendid hiding places and Ōta Shrine is seldom without its band of renegade little people laughing and running beneath the sacred cypresses.

HEIHACHI-JAYA

inn (ryokan), restaurant

8–1 Kawagishi-chō, Yamabana, Sakyō-ku

左京区山端川岸町8–1　☎ (075) 781–5008

CHECK-IN: 11 A.M. ▪ CHECK-OUT: 9 A.M. ▪ CLOSED: 4th Thursday ▪ RATES: ¥13,000 (w/2 meals); bath only, ¥500, plus ¥400 for use of *yukata* ▪ RESTAURANT OPEN: 11 A.M.–9 P.M. (seating until 8) ▪ CLOSED: 4th Thursday ▪ PRICES: Lunch from ¥2,500, dinner from ¥7,000 ▪ CREDIT: DC, JCB, MC, MIL, VISA

Four hundred years ago footsore fish peddlers returning to Kyoto after the twenty-four-hour trek from the Japan Sea were relieved to find Heihachi-jaya at the foot of the mountains, just where they'd left it, welcoming them with tea and barley rice, and a place to rest their heavy loads.

Heihachi-jaya still offers weary travelers the same promise of comfort and a good meal. Hugging the east bank of the Takano River, the old roadhouse on the northeast outskirts of Kyoto is now an inn and restaurant serving *kaiseki*-style freshwater fish cuisine and the barley rice and tea for which they were known centuries ago. Entering the moss-covered Kigyūmon Gate, which once belonged to a rural Zen temple, you leave the city behind and stroll through a lush garden into a quiet world that seems to belong to a different time. During the Edo period this inn was the popular haunt of samurai and wealthy merchants, who knew of the inn's reputation for the best fish cuisine in the capital. Yamabana Heihachi-jaya, the inn's for-

mal name, means "Heihachi Teahouse at the foot of the mountains." Located on what was once the only road between Kyoto and the best fishing spots on the Japan Sea, it was the first stop for peddlers on their return trip to the capital; hence the inn received the freshest fish. When the railroad connecting Kyoto with the coast was built in the Meiji period, the peddlers no longer had to make the arduous journey. Heihachi-jaya began serving freshwater fish around the turn of the century, and now offers both ocean fish (*wakasa kaiseki*) and river fish (*seiryū kaiseki*) cuisine.

One of the unique features of Heihachi-jaya is the delightful *kamaburo*, an old-fashioned Japanese-style clay sauna, heated from below the floor by pine wood from the nearby forest. The *kamaburo* originated just north of here in Yase several centuries ago as a means of curing the battle scars of a young emperor. Sightseeing "battle scars" can also be cured in the comfortable temperatures of the *kamaburo*, particularly when taken in combination with a fine meal at Heihachi-jaya. Have a relaxing sauna, don a cotton *yukata* robe, stroll back through the garden to a private room overlooking the Takano River, and enjoy a *kaiseki* meal and the full beauty of an evening in northern Kyoto. The *sansai* (or mountain greens), fresh-grilled fish, and barley rice for which Heihachi-jaya is famous taste even better after the soothing sauna.

Though most of the original guest rooms were washed away during a terrible flood in 1789, the kitchen facing the highway was saved, and the original stone floors and giant rafters are just as they were in the Edo period. Peek inside as you pass by for a glimpse of the *daidokoro*, or kitchen, the heart of a traditional Japanese restaurant, where *sashimi* is sliced and rice boiled in the same way it has been for generations.

All the amenities of sauna and private room are available not only to overnight guests, but also to guests who come for lunch only, though reservations are a good idea. Guests without reservations will be offered seats in the spacious central dining room which also overlooks the Takano and garden, if private rooms are not available. Away from the noise and confusion of midtown, Heihachi-jaya offers fine food, a relaxing sauna, lush gardens, and a place to take off your shoes, unwind, and stay awhile.

KIKAKU-TEI
inn (ryokan), restaurant

55 Higashiyama-chō, Kamitakano, Sakyō-ku
左京区上高野東山町55　☎(075) 781–4001

CHECK-IN: 3 P.M. ■ CHECK-OUT: 10 A.M. ■ RATES: From ¥15,000 (w/2 meals) ■ RESTAURANT
OPEN: 11 A.M.–6 P.M. (reservations required) ■ CLOSED: 2 days a month ■ PRICES: From ¥8,000 ■
CREDIT: Major cards

Yase is a small rural town that clings to the foot of Mt. Hiei in the northeast corner of Kyoto like a shy child clutching her mother's apron strings. The single narrow road that leads to Yase and to Ōhara beyond was once the only trade route between the ancient capital and the Japan Sea. The old road through the mountain pass was arduous and exhausting.

For centuries Yase has been known as a place to relax, to recover, to enjoy at the end of a long journey. The name Yase literally means "eight springs," for here a number of small streams flow into the Takano River as it makes its way to the Kamo River in the heart of Kyoto. But local legends tell of a different origin to the village's name. Once in the seventh century after the death of the emperor Tenji, the armies of the emperor's illegitimate son fought his brother for control of the throne. The brother (later known as Emperor Tenmu) won, but not without suffering a near-fatal arrow wound in the back. The battle took place at Ōmi on the other side of the mountain near Lake Biwa, and his men carried their dying lord over the mountains to safety in a tiny village by a river and stayed with him until he recovered. The villagers say what pulled him through was the *kamaburo*, an ovenlike steambath in which he could lie flat on his stomach while his arrow wound healed. The village became known thereafter as Yase, or "arrow-in-the-back," written with different Chinese characters from those used today in the town's name. Both the baths and the legend persist, however, and Yase has kept its reputation as a place to escape to, if now only from the heat and commotion of the city below.

Kikaku-tei is a *kamaburo* inn, hidden at the edge of the forest beside the Takano River in Yase. It was once the elegant villa of Hiroshi Tanaka, the industrial magnate who founded the famous Miyako Hotel in Kyoto. Among other things, he owned Kyoto's first electric power company and established the Keifuku train line that runs from Demachi (where the

Takano and Kamogawa rivers meet in Kyoto) to Kurama (in the mountains north of the city) and to Yase, just across the river from Kikaku-tei.

The Keifuku train has thankfully never really been modernized. You sit on velvet-covered seats as the old one-car electric train rumbles up out of the city to Yase at the end of the short line. It takes about twenty minutes. Climbing down from the platform you walk a few meters to a creaky old footbridge that (hopefully) takes you across the Takano River to a dirt path leading to the right, past a small waterfall, and on to the inn. Stone walls surround the former villa, and a single tile-roofed gateway leads enticingly up the stone steps and out of the real world. In "borrowed landscape" style, the gardens, though carefully tended, seem a part of the forest on the mountainside to which Kikaku-tei clings. Giant maple trees hide the secluded inn from view as you begin to climb the mossy steps.

The rooms in the north wing are smaller and on more of a personal scale than the luxurious main rooms in the south wing. At the end of the corridor in the north wing is a beautifully designed tearoom in which the former mistress of the house entertained friends at tea ceremonies overlooking the Tsurukame (Crane and Turtle) Garden with its small pond, stone lanterns, and canopy of maple trees.

The south wing (originally the main house) is separated by a long corridor leading across more garden so that every room in the villa has a sweeping view. The largest, most luxuriously appointed room is downstairs on the south side, with glass doors that face the main garden on two sides, giving it an expansive air of extravagance.

Kikaku-tei was turned into a *ryokan* after the owners passed away. The old villa seems a bit disgruntled at having been turned into an inn. Not as polished perhaps as some of its prima donna counterparts in midtown, Kikaku-tei speaks with the voice of an era in Japanese history, not so very long ago, when the very wealthy few lived a life of sequestered elegance and luxury away from the eyes and out of the reach of the majority of the poor.

The *kamaburo* at Kikaku-tei can be used anytime, before or after dinner and again in the morning if the guest so chooses. Not as hot as a Swedish sauna, the round, clay, oven-shaped *kamaburo* is the original Japanese way to unwind and heal your wounds, be they sore feet or overtaxed senses.

The meals at Kikaku-tei feature freshwater fish in season, whether as a part of a full-course *kaiseki* meal, or in *kamayaki*, the one-pot specialty of the house—a bountiful feast of seafood, mushrooms, and vegetables simmered in a delicious broth at your table. (*Kamaburo* privileges are also available to guests who come only for dinner, but reservations are required.)

ICHIWA rice cakes

いち和

69 Imamiya-chō, Murasakino, Kita-ku
北区紫野今宮町69　☎(075) 492–6852

OPEN: 10 A.M.–sunset ■ CLOSED: Wednesdays ■ PRICES: ¥400

Mochi wa mochiya (Leave rice cakes to the rice cake makers)

"Old" is a relative term. Two hundred years is about as old as you can get in America; a thousand years is "pretty old" in Japan. Ichiwa, a shop that has served grilled *mochi* (rice cakes) in sweet sauce to visitors to Imamiya Shrine since the Heian period, is pretty old by any standard.

Mrs. Hasegawa, at 74, is old too, but doesn't seem to mind. She bustles back and forth between her wood-burning cookstove in back and the charcoal grill out front, endlessly turning the little skewers of *aburi mochi* in winter snow and summer thunderstorm as she has all her life. "*Binbō hima nashi* (the poor have no time to spare)," says Mrs. Hasegawa as she rushes out, wiping her hands on her apron, to welcome customers with a hearty "*O-koshi-yasu*" and usher them to a seat beside the little garden in back, said to have been designed by Kobori Enshū, the famous tea master and landscape garden designer of the early seven-teenth century. Even the tea-caddy-shaped stone water basin in the old garden attests to Ichiwa's long associa-tion with the masters of tea. The crystal-clear water, drawn from the an-cient well at the center of the shop, has been sought after by tea people for centuries. The daughter of the head-master of Urasenke, the world-famous school of tea, is even rumored to have a sweet tooth when it comes to Mrs. Hasegawa's tasty *aburi mochi*.

Aburi mochi are cakes of rice flour dough charcoal grilled and dipped in sweet *miso* sauce. The bamboo skewers on which the *mochi* is placed for grilling are split by hand from green bamboo stalks whenever there is a spare moment at Ichiwa. Sixteen skewers are used with every serving, which keeps the Hasegawas busy all the time.

Aburi mochi has been connected with a very old festival held at Im-amiya Shrine, outside the gates of which Ichiwa has stood for centuries.

Yasurai Matsuri, celebrated on the first Sunday in April at Imamiya

Shrine, is another such festival dating from the ninth century, intended to pacify the spirits of the falling cherry blossoms, which were thought to cause epidemics. Dressed in red and black wigs representing demons, the participants beat their drums and chant "Flowers rest in peace!" with great conviction.

Sekihan, rice with red azuki beans served at festive occasions (in this case with flower petals on top), and a skewer of *aburi mochi* was said to be all that was needed to ward off disease till the following year. Ichiwa sells *aburi*

mochi every day of the year now, but their history is tied to that of this ancient shrine and the festival still held here every year in spring. (Imamiya Shrine was dedicated to the gods on this site in the year 1001 following an epidemic that took the lives of thousands. The death toll was so high that there is record of bodies being carried to Osaka, twenty-five miles to the south, to be cast into the Inland Sea.)

Aside from a chance to see this three-hundred-year-old building and taste the delicious sweet *mochi*, Mrs. Hasegawa herself is worth the trip to the north of Daitoku-ji. When questioned about the equally old and marvelous *aburi mochi* shop, Kazari-ya, just across the way, she whispered, "Yes, they're very old too, but the shop changed hands once a few years ago" (two hundred years to be exact), as if she were letting us in on a recent neighborhood scandal. She is justifiably proud of her twenty-three-generation heritage, and her daughter and granddaughter work beside her every day, reassuring her that, unlike some of the other old shops, Ichiwa has a future. For Mrs. Hasegawa "old" is certainly a relative phenomenon.

ISODA nattō

磯
田

41 Shimomonzen-chō, Murasakino, Kita-ku
北区紫野下門前町41 ☎(075) 491–7617
OPEN: Daily, 8 A.M.–8 P.M. ■ PRICES: ¥500–¥2,000

Even a veteran foreign in Japan, when asked which Japanese food he could live without, will inevitably answer "*nattō*." The viscous texture and piercing odor of fermented soybeans doesn't even appeal to all Japanese, though people from Tokyo seem braver in this regard than those from Kyoto.

The specialty of the house at Isoda's bears the name *nattō*, but that's where the resemblance stops when it comes to flavor. Daitoku-ji *nattō* is a Kyoto treat that comes in a small wooden box, has the salty, rich flavor of soy, keeps for a year, and will permanently ruin your taste for peanuts with beer.

In business for centuries, Isoda has no need of a flashy signboard—people who know Daitoku-ji *nattō* know where to go. Like many old Kyoto shops, Isoda never advertises. A tiny bowl of the addictive little beans in the window to the left of the doorway is all Isoda needs to inform its customers that this is the home of Daitoku-ji *nattō* (and of the Isoda family since the late fifteenth century).

When the founder of Daitoku-ji came to Kyoto in the early fourteenth century, he brought with him an entourage of soldiers to protect the new center of the Rinzai sect of Zen. One of the Isodas' ancestors was a guard who not only defended the controversial temple, but acted as a servant to the powerful priests who lived there.

After the temple was destroyed in the Ōnin Wars (1467–77), an eccentric Zen priest named Ikkyū supervised the reconstruction of the temple and became its forty-seventh (and most celebrated) abbot. According to legend, it was Ikkyū who introduced the Chinese Buddhist recipe for this compact, high-protein treat that could easily be taken along as a snack by mendicant priests for fortification them on their way around the countryside begging for alms.

The original recipe for Daitoku-ji *nattō* (the one still used at Isoda) is a simple, natural process: an old-style cookstove is used to boil dried soybeans in water in a giant cast-iron vat for five or six hours and then left to

cool overnight; the beans are then drained and rolled in barley flour in wooden flats, where they are kept for five or six days until a fuzzy white mold forms, indicating that the fermentation process has begun; next, they are placed in large, round, wooden buckets and stirred with salt water (the stirring is repeated off and on for an additional five or six days). From here the beans are placed outside in the direct sunlight in the courtyard at the rear of the Isoda home. They are left to ferment and dry for one to two months, stirred several times a day until they separate into individual beans again (the viscous consistency gone), and are determined to be the proper color and texture to be packaged.

Because warm weather and natural sunlight are required, Daitoku-ji *nattō* can only be made during the summer months, most often in August after the rainy season has let up. The entire process is regulated by experience, rather than timers and gauges. There are no temperature controls or humidity regulators, and the not infrequent Kyoto summer thunderstorms keep the Isodas running around with umbrella-shaped tin lids to keep each batch dry. They produce enough in a few months to last all year, though they have been known to sell out by July of the following year if regular customers let their addiction get the best of them.

Even the famous tea master Sen no Rikyū is said to have been a fervent fan of the salty morsels. Because of the many tea people who frequent Isoda, they also make two kinds of dry confectionery, or *higashi*, which contain tiny bits of *nattō* and are served with ceremonial tea.

Chūgo Isoda, the present owner and a seventeenth-generation *nattō* maker, still keeps an iron-pointed halberd that has been in the family since his forefathers spent their days defending the famous neighboring temple. He and his wife work together every day during the sweltering Kyoto summers, boiling and stirring their beans. In the evenings they retire to the main room of their house, just behind the split curtain that separates the shop front from the kitchen in back. But Isoda-san doesn't eat *nattō* with his evening glass of beer. "Enough is enough," he says, wiping the sweat from his brow in the midday heat. "They're good, but enough is enough."

TARUDEN
buckets and casks

332 Higashi Yashiro-chō, Ōmiya Nishi-iru, Rosan-ji-dōri, Kamigyō-ku
上京区盧山寺通大宮西入東社町332　☎(075) 431-3087

OPEN: Daily, 8 A.M.–8 P.M.

It is a sizzling summer afternoon in the middle of the city and Tomii-san draws an ice-cold bucket of water from his well for his foreign interviewer to refresh her face and hands. He props up an electric fan on top of a giant wooden washtub, sits me down in front of it, and asks me what I'd like to know. "Tell me about the man in the picture," I say, pointing to the emaciated figure in white robes in the photo on the wall in back. "Oh, that's my friend Sakai-san. He's a holy man." Sakai-san had just completed a thousand-day austerity, called *sennichi kaihō gyō*, in which he walked a circuit of twenty-five miles a night around Mt. Hiei (north of Kyoto) for a thousand nights over a period of seven years. During the final stage of fasting and prayer, Sakai-san carried a pair of Taruden's wooden buckets suspended on a pole over his shoulder from a well to a sacred site where a purification ritual was performed. Having made the buckets that Sakai-san carried is one of the things Tomii-san is proudest of.

You'll find Tomii-san to be a very down-to-earth person, but his family has always had a connection with the world of spirits. The family well stood inside the precincts of an old shrine at one time and provided water for the purification of its worshippers. Over 120 years ago, Tomii-san's great-grandfather started to make buckets here in this same building.

Today one of his best customers is the local Tōei Movie Studio, which places regular orders for old-style buckets to be used as props in samurai dramas (though Tomii-san would rather see his buckets used for the simple purpose for which they were intended: as bath buckets, washtubs, and saké containers).

A middle-aged neighbor appeared as we sat talking. She announced that her eighty-year-old mother could no longer bear to be without a wooden washtub. Tomii-san was out of washtubs that day and apologized. Spying the used tub on top of which the fan was perched, she said, "Well, how about that one?" Perhaps understanding how adamant an eighty-year-old grandmother can be, Tomii-san extricated the large tub, doused it with well water, scrubbed it down with a bristle brush, and tied it to the back of her bicycle. "I know what you mean," he said. "The old folks just don't believe that these newfangled washing machines can get a collar clean enough." As his customer peddled off with a satisfied expression, he turned to me with scrub brush in hand and said, "I haven't been sick one day in forty years. It's because I use one of these old scrub brushes on my back!"

Both Tomii-san and his buckets are sturdy. His cedar bath buckets last thirty or forty years with daily use, if properly dried in the sun whenever possible. The lidded casks (*taru*) for storage and carrying buckets (*oke*) with handles are made from designs and techniques described by his great-grandfather in an old notebook, one of his prized possessions. Special hand-made curved planes called *kanna* form the exact angle of each curved stave depending on the diameter of the particular bucket to be made. Like most traditional woodworkers in Japan,

Tomii-san makes all his tools himself. The staves are held together by tiny bamboo dowels joining every seam. The workmanship must be perfect to create a bucket that holds water even before the bamboo or copper ring is put around it for extra strength.

Some of Taruden's buckets are used by Urasenke, the world-famous tea ceremony school just across Horikawa Street to the east, in preparation for each New Year's ceremony. Bucket-shaped flower vases are also popular with local tea masters in search of objects that possess a sense of simplicity and unpretentious dignity. Taruden makes several different shapes and sizes of flower vases in cypress (*sawara*), all with a natural unvarnished finish.

Taruden is located in the heart of the Nishijin textile district, and the rhythmic sound of looms can be heard all over the neighborhood. Most of the larger weaving companies abandoned hand-weaving for the Jacquard loom nearly a century ago, and out of the twenty thousand looms in Nishijin, the weaver next door to Taruden is one of only twenty-five hundred that still use hand-looms.

Tomii-san, unfortunately, has no son and no apprentice to carry on his obsolete trade. But meeting him now and visiting his two-hundred-year-old shop with the bright red buckets out front (his only "signboard") offers reassurance, if only temporarily, that you haven't arrived in Kyoto too late.

IZUSEN Buddhist temple food

4 Daitoku-ji-chō, Murasakino, Kita-ku

北区紫野大徳寺町4

☎ (075) 491-6665

OPEN: Daily, 11 A.M.–5 P.M. ▪ PRICES: ¥2,200–¥4,800

Izusen is a restaurant that serves *shōjin-ryōri*, or Zen temple meals, on the grounds of a sub-temple of Daitoku-ji called Daiji-in. The restaurant itself has facilities for large groups as well as individuals, but a delicious meal can be enjoyed at a table in the garden in quiet, natural surroundings (weather permitting). Meals are served in a set of red lacquered bowls in the shape of *teppatsu*, or priest's begging bowls, that can be stacked one inside the other when the meal is finished. On the edge of the garden which leads to Daiji-in is the "grave" of the writing brush of Murasaki Shikibu, the author of *The Tale of Genji*. Prices are reasonable and reservations are not required (but a good idea in spring and fall).

IKKYŪ Buddhist temple food

20 Daitoku-ji-monzen, Murasakino, Kita-ku

北区紫野大徳寺門前20

☎ (075) 493-0019

OPEN: 12 noon–8 P.M. (seating until 6); shop, 8 A.M.–8 P.M. ▪ CLOSED: Periodically ▪ PRICES: Meals from ¥6,000

The most famous Buddhist temple food (*shōjin-ryōri*) restaurant in Kyoto, located outside the east gate of Daitoku-ji. The food is excellent, but the portions are small and the prices are high. The shop has a long history of serving the temple priests at Daitoku-ji but the building has recently been remodeled and, though beautifully appointed, has lost the fine patina and atmosphere that its ripe old age once lent it. Reservations are a must.

HINODE-YA kimono

106 Kakai-in-chō, Teranouchi-sagaru, Ōmiya-dōri, Kamigyō-ku

上京区大宮通寺之内下ル花開院町106

☎ (075) 441-1437

OPEN: 10 A.M.–8 P.M. ▪ CLOSED: Thursdays ▪ CREDIT: DC, JCB, UC, VISA

In Nishijin, famous for weaving in Kyoto since the sixteenth century, it is not easy to find a shop that sells fabrics. Most of the area's twenty thousand looms are hired by major wholesalers, who in turn resell their goods to *gofuku-ya*, or retail kimono shops, most of which are located in the area west of Karasuma below Oike-dōri. Hinode-ya is an exception and they have been in business here in the middle of the Nishijin district since the Meiji period. They sell all kinds of fabrics, primarily in the narrow width used for kimono. Although most *gofuku-ya* sell only by the full bolt length needed to make a kimono, Hinode-ya also sells by the meter off the bolt, thanks to the owner's young daughter, who is trying to adjust the traditional family business to fit the times. They also offer *yukata* (light summer kimono) and *monpe*, the traditional garb of farm women.

MYŌREN-JI temple lodgings

Teranouchi Nishi-iru, Horikawa-dōri, Kamigyō-ku

上京区堀川通寺之内西入

☎ (075) 451–3527

CURFEW: 8 P.M. ▪ RATES: ¥3,000 (w/breakfast and ticket for public bath)

Friendly lodgings in a thirteenth-century temple of the Hokke sect. The old bell tower is noteworthy, and the rooms of the *shukubō* (lodgings) overlook a sand and stone garden of which the temple is proud. Make reservations by postcard well in advance because temple activities take precedence over outside lodgers. The lady (her foreign guests call her Chizuko-san) who handles the *shukubō* is kind and helpful. She learned English on her own to be of help to the many young foreigners who have sought rooms at Myōren-ji in the last few years. Sutra reading (*o-kyō*) from 6:30 A.M., a fine way to start the day, but not mandatory.

SEISHŌ-DŌ YAMASHITA
tea utensils

Teranouchi-agaru, Ogawa-dōri, Kamigyō-ku

上京区小川通寺之内上ル

☎ (075) 431–1366

OPEN: Daily, 9 A.M.–5 P.M.

On the road which leads to the gates of the two most famous schools of tea ceremony in Japan, Urasenke and Omotesenke, Seishō-dō has been selling tea utensils since 1847. From the most exquisite antique tea bowls worth hundreds of thousands of yen to the smallest tea accessories, a set of tiny wooden forks for slicing tea cakes, Seishō-dō is the place to browse or to search for a particular item to complement a collection of tea utensils. Stroll through this neighborhood past the grounds of Urasenke to Hōkyō-ji (famous for its exhibition of antique Japanese dolls in March and October) or to nearby Myōken-ji (see separate listing), which provides overnight accommodations and a sample of temple life.

MYŌKEN-JI temple lodgings

Teranouchi Higashi-iru, Horikawa-dōri, Kamigyō-ku

上京区堀川通寺之内東入

☎ (075) 414–0808, 431–6828

CURFEW: 9 P.M. ▪ RATES: ¥3,500 (w/ breakfast)

Accommodations in a temple of the Nichiren sect founded over 650 years ago. You may have to share a large room with other travelers if the temple is crowded, but private rooms are available if you send a postcard ahead requesting reservations. Unlike most modern-day inns, the rooms have no TVs or other gadgetry to mar the traditional beauty. They overlook a mossy garden that's as fine as any you'll find in one of Kyoto's expensive inns. The very low price includes a simple Zen-style breakfast. Bath facilities are available.

RAKU-SEI

Western Kyoto

Arashiyama . . . the name equals "autumn" in the minds of anyone who has ever visited this beautiful ravine in November. The steep mountain slopes with their seasonal wardrobes of crimson and green have been the favorite haunt of Japanese emperors for centuries. The Togetsu-kyō, the bridge that spans the wide Ōi River, marks the center of this area.

From this bridge north, the fields and bamboo groves of Sagano, dotted with the thatched rooftops of a dozen small country temples, stretch past Tenryū-ji temple with its dragon ceiling, all the way to the torii gate which leads to Atago Shrine. Farther north is Ninna-ji, with its pair of snarling carved Niō guarding the gate; Ryōan-ji, with its world-famous stone garden; and Kinkaku-ji, the Gold Pavilion built by Shogun Ashikaga Yoshimitsu in the fourteenth century.

Raku-sei, renowned for its scenic beauty, was also a place of exile for court ladies who fell out of favor with their lords. The melancholy aura of small temples like Giō-ji, named after one such lady who shaved her head and lived out her years here in shame, have given Raku-sei a wistful feeling of romance that appeals to today's young women, who flock here every year to share in the timeless sentiment of unrequited love that seems to pervade the western hills. The quiet mountains, bamboo forests, rivers, and fields with the many small country temples, restaurants, and inns make this area one of the best in Kyoto for a leisurely stroll away from the noisy city.

HIRANO-YA
sweetfish (ayu)

16 Sennō-chō, Saga Toriimoto, Ukyō-ku
右京区嵯峨鳥居本仙翁町16　☎(075) 861–0359

OPEN: Daily, 11 A.M.–9 P.M. ▪ PRICES: ¥3,500–¥15,000 ▪ CREDIT: MC

Smoke rises in the air above thatched rooftops at sunset. Below, the light of the bath fire glows in the darkness. A single cricket perseveres on the edge of winter, though the sound of footsteps warns him to be silent (he is, after all, alone now). Steep-sloped mountains contain the ancient valley, and the last few farmers trudge home from their rice fields, another year's work almost done.

Sagano in the western part of Kyoto was once nothing more (or less) than a country field. To find such a pastoral scene now, one must travel beyond the mountain ridges that surround the former capital city to the more remote rural areas that remain. Shūzan is one such place, Hanase another. Ōhara, though a popular tourist destination, still retains much of its rustic charm. But inside the city limits of Kyoto, there is hardly a scrap of countryside left untouched by urban sprawl. Sagano is perhaps the last area in which vestiges of rice fields and farmhouses can still be found at all in Kyoto.

Just inside the vermilion *torii* gate

that leads up the mountainside to Atago Shrine on the northwest edge of Sagano stands a four-hundred-year-old thatched teahouse called Hirano-ya.

Grilled *ayu*, a small freshwater fish, is the specialty of the house now, but long ago a cup of tea and a skewer of *shinko dango*, a popular local rice confection, were the treats for which Hirano-ya was known. For centuries, their homemade *dango* provided shrine worshipers with the encouragement to tackle the steep, two-hour climb to the top of Atago-san, the mountain on which the god who puts out fires dwells.

Fire has always been the most dreaded affliction in Kyoto, where the houses were built of wood with shared walls on two sides. On more than one occasion fire has destroyed the entire city in a matter of hours, so it became customary for every citizen to climb the hill once a month to plead with the cantankerous god of fire for mercy.

Though this custom has given way to a once-a-year symbolic climb on July 31, the pair of old teahouses at the

base of the hill beside the *torii* still offer rest and nourishment to faithful worshipers and to anyone who enjoys a fresh *ayu* meal served in gracious traditional country style.

The *ayu* served at Hirano-ya are caught in the nearby Hōzugawa river, brought live by fishermen and placed in the large pond out back. No refrigerator is used, so each morning just enough fish are caught from the pond to last the day (a process you can watch from the open veranda overlooking not only the pond but a backdrop of maple trees whose tiny star-shaped leaves form a jigsaw puzzle with the sky).

The *ayu* meal served *kaiseki* style is expensive. But the smell of freshly caught fish grilling over charcoal in the kitchen below and the rustic beauty of this two-hundred-year-old farmhouse with its dark, curving beams and heavy thatched roof is just about the only taste of traditional Japanese countryside this side of Mt. Atago. *Ayu* season is from May through October, and a full-course *ayu* meal runs ¥10,000. In the fall the *yudōfu-no-okimari* lunch of tofu simmered in a ceramic pot at your table is available at a much more reasonable ¥3,500. (For a brief country pause, the original *shinko dango* are still made fresh every morning and served with green tea at pilgrims' prices.)

The unusual Saga paper lanterns that light each room at Hirano-ya are a special source of pride for Tamiko Inoue, the thirteenth-generation proprietress of the old restaurant. It is difficult to find rustic lanterns like these, and she must order them from the last craftsman in the area who still knows how to weave the bamboo spines and coat the handmade paper with tannin the way they were made in the old days. Giant and unevenly constructed, they glow with a soft amber light that sets the mood at Hirano-ya, a quality described as *soboku* in Japanese, the artless beauty of things that belong to the countryside.

Kyoto Prefecture includes miles and miles of breathtaking farmland that extends all the way to the Japan Sea. After lunch under the high thatched roof of the old teahouse, a short drive through the tunnel to the west (or a hike over the hillside trail) will lead you to Kiyotaki, a country village from which you can begin a walk that leads along the banks of a river out into the hills beyond. Or drive up through the Arashiyama Takao Parkway to Highway 162, which, in three hours, will take you down winding mountain roads lined with Kitayama cedar (the trees that are so carefully groomed to decorate the interiors of Kyoto homes) to the Japan Sea. Valleys wedged between steep, cedar-covered mountains reveal tiny farm villages around every bend, scenes not long for this increasingly urbanizing world.

KOTŌ-EN
Shigaraki ware

15–2 Chōjin-chō, Saga Nison-in-monzen-kita, Ukyō-ku (Near Rakushi-en)
右京区嵯峨二尊院門前北長神町（楽只苑そば） ☎ (075) 872–2134
OPEN: Daily, 9 A.M.–5 P.M.

A hundred-odd ceramic *tanuki* (the legendary barrel-bellied raccoon dogs of Japan) from six feet high to pocket sized lined up in a courtyard in the middle of the bamboo forests of Sagano is enough to charm any traveler to stray for just a moment from his path. That's the secret of the wily *tanuki*, who has been seducing unwary strangers with his magical powers for centuries. Able to transform himself at the blink of an eye into a beautiful maiden or an ugly old hag, the *tanuki* is not to be trusted. Mischievous rather than evil, he has a whimsical turn to his dubious character that has managed to endear him to the hearts of even the most circumspect Japanese. A popular symbol with Kyoto merchants, the *tanuki* can often be found outside the doorways of the city's old shops, placed there perhaps in the hopes that some of the creature's crafty ways will rub off on its master.

Kotō-en, a pottery shop in the middle of Sagano in western Kyoto, is known for the comical covey of *tanuki*

in its courtyard, as well as for the wide variety of Shigaraki ceramics on display inside. Kotō-en is a Kyoto branch of the Sōtō-en kilns in Shigaraki, a famous pottery village since the Middle Ages in Japan. Built in the Edo period, the climbing kiln (or *noborigama*) at Sōtō-en is one of the largest kilns in Japan, producing glazed and unglazed stoneware from the coarse, reddish clay taken from the surrounding hillside.

Though pottery making in the Shigaraki area dates back nearly twelve hundred years, Shigaraki ware rose to its height during the Muromachi and Momoyama periods when the natural, rustic character of its ash-glazed finish came to the attention of tea masters in search of *wabi*, the simple, unaffected quality that was considered essential to the practice of tea ceremony.

Shigaraki ware still flourishes today, although it has undergone as many changes as the *tanuki* himself in the centuries it has been in production. The pottery is now popular as everyday ware (mugs, *nabe* cooking pots, and *ueki-bachi* planters), but the Shigaraki kilns still produce some of the beautiful natural-glaze tea wares for which the village became famous.

A short stroll through the courtyard to the display room will introduce you to the incorrigible Tanuki-san in almost every form imaginable. Long a symbol of good luck and happiness, the *tanuki* has become a trademark of the ancient kilns at Shigaraki in recent years. Inside the shop you'll find vases, tea bowls, coffee cups, serving platters, dish sets, ashtrays, and even chopstick rests (*hashi-oki*), all at the most reasonable prices in town.

(It is possible to visit the kilns at Sōtō-en in Shigaraki by bus or train. See Day Trips.)

Tanuki

The *tanuki*, apart from his legendary escapades, is a real-life creature. A member of the badger family, the *tanuki* (raccoon dog) has often been known to pester farmers and even suburban dwellers when in search of food to fill his insatiable belly. The hair of the *tanuki* is prized for use in the finest paintbrushes (almost as much as its clever hide is prized by irate farmers).

His mythological reputation is even more notorious than his name as an incorrigible farm pest, and over the ages these eight special "charms" have been officially attributed to this popular character:

1. the umbrella hat—a symbol of protection against accidents and mishaps.
2. the big round eyes—a reminder to be wary of all that is around you.
3. the whimsical face—a reminder to be amiable and keep smiling.
4. the saké bottle—*tanuki* wisdom says: if you have the money to buy saké, you should have the good manners to know how to hold your liquor.
5. the credit book—reminds the heavy drinker that his local saké shop extends him credit, so he in turn should learn the importance of trust.
6. the big belly—Japanese decisions are made from the gut (*hara o kimeru*); remember to think well before making a decision and to have the courage to stick to your decision.
7. the stalwart tail—anything as determined as a *tanuki* tail is to stand straight and tall should find nothing but success ahead.
8. the privates—last but impossible to overlook, the *kinbukuro*, which literally means money bags, in slang refers to the scrotum—the crafty badger's last word on the subject: don't be a miser, buy a *tanuki*. . . .

NISHIKI kaiseki cuisine

Nakanoshima-kōen-uchi, Arashiyama, Ukyō-ku

右京区嵐山中之島公園内 ☎ (075) 871–8888, 881–8888

OPEN: 11 A.M.–9 P.M. ■ CLOSED: Tuesdays ■ PRICES: ¥3,500–¥9,500

"*Obake deshō*," her employees tease, suspecting she's really just a ghost. But at 91, Ine Tanaka is the heartiest spirit I've ever had the pleasure to meet. For over forty years she has been the proprietress of one of Kyoto's most popular restaurants, and the story of her life is as amazing as her *kaiseki* menu is delicious.

"Actually, I was born in Tokyo," she told me, "so people around here consider me a kind of foreigner. I married a man whose family owned a pair of successful tempura restaurants. He threw me out when I didn't bear him any children. That's the way it was in those days: the man's word was law. I had no choice but to leave.

"I ended up staying in Osaka with his folks, no less, to help them manage the restaurant. As could be expected, we didn't get along, and when I asked them if they'd consider just selling the place to me, I think they agreed just to get rid of me. They wanted ¥3,000, which was a fortune before the war. I rounded up ten people I knew and talked them into loaning me ¥300 each. In

no time my place was one of the best tempura restaurants around. Until the bombings, that is. (Did you say you were an American, dear?) Well, they got me. The place burned to the ground. Decided it was time to move to a quieter town. I wound up staying at a rundown old inn in Kyoto out on a sandbar in the middle of the river in Arashiyama. The old couple who owned it were looking for someone to take it off their hands, so I volunteered. (Had to borrow the money again, mind you.) Little by little I pulled the place together and opened another restaurant right here."

Ine Tanaka still bustles around the corridors at Nishiki every day, bowing to customers and barking orders at the maids to straighten the shoes the guests have left in a jumble by the doorway. "You have to be on them every minute," she whispers again. "That's the only way to be sure the place is run the way you want it." A dozen young cooks scurry back and forth worriedly as the tiny gray-haired rear admiral in kimono scrutinizes the

sashimi slicing. Her restaurant serves three hundred people a day, and there is no time for mistakes.

Apart from renovation done on the one-hundred-year-old inn, the traditional tatami rooms literally perched out over the Ōi River are much the same as they used to be. This area is part of a historic preservation district; the rooms at Nishiki sprawl low along the riverbank, half hidden behind the high bamboo fence that surrounds the entire place, in keeping with the local style. Reservations are a must, though you may have a chance without them if you arrive before 11 A.M.

Like her life, Tanaka-san has played her menu by ear. It is *kaiseki* style with all the delicate courses, but an old-fashioned workman's lacquered lunch box with drawers (a work of "found art" discovered in a neighborhood junk shop by Tanaka-san's adopted son) forms the unique centerpiece, making the meal an eclectic cross between formal *kaiseki* and a deluxe *bentō* box lunch. It is called *o-shuku-zen*, a name whose Chinese characters refer romantically to an inn which serves meals amid the cherry blossoms.

The basic seven-course *o-shuku-zen* is only ¥3,000, the most reasonable price in town for a *kaiseki*-style meal of such proportions. Every month the ingredients are changed completely to match the season, and Tanaka-san's son prepares a special booklet (in Japanese) every month that describes every course with exacting detail for customers to peruse while they are waiting. The son, now sixty, was among the first group of young men who came to work in Tanaka-san's kitchen; she knew from the start that he would be the one to take over when she got too old . . . if that day ever comes (which appears doubtful). At present he is the owner of his own chain of traditional cooking schools.

A sample menu for the month of July featured such seasonal treats as *ayu no shio-yaki*, small freshwater white fish, salted and grilled; *karashi-dōfu*, a spicy local tofu dish; and *age-nasubi*, fried eggplant in *miso* sauce, served in a silver eggplant-shaped container. The top shelf of the *o-shuku-zen bentō* box was decorated with crosshatched twigs of bamboo on which "bloomed" three miniature paper-thin porcelain bowls, the shape of morning glories (the flower of the season) in soft blues and pinks, filled with tiny portions of seafood delicacies such as sea urchin and baby clams.

Nishiki has become a popular afternoon spot, particularly with women, an unusual phenomenon in Kyoto, where restaurants were once the exclusive domain of men.

One final question: What do you think about women's lib? "Women's lib?" she cackled. "Good heavens, I'm an old lady . . . what would I know about a thing like that!"

INOUE
bed and breakfast (minshuku)

1 Fujinoki-chō, Saga Shaka-dō, Ukyō-ku
右京区嵯峨釈迦堂藤木町1
☎ (075) 871-3335

CHECK-IN: 4 P.M. ■ CHECK-OUT: 10 A.M. ■
CLOSED: 1st & 3rd Tuesdays ■ RATES: ¥4,000
(w/breakfast), ¥5,000 (w/2 meals)

Constructed in the late Edo period as a farmer's house. The present owner is a landscape gardener and has done the grounds himself. It was a *kaya-buki* (thatched-roof) house originally, but fire ordinances forced them to switch to tile, though they have preserved the shape of the roof. The Inoues have preserved the interior with its heavy wooden doors and dark beams. They opened their house as a *minshuku* (a private house that provides rooms for guests) at the request of foreigners who were attracted by the beautiful old house and inquired about the possibility of staying a night. Cameras and bicycles (both handy items in the Arashiyama–Sagano district) are available to guests on a rental basis.

The menu includes several dishes made from the tofu at Morika, a famous tofu maker which is located in this neighborhood.

SAGA NINGYŌ NO MISE
Saga dolls, clay toys

2 Ogurayama-chō, Saga, Ukyō-ku
右京区嵯峨小倉山町2 ☎ (075) 871-7141

OPEN: 10 A.M.–5 P.M. ■ CLOSED: Periodically

Saga ningyō, or Saga dolls, originally referred to an old type of wooden figure that was coated with a white shell paste, elaborately painted and edged in gold. Though true Saga dolls are no longer made, the Iura family makes small clay figures (*tsuchi ningyō*) that retain a touch of the refinement their predecessors were noted for. The Iuras have been making these small clay figures here beside the rice fields in front of the thatched poet's hut known as Rakushisha since the late Edo period. The figures are miniatures of the twelve animals of the Chinese zodiac: the cock, the dog, the dragon, the horse, the monkey, the ox, the rabbit, the rat, the sheep, the snake, the tiger, and the boar. Each year in a cycle of twelve has the name of an animal in the zodiac (1985 was the Year of the Ox, 1986 the Year of the Tiger, and 1987, the Year of the Rabbit). Your character is said to be related to the animal of the year in which you were born. Each little figure at the Iuras' shop is sold in a tiny wooden box with its name and the shop's stamp on the lid.

PENSION KOKYŌ
inn, restaurant

1–4 Tateishi-chō, Saga Tenryū-ji, Ukyō-ku

右京区嵯峨天竜寺立石町1-4

☎ (075) 882–1817, 861–0278

CHECK-IN: 1 P.M. ■ CHECK-OUT: 10 A.M. ■ CLOSED: Periodically ■ RATES: From ¥5,000 (w/breakfast) ■ RESTAURANT OPEN: 10:30 A.M.–8:30 P.M. (seating until 8) ■ CLOSED: Periodically ■ PRICES: From ¥1,400, *kaiseki* from ¥6,000

A tile-roofed gateway leads to this interesting pension housed in a hundred-year-old building constructed in the Meiji period. Inside the decor is "antique"—this time Western to complement the Japanese-style exterior. (Both Japanese and Western meals are served.) A two-minute walk from Keifuku Arashiyama Station, north of the entrance to Tenryū-ji temple. The atmosphere is quiet and comfortable, as the name Kokyō, or hometown, suggests.

SAGA NO SATO bed and breakfast (minshuku), restaurant

46–2 Kitatsukurimichi-chō, Saga Tenryū-ji, Ukyō-ku

右京区嵯峨天竜寺北造路町46-2

☎ (075) 882–0623 (English spoken)

CHECK-IN: 3 P.M.–10 P.M. ■ CHECK-OUT: 10 A.M. ■ RATES: From ¥5,000 (w/2 meals), no dinner on Tuesdays

An inexpensive and popular *minshuku* just north of the main entrance to Tenryū-ji on the opposite side of the street. Serves a variety of meals in-

cluding *yudōfu*, *shabu-shabu*, and *bentō* (the price of a room depends on the meal). A Western-style coffee shop of the same name is located just to the left of the entrance and has become a fashionable spot for young people to stop for coffee while sightseeing in Arashiyama. This *minshuku* was the former home of actor Shintarō Katsu (of the Zatōichi series) and his wife, actress Tamao Nakamura. The famous movie star couple had the garden and tearooms designed to their own unique taste, and the house became a gathering place for their many film industry friends, who frequently stayed overnight. Popular with young people, Saga no Sato is almost always a lively place, and advance reservations are a must in spring and fall.

SAGANO yudōfu restaurant

45 Susuki-no-baba-chō, Saga Tenryū-ji, Ukyō-ku

右京区嵯峨天竜寺芒ノ馬場町45
☎ (075) 871-6947

OPEN: Daily, 11 A.M.–8 P.M. (last order, 7 P.M.), private rooms, 11:30 A.M.–7 P.M. (seating until 5:30) ▪ PRICES: ¥2,500

Hidden in the bamboo forest just south of Tenryū-ji is a beautifully designed restaurant serving *yudōfu*, a popular Kyoto dish featuring simmered tofu and a number of side dishes for a reasonable price. It is difficult to say whether this restaurant is in the middle of the forest, or the forest is in the middle of the restaurant—everywhere you look there are towering stands of bamboo. The walls in the main building are lined with *some-tsuke* blue-on-white porcelain bowls and platters. The gravel path that leads to the entrance is guarded by twelve large stone figures which were brought back by Hideyoshi from his sixteenth-century invasion of Korea. On the north end of the modern tile-roofed building there is a sand and stone garden that is unequaled by any in Japan—not for its extraordinary beauty, but for the submarine enshrined in the center. It is one of the suicide subs used in World War II and was placed there by the peace-loving owner of Sagano as a monument to the tragedy of war and a reminder of the importance of peace.

KOGŌ-AN restaurant

3–16 Susuki-no-baba-chō, Saga Tenryū-ji, Ukyō-ku
右京区嵯峨天竜寺芒ノ馬場町3-16
☎ (075) 861-0556

OPEN: 11 A.M.–4 P.M.; 5 P.M.–9 P.M. ▪ CLOSED: Thursdays ▪ PRICES: ¥2,500–¥6,000, *kaiseki* from ¥10,000

Beautiful pavilions overlooking gardens, with the borrowed scenery of the steep slopes of Arashiyama, serving *o-usu* (tea-ceremony tea for ¥800), mini-*kaiseki*, and formal full-course *kaiseki* at very reasonable prices in a villa-like setting on the north bank of the Ōi River. Reservations are required in the evening and for *kaiseki*.

RAKU-NAN

Southern Kyoto

Raku-nan is the only side unprotected by mountains, and the main transportation route to the old port of Sakai (now Osaka) on the Inland Sea to the south. The old highway used by samurai and peddlers in the Edo period still exists, as do the post towns along the way like Fushimi. Fushimi Inari is the home of a shrine to the rice goddess which predates the founding of Heian-kyō in 794 and still attracts thousands of merchants and businessmen who pray for a successful year during its festival every February. Fushimi Momoyama, formerly a castle town at the foot of Toyotomi Hideyoshi's great sixteenth-century fortress Fushimi-jō, is now one of the two biggest saké producing towns in Japan, with thirty-seven different breweries (see page 211) within walking distance of each other along a canal that was once a main thoroughfare for the flat-boats that carried goods back and forth from Kyoto to Sakai. It takes just fifteen minutes to reach Fushimi by local express from Sanjō-Keihan Station, but this nonetheless puts Fushimi outside the normal tourist path. Raku-nan belongs to the common people. It has never had the frills and finery of areas in the north that were in closer proximity to the Imperial Palace. This is where "the people" lived—and still live. Industrial, straightforward, and real, it is seldom included on tourist routes. If you are looking for a side of Kyoto that hasn't been tinted for the travel posters, Fushimi is the place to find it.

SOUTHERN KYOTO

JŪJŌ

to Sanjō

KINTETSU KYOTO LINE

KAMO RIVER

Route 24

●1

FUSHIMI INARI

3
○
INARI

Fushimi Inari
⛩ Shrine

Mt. Inari
△

KAMI
TOBAGUCHI

MINAMI-KU

FUKAKUSA

Nara Kaidō

KEIHAN LINE

Route 1

to Osaka

Meishin Expressway

FUJIMORI

Takeda Kaidō

TAKEDA

NANASE RIVER

Kyōmachi-dōri

⛩ Fujinomori
Shrine

SUMIZOME

FUSHIMI-KU

JNR NARA LINE

FUSHIMI

Tsuchihashi-dōri

SHIN TAKASE RIVER

FUSHIMI CANAL

4○

Tanbabashi-dōri

TANBA-
BASHI

Fushimi
Momoyama
Castle

5○

Mōribashi-dōri

6○

Ōtesuji

7
●OFUSHIMI
MOMOYAMA

9○

○10

●8

MOMO-
YAMA
GORYŌ-MAE

MOMOYAMA

to Nara

MOMOYAMA
MINAMI-
GUCHI

KEIHAN UJI LINE

to Uji

●2

CHŪSHOJIMA

KANGETSU-
KYŌ

Kangetsu
Bridge

UJI RIVER

to Yodoyabashi

0
0   500 m

1/2 mile

TANKA Fushimi dolls

伏見人形窯元

丹 嘉

22–504 Hon-chō, Higashiyama-ku
東山区本町22–504　☎(075) 561–1627
OPEN: 8 A.M.–4:30 P.M. ■ CLOSED: Sundays, holidays

Wherever you find a pair of perky-eared stone foxes (whose inscrutable demeanor bears a suspicious resemblance to the small, bushy-tailed house dogs chained to many Kyoto doorways), you know you are standing before the precincts of one of Japan's forty thousand Inari shrines. The vigilant foxes, one perched purposefully on either side of the brilliant vermilion *torii* gate, are the messengers of the rice goddess enshrined within, a revered spirit in a traditionally agrarian country whose staple food has always been rice.

Since the eighth century, Inari-san, as the shrine is affectionately known, has belonged to the common people—to the farmers, of course, whose lives once hung in the balance on the basis of the number of rice bales they were able to pay the feudal lords to allow them to keep on toiling; later to the merchants whose profits helped hold society together in times of war and political upheaval; and finally to the businessmen and industrialists who run the country today. Every year in

February during the shrine's annual festival, the young *miko* priestesses literally rake up hundreds of thousands of yen in contributions to the goddess of rice, who seems to have become the goddess of yen. The hundreds of symbolic *torii* gates which lead up the mountain to the heart of the shrine commemorate sizable donations made by hundreds of local shopkeepers and national corporations alike. A walk through the brilliant tunnel of vermilion is magic enough to draw tourists and photographers to Fushimi Inari year round.

The path leading up the hill to Inari Shrine is lined from end to end with shops selling all manner of amulets and Shinto paraphernalia to pilgrims and sightseers alike. Tanka was there, long before any of the rest, making and selling Fushimi *ningyō*, the painted clay dolls that are both colorful souvenirs and symbols of good luck at the shrine.

Fushimi dolls depict characters from folk tales (Kintarō, Momotarō, and Manjūkui-no-ko) or from the

Seven Gods of Good Luck (Hotei, Ebisu, or Daikoku). Some, like the heroic folk character Kintarō, are given as gifts of congratulations upon the birth of a baby boy with the wish that he will grow up strong and honorable like the legendary character the doll represents. These, like most Japanese dolls, are not meant to be played with, but to be displayed as protective objects or symbols of good luck.

At Tanka, Ōnishi-san makes Fushimi dolls from the same molds cut by his ancestors four hundred years ago. These are said to have been the prototypes for all the clay dolls made throughout Japan today. *Tsuchi-ningyō*, or clay dolls, have become popular regional souvenirs in rural towns from Hokkaido to Kyushu in hundreds of different forms and designs.

Tanka has over eight hundred original molds to choose from, and samples of many of these are displayed in a glass case that covers the entire south wall. (He doesn't keep them all in stock however, and although special dolls can be custom ordered, this year's selection is in a display case in the center of the room.) Each year Ōnishi-san also makes up a large order of the "animal of the year," according to the Oriental zodiac.

The dark, burnished-looking shapes that inhabit the display case on the north wall are not the goblins they appear to be, but are in fact some of Tanka's original centuries-old molds. Ōnishi-san brought out one for us to examine, pointing out the stamp on the base. Tenshō 3, it said—1576.

The shop building itself is characteristic of Fushimi-style architecture with its slightly curved, expansive tile rooftops. Note the row of roof guard-

ian figures. Shōki, the bearded warrior with the sword, is the most common in Kyoto, but at Tanka, the figures include an array of chubby urchins and horned devils that only a master mold-maker like Ōnishi could have devised. Constructed over two hundred years ago, the building is older than many in Kyoto, having survived the dreadful series of fires that destroyed much of the city proper.

One of the most popular dolls at Tanka now is called Manjūkui-no-ko, a standing figure of a boy who holds half of a *manjū*, or bean cake, in each chubby hand. This enigmatic figure is the perfect statement of the wisdom of an Eastern Solomon:

A young boy, wiser than his years, was asked by his quarreling parents to choose which one of them he liked best. He paused thoughtfully, picked up a knife and cut the *manjū* he was holding in his hand in two. He held out the two slices to his parents and asked: "Which half of this bean cake is sweeter?" Out of the mouths of babes . . .

GEKKEIKAN
saké brewery

247 Minamihama-chō, Fushimi-ku
伏見区南浜町247　☎(075) 611–0111

OPEN: 8:30 A.M.–5 P.M.

Yoi niya moto suri yonaka nya koshiki

Ara, yoi-se yoi-se

Asa no araiba ga nakenya yoi

Asa no araiba ga nakenya yoi

Asa no araiba ga nakenya yoi.

So sang the saké makers of Fushimi as they toiled through the night stirring fermenting rice with long-handled wooden paddles, preparing the *moto*, or yeast mash, for the next step in the marathon task of making saké, the traditional rice brew of Japan.

The song tells of a young man who wanted all his life to be able to work in the great saké breweries of Fushimi. When his lucky break finally comes and he finds himself toiling all through the cold winter night over steaming tubs of rice, he has second thoughts. He bemoans the icy mornings when he has to wash the rice and wishes he hadn't been quite so hasty in his choice of employment. In the end, he muses, his efforts will be turned into delicious Fushimi saké, but there is a touch of irony that implies he'll never be the one to taste it.

Since the seventeenth century, the great saké breweries (*kura*) of Fushimi have hired farmers to come to Kyoto during their idle winter months to make what was once the saké of samurai.

The eldest, most experienced of these workers were known as *tōji*, the master brewers, who brought with them the hard-earned knowledge of generations of saké makers who spent one hundred days of constant, back-breaking work each year to make Fushimi one of the main centers of saké production in Japan today. Although some of the saké companies now have modern factories elaborately temperature-controlled to produce saké year round, many of the smaller makers still employ the *tōji* each year from the same families that have worked in their *kura* for centuries.

Gekkeikan, the number-one-selling saké in the world, hasn't forgotten the debt they owe the *tōji*, who have served their company faithfully for over three hundred years. Although they now possess the most advanced, best-equipped brewery in the country, Ōkura (the company that produces Gekkeikan) still insists on maintaining the original old tile-roofed *kura* in which their *tōji* have worked for centuries. Beside a willow-lined canal not far from the Keihan station at Chūshojima (fifteen minutes south of Kyoto), the huge tile-roofed *kura* of Gekkeikan still produce a limited amount of *tezukuri*, or "handmade," saké just as they have since 1637.

When Rokurouemon Ōkura first opened his brewery in Fushimi 350 years ago, he was one of many competing for the favor of the Tokugawa shogunate in an area that was already one of the two biggest saké producers in the country (the other being Nada near Osaka in the south).

Fushimi is located at the convergence of three major rivers, the Yodo, the Kamo, and the Katsura, and was a convenient stop for boatmen and traders plying the waterways and highways between Kyoto and Osaka. Fushimi was a saké brewer's dream—it had river access with which to bring the best rice available from Himeji; it

had the chilly winters necessary for conducting the world's most finicky brewing process; and not only did it have some of the best underground spring water available, but it had a castle full of thirsty samurai, possibly seventeenth-century Japan's most avid saké fans.

In 1905, when renewed commerce with the West was in full swing, the Ōkura family named its saké Gekkeikan, a name which means "laurel wreath" (as the illustration on the label still indicates) to symbolize the Olympian heights to which the company aspired. In 1914, Gekkeikan was designated a purveyor to the imperial household.

Stop at one of the many liquor stores on the arcade that leads west from Fushimi Momoyama Station on the Keihan Line. There you can find all thirty-eight brands of saké produced in Fushimi, as well as a number of gift sets from Gekkeikan. A single bottle of *junmai-shu* (100 percent rice saké, with no extra sugar or alcohol, added) sells for ¥2,500; a two-bottle set of dry (*karakuchi*) and sweet (*amakuchi*) saké for ¥4,000. A saké cask (*komokaburi*) complete with a saké decanter (*tokkuri*) and a pair of matching saké cups (*choko*) can be had for ¥3,500 to ¥5,000.

Wander around the backstreets near the canal where Gekkeikan's old *kura* still stand and visit their museum, the Ōkura Kinenkan, for a look at how saké was made four centuries ago.

Gekkeikan offers individual and group tours in English. Reservations should be made two to three days in advance to guarantee an English-speaking guide. The tour takes an hour and the last one begins around 3 P.M.

SMALL BREWERIES IN FUSHIMI

Of the thirty-seven saké brewers in Fushimi, a few small places are worth a visit, although tours are available only by making special arrangements well in advance. Neighborhood liquor stores sometimes arrange annual tours with ten or so of their best customers, and a call to the brewery may help you get in on one of these. Saké is brewed only during the winter months, from October through March; no tours are conducted in the off-season. Not all saké brewers have retail shops (Gekkeikan does not). The Tsunoyoshi Saké Shop on Nishiki Market Street in downtown Kyoto carries most Fushimi brands (and a wide selection of ji-zake, or local saké, from small rural breweries all over Japan). A sampling of saké brewers can be found in the following list (S4–S6, S9).

S3

TAMA-YA
inn (ryokan), restaurant

73 Inari-onmae-chō, Fukakusa, Fushimi-ku (Fushimi-inari-sandō-kado)

伏見区深草稲荷御前町73（伏見稲荷参道角）

☎ (075) 641-0103 ∎

CHECK-IN: 4 P.M. ∎ CHECK-OUT: 10 A.M. ∎ RATES: From ¥9,500 per person (w/2 meals), from ¥9,000 per person for 2 or more (w/2 meals) ∎ CLOSED: 3 days a month ∎ RESTAURANT OPEN: 11 A.M.–6 P.M., private rooms (reservation required) 11:30 A.M.–8:30/9:30 P.M. (seating until 6:30) ∎ CLOSED: 3 days a month

Tama-ya is an old inn and restaurant where *daimyō* and their samurai stayed in their travels on what was the only road from Kyoto to Osaka during the Edo period. Many of the inn's guests are visitors to Fushimi Inari Shrine, beside whose gateway the inn is situated. Not as expensive as many of the inns in downtown Kyoto, the rooms in this one-hundred-year-old building have not yet been "modified" for the tourist trade. Beautiful gardens, long, squeaky wooden corridors, and the feeling that you have stumbled into a musty corner of the past. The room just inside the entrance serves inexpensive *bentō* lunch boxes, but reservations are required for their *kaiseki* dinners served in private rooms (*o-zashiki*) in the evenings.

S4

SHŌTOKU saké

Shōtoku Shuzō Ltd., 16 Butai-chō, Fushimi-ku

伏見区舞台町16

☎ (075) 611-0296

OPEN: 8:15 A.M.–4:45 P.M. ∎ CLOSED: Sundays, holidays, some Saturdays May–Aug.

During the Edo period, this brewery was located at Kawaramachi-Shijō, right in the center of downtown Kyoto. They moved to Fushimi during the Meiji period, where their brewery now produces some of the finest saké in Fushimi. The owner graduated with a degree in agricultural science, and is noted for his research on the propagation of rice, a background that must come in handy to a rice-wine maker. Shōtoku *junmai-shu*, or "pure saké," is noted for its pleasant aroma and slightly *karakuchi*, or dry, flavor. Many of the drinking establishments along Pontochō have been serving Shōtoku saké for generations, and Pontochō is one of the best places to sample it. Bottles may be purchased at the brewery.

TAMA-NO-HIKARI saké

Tama-no-hikari Shuzō Ltd., 545–2 Higashisakai-machi, Fushimi-ku

伏見区東堺町545-2

☎ (075) 611–4283

OPEN: 8 A.M.–5 P.M. ■ CLOSED: Sundays, holidays

This brewery has been making saké since 1673. Formerly located in Wakayama Prefecture, where the Kishū-ke (a branch of the Tokugawa shogunate family) were among their customers. After their brewery was destroyed during World War II, they moved to Fushimi, where they carry on their three-hundred-year-old family tradition. Their *junmai-shu* (100-percent rice wine) is noted for its fragrance and slightly tangy flavor. Although Tama-no-hikari is one of Fushimi's finest sakés, it has an official *nikyū*, or second-class government rating. In fact, only large breweries seek the *tokkyū*, or special top class, rating because of the higher tax imposed on saké with this rank. Bottles may be purchased on the premises. Takasebune, the tempura restaurant (see separate entry), pours Tama-no-hikari.

HINODE-ZAKARI saké

Matsumoto Shuzō Ltd., 7 Daikoku-chō, Yokoōji Misu, Fushimi-ku

伏見区横大路三栖大黒町7

☎ (075) 611–1238

OPEN: 8 A.M.–5 P.M. ■ CLOSED: Sundays, holidays ■ PRICES: From ¥1,600

This saké-brewing family came to Kyoto from Ōmi during the Edo period. They have been brewing saké in Fushimi for two hundred years, and their master brewer Osamu Imatsu has won awards for his *junmai-shu*, or 100-percent rice saké, brewed in the traditional way. A limited amount of *junmai-shu* is brewed each winter and is *amakuchi*, the sweet type for which Fushimi became famous. It is especially good when served with tempura. Bottles may be purchased on the premises.

AZUMA sushi

762 Higashiōte-chō, Fushimi-ku

伏見区東大手町762

☎ (075) 611–1379 (English spoken)

OPEN: 10:30 A.M.–8 P.M. ■ CLOSED: Thursdays ■ PRICES: ¥650–¥3,000 ■ CREDIT: UC, VISA

On the arcade just west of Fushimi Momoyama Station. Serves the best sushi in Fushimi, with plastic samples of the menu outside in the display window, making it easy to order. This is an excellent place to sample Gekkeikan saké while you are in Fushimi.

TORISEI yakitori and saké

186 Kamiaburagake-chō, Fushimi-ku

伏見区上油掛町186

☎ (075) 622–5533

OPEN: 11 A.M.–2 P.M., 6 P.M.–10:50 P.M. ■ CLOSED: Mondays ■ PRICES: ¥100–¥3,200

A *yakitori* (skewered morsels of grilled chicken) restaurant that is owned by Yamamoto Honke (see S9), the makers of Shinsei saké, and shares one of the Yamamoto *kura*. They serve a chicken-and-rice dish called *tori-meshi*, a chicken noodle soup called *tori-rāmen* for lunch, and regular *yakitori* fare in the evenings. This is an excellent place to sample Shinsei saké.

S9

YAMAMOTO HONKE saké

36-1 Kamiaburagake-chō, Fushimi-ku
伏見区上油掛町36-1
☎ (075) 611-0211

OPEN: 8:30 A.M.–5 P.M. ■ CLOSED: Sundays, holidays, Saturdays & Sundays Mar.–Oct.

In business since 1688 as a retail shop for saké, *miso*, and salt, Yamamoto Honke started making its own saké during the Meiji period and is now one of the most popular brewers in Fushimi. Their brand name is Shinsei and it can be purchased at almost any liquor store in Fushimi or Kyoto, or directly from their head office around the corner from their *kura* storehouses. (To sample Shinsei, see Torisei, S8.)

S10

TERADA-YA inn (ryokan)

263 Minamihama-chō, Fushimi-ku

伏見区南浜町263
☎ (075) 611–1223/4, 611–0710, 622–0243

CHECK-IN: 6 P.M. ■ CHECK-OUT: 9 A.M. ■ RATES: ¥5,000 (w/breakfast)

This *ryokan* is famous as the scene of a fight between Sakamoto Ryōma (a loyalist who sought to overthrow the Tokugawa shogunate and restore the emperor to power in 1866) and samurai troops of the shogun. He was assassinated a year later at the age of thirty-two. The inn has been kept intact since Sakamoto's day, complete with nicks in the woodwork that commemorate the famous sword fight. From 10 A.M. to 4 P.M. Terada-ya is open to the public as a museum, so guests staying at the inn may only use their rooms at night. Very inexpensive and popular with history buffs and students, who are its most frequent guests. An interesting place to visit while you're in Fushimi.

Getting Around

Finding your way around an unfamiliar city can be a trying and time-consuming task, even when language is not a problem. Fortunately, Kyoto has one of the finest information centers in the world. Whether you are looking for a place to practice Zen meditation or for the best steak dinner in town, the Tourist Information Center (TIC), on Karasuma-dōri, a half a block north of Kyoto Station, can tell you everything you need to know. City maps, transportation information, current exhibitions, hotel and inn reservations, and even volunteer guides are available here from 9 A.M. to 5 P.M., Monday

Aerial view of Central Kyoto

through Friday, and from 9 A.M. to noon on Saturdays. (On Sundays, or anytime, you can call the Japan Travel Phone at [075] 371-5649 for information or assistance of any kind in English.)

There are two helpful periodicals available at most hotels and at the Maruzen Book Store downtown ([075] 241-1062 Kawaramachi-dōri): the *Kyoto Monthly Guide* (also available at the TIC) gives information on exhibitions and festivals and other current events in Kyoto, and the *Kansai Time Out* offers everything from movie listings to *sumō* wrestling matches in the Kansai area, which includes Kobe, Osaka, and Nara.

Kyoto has an excellent public transit system. It is cheap and easily navigable with one of the plentiful tourist maps available around the city at hotels, the TIC, and other outlets.

Kyoto has five train companies, six bus companies, one subway line, and more taxis than any other city in Japan. The trains can be very useful for destinations on the outskirts of the city (Arashiyama, Yase, Kibune, or Fushimi) or for traveling to Nara, Osaka, or Kobe. TIC has excellent maps with complete bus and train information on the back. Most of the buses, however, do not have destinations written in English, and stops are announced in Japanese. Buses are often overcrowded, and for someone with only a few days to spend in Kyoto, much time will be wasted in trying to locate bus stops, waiting for the bus, and praying you'll be able to figure out when and where to get off.

Within the city limits, taxis are a good alternative. From downtown (Kawaramachi-Sanjō) to anywhere in the city the fare will not exceed ¥2,000, and in many cases it will be less than ¥1,000. The drivers are honest, do not expect to be tipped, and are rarely guilty of taking you "the long way around." Few of the taxi drivers in Kyoto speak English, so it is a good idea to have the location you wish to reach written down in Japanese (your hotel clerk will be glad to do this for you). All of the shop addresses in this book are listed in both English and Japanese.

For exploring the backstreets, bicycles are a popular option, and there are several places that rent them. Kawabata-dōri, the road that runs north of Sanjō Station on the east bank of the Kamo River, has several good rent-a-cycle shops. One of these, Keihan Rent-a-Cycle ([075] 761–4892), has locations all over the city so that you can pick up a bicycle in one place and drop it off at your destination.

One extra piece of advice on seeing Kyoto is to not try to see it all if your time is limited. The guided tours will run you all over town from Famous Temple to Famous Temple in a thorough (and thoroughly exhausting) five hours. If you have only one day, visit Raku-tō, which has more splendid temples, shops, and museums than you could see in a week. If you have two days, try Raku-tō and Raku-chū, the central district. In three days, the western sector, Raku-sei, with Arashiyama and Sagano could be added. With more time, Raku-hoku in the north, and Raku-nan in the south would take at least a day each to explore.

Walking is by far the best way to search for the heart of Kyoto. With a comfortable pair of shoes, you can discover all the little alleyways and niches that make this city one of the most intriguing in the world. Since Kyoto is still a safe place to wander, you can stroll through any quarter without fear of having your pockets picked or being otherwise assaulted. (Even after dark in the middle of the entertainment district in Gion the streets are safe.) Most of the shops in this book were found on foot, and it is the author's hope that you will use this guide to lead you into areas that you can explore on your own.

Walks through Old Kyoto

There are several old neighborhoods in Kyoto where the streets are lined with old houses and shops that have remained relatively unchanged for the last hundred years. Some of these areas have been designated historic preservation districts, and a few of the houses and shops along their narrow streets have been named cultural assets. The long blocks of old wood-frame houses that open directly onto the street in traditional Kyoto style are called machi-nami, *or urban row houses. Largely due to the efforts of local citizens (and the Department of Architecture at Kyoto University), these neighborhoods now have building regulations and receive financial assistance from the city or prefectural government.*

A walk through one of the historic machi-nami *districts takes you away from the bustle and traffic of the twentieth century for a moment to experience what life was like for the citizens of Kyoto a century ago.*

GION-SHINBASHI. The heart of Kyoto's most famous geisha quarter is within a five-minute walk of the center of town. South of Shijō along Hanamikoji-dōri are rows of old "teahouses" to which the sound of *shamisen* music and the exotic delights of the "floating world" nighttime entertainment still belong. On the corner you'll find the rust-colored walls of Ichiriki, a two-hundred-year-old teahouse in which the leader of the forty-seven samurai is said to have plotted to avenge his master's downfall by assassinating the arrogant shogun retainer responsible. Ichiriki is one of the teahouses in Gion that requires a personal introduction from a respected customer for reservations. No amount of money will get you past the gate without it.

Wandering the side streets, even late at night, is still safe in Kyoto, perhaps safer now than it ever was in the raucous eighteenth century when this district was in its heyday. You may pass an apprentice geisha (*maiko*) dressed in elaborate kimono, with her long brocade sash, her face painted white, her hair adorned with costly ornaments, clip-clopping past you in platform *geta*.

North of Shijō along the Shirakawa river is the Shinbashi district. Weeping willows and *sudare* blinds have become symbolic of this triangle of teahouses beside the old canal. As you walk down the narrow street one block north of the canal, you'll pass a miniature shrine to the Buddhist deity Jizō, protector of children and patron saint of every neighborhood in Kyoto. The women who run the teahouses of Shinbashi take turns tending the shrine, cleaning it carefully and offering fresh flowers each day. (Eastern Kyoto.)

HONGAN-JI. Between Nishi Hongan-ji and Higashi Hongan-ji temples, two powerful schools of the Jōdo sect of Buddhism, there is an area called a *monzen-machi*, or temple-gate town, that abounds with old shops dealing in religious articles such as prayer beads, home shrines, altar cloths, candles, and incense. The two temples are located just north of Kyoto Station and draw thousands of devotees each year on pilgrimages from the countryside, eager to buy religious articles to take back to the temples in their hometowns. Walking east from the central gate of Nishi Hongan-ji, you'll pass dozens of shops and old *ryokan* that have been offering accommodations to visitors to the temples for centuries. (Central Kyoto, south.)

KAMIGAMO. The area in the north of Kyoto that surrounds Kamigamo Shrine is one of the oldest in the city. The shrine itself predates the founding of the capital, having been dedicated to the god of thunder and rain long before Emperor Kanmu took up residence in Kyoto in 794. One of Kyoto's oldest festivals, the Aoi Matsuri, started here in the sixth century when a series of disastrous floods were thought to have been the result of the emperor's neglect of the thunder god. Every year on May 15 an imperial messenger visits the shrine in an elaborate procession to perform solemn rites to appease the god.

The shrine was built by the Kamo clan, one of the two main clans that inhabited this valley before Kanmu arrived. According to records from the seventeenth century, over 275 households belonging to descendants of this family (who were also priests of the shrine) formed a *shaké-machi*, a township that centered around the shrine to protect it and administer its affairs. The canal that leads east in front of the shrine is part of an original network of canals that acted as both a protective moat and an irrigation system. It is still lined with the clay-walled family residences of the *shaké-machi*, some of which trace their history back to the time of the first generation of priests. The area is also famous for its rice fields and small farms, and local women with their heavy vegetable carts can still be seen making the rounds of nearby neighborhoods, particularly the Nishijin weaving district. The pond in front of Ōta Shrine about six hundred yards east of Kamigamo Shrine is famous for its gorgeous irises which bloom each year in May. (Northern Kyoto.)

NISHIJIN. Kyoto's famous textile district where the fabulous brocade *obi* sashes are woven and the kimono fabrics are dyed. Since the early sixteenth century a guild of weavers and dyers has existed in this neighborhood and the dark, heavily gridded façades of their houses still line its narrow backstreets. Most of the textiles are sold under the name of famous wholesalers, though production is divided among hundreds of local craftsmen, who specialize in only a part of the whole process (like dyeing threads or preparing warps for weaving). The sound of thousands of looms can be heard echoing down the narrow alleyways of Nishijin as you walk along, although the workshops remain hidden behind the *senbon-gōshi*, or "thousand-fingered," wooden-slatted windows that hide the way of life of their inhabitants from public view. Peeking through half-open doorways of the textile workers' homes will give you a glimpse behind the scenes at one of Kyoto's most treasured old crafts. (Northern Kyoto; area cordoned off by Kitaōji-dōri and Horikawa-dōri.)

NINENZAKA and SANNENZAKA. Walking south from Maruyama Park toward Kiyomizu Temple you'll find an area of old shops and crumbly-walled temples that is one of the most popular in Kyoto for a Sunday afternoon stroll. The cobbled slopes leading up to the thousand-year-old temple are lined with *monzen-jaya*, or temple-gate tea shops, that have been serving refreshments to pilgrims and sightseers for centuries. A recent surge of interest in the area has prompted many local shopkeepers to remodel their old shops to accommodate the influx of tourists, and many now have a coat of paint and a facelift that robs the original of the dignity and *sabi*, "the beauty of rust," they once possessed. Until recently this area was also a booming ceramics center producing Kiyomizu ware, the painted wares for which Kyoto is famous. Many pottery shops still exist in the area, though the kilns have all moved to the suburbs in accordance with new pollution control laws. Dozens of shops selling antiques, pottery, and Buddhist articles and a number of fine restaurants crowd the narrow streets leading up to Kiyomizu Temple. A brief detour to the west to see Yasaka Pagoda will take you down quieter side streets in a very old neighborhood. Don't miss Ishibekōji, a small alley across from the entrance to Kodai-ji temple. This cobbled street with its high stone walls is lined with teahouses where geisha from Gion come each evening to entertain their guests. During the daytime it is practically deserted, except for an occasional sightseer who has wandered off the main path. (Eastern Kyoto.)

SAGANO TORIIMOTO. The orange *torii* gate of Atago Shrine in the western suburbs of Kyoto is the focal point of a row of *minka*, or rural houses, many of them thatched, that line the road leading through the gate to the old shrine dedicated to the god who puts out fires. The constant danger of fire in the ancient capital precipitated a custom that encouraged everyone in Kyoto to visit this shrine once a month. A festival held once a year in July still draws believers to make the steep three-hour climb up the mountain to gain the favor of this important local deity. The two thatched teahouses on

either side of the *torii* have been there for four hundred years selling a special kind of sweet called *shinko-dango* to fortify pilgrims on their uphill trek. They now serve *ayu*, a popular local river fish, grilled in *kaiseki* style (see listing for Hirano-ya, W1).

The graveyard at Adashino Nenbutsu-ji with its thousands of stone grave markers nearby also attracts a large number of visitors to this area. Take the turnoff about halfway down the road from the *torii* gate that leads to Arashiyama in the south. This road winds through the rice fields and bamboo forests, past the minor temples and shrines of yet another historic preservation district noted for its rural beauty. The road leads eventually to Arashiyama and the Tōgetsu Bridge that marks its center. It takes a full day to walk from *torii* to bridge, so many people prefer to rent bicycles at a shop near the bridge. A leisurely ride takes you to the shrine gate in half the time. The hundreds of crimson maple trees in Arashiyama make this area a popular tourist attraction in the fall. (Western Kyoto.)

Day Trips to the Countryside

Within a few hours by train or bus from Kyoto there are several towns and villages worth visiting, particularly if you are interested in pottery, papermaking, green tea, saké, or just beautiful countryside.

FUSHIMI. Located at the spot where the Yodo River meets the Takase River, Fushimi was originally a rest stop for boatmen traveling between Kyoto and Osaka. The northern part of Fushimi is called Fushimi Inari and is the location of an old shrine to the god of the harvest. Every year people still flock to Fushimi Inari Shrine around New Year's to pray for a prosperous year (whether their business is rice farming or micro-chip manufacturing). A road that was part of the Tōkaidō Highway built by the Tokugawa shogunate during the Edo period passes through Fushimi Inari, and some of the old shops and inns still exist, practically unchanged from the days when the feudal lords and their entourages used the highway.

Fushimi Momoyama, a bit farther south, was the site of one of Toyotomi Hideyoshi's castles in the sixteenth century. The location of the Yodo River, the availability of fresh water, and the proximity of a castle full of thirsty samurai made this castle town, or *jōka-machi*, the perfect place for brewing saké, for which this area is still famous. The old storehouses of the saké brewers have been preserved along the canal here, and some brewers give tours (by appointment only) for a glimpse of how saké is made. Terada-ya (see separate listing), an old inn in this area, now operates as a museum during the daytime (making accommodations inconvenient, but reasonable). It is famous as the hideout of Sakamoto Ryōma, one of the principal plotters of the Meiji Restoration in the 1860s, and mementos of his stay are on display throughout the inn. (See also S4–S6 and S9.)

Twenty minutes by Keihan Line from Sanjō Station. Fare: ¥180.

KURODANI. A beautiful paper-making village three hours north of Kyoto by bus from the Gion Terminal. Everyone in this village seems to be related—if there's a wedding, the whole town closes up. But when it's open you can see the village women rinsing reeds in the stream as has been done for centuries. Recently a small museum and shop were opened. The different kinds of paper are displayed and may be purchased. The rural setting and still-authentic nature of this little town make the long bus ride well worth it.

Two and a half hours by Kyoto Kōtsū bus from Gion Terminal (check with the TIC for departure times). Fare: ¥1,150.

ŌHARA. Few people miss the chance to visit this small town in the northeast of Kyoto if they have even half a day extra to spend. Just a forty-minute bus ride takes you to the foot of a hill that leads to the secluded temple Sanzen-in, founded in 860, and to Jakko-in, a nunnery to which the empress Kenreimon fled in 1185 after the death of her son, the emperor Antoku. The women of Ōhara (Ōhara-me) are noted for the colorful farm costumes they wear and the heavy loads they once carried on their heads. Weekdays are best for trips to this popular nearby town, also noted for its delicious home-grown pickles.

Forty minutes by city bus #5 from Sanjō Station. Fare: ¥350.

SHIGARAKI. This still-booming pottery village is one of the oldest in Japan and the site of an imperial palace in the eighth century before the capital was moved to Kyoto. The salt-glaze ceramics of Shigaraki were once among the favorites of the tea master Sen no Rikyū, who praised their rustic beauty. There is a museum in the center of town which has a fine collection of old Shigaraki ware, and several major kilns which are open to the public. All are within walking distance of the station. A few individual potters continue to fashion tea wares, while the major kilns produce everyday wares such as cooking pots (*donabe*), vases, coffee cups, saké sets, and even *tanuki* raccoon dogs and frogs as garden ornaments.

Two hours from Kyoto Station. Take the Tōkaidō Line to Ishiyama. Change to a local bus at Ishiyama. Fare: ¥1,020.

UJI. This old town forty minutes to the southeast of Kyoto has been famous for centuries for the production of the finest green tea in Japan. From the train station you can easily locate the famous Uji Bridge, the oldest stone bridge of its kind in Japan, and walk up the gentle slope towards the temple Byōdō-in, one of the only examples left of the graceful architecture of the Heian period. All along the road that leads to the temple you'll find shops that sell the famous local tea. Buy a container of *sencha*, the high-quality green-leaf tea, or one of *matcha*, the powdered green tea of the tea ceremony.

Forty minutes by Keihan Line from Sanjō Station. Fare: ¥250.

A Few Special Places to Hide

A few special places in Kyoto always offer a peaceful moment or two, even in the height of tourist season—places a bit out of the way (and out of the ordinary) that come as a welcome change of pace when the city's two thousand temples and shrines start melting together in your mind.

HAKUSASON-SŌ. The private villa of the painter Kansetsu Hashimoto built in 1916. Stroll through the lush garden, past a quiet pavilion and teahouse along the edge of a pond full of colorful *koi*. Have a bowl of *matcha* and a traditional tea cake in a tatami room overlooking the pond. Visit the small gallery in back which contains some of Hashimoto's works and objects from his collection of ancient European and Middle Eastern art. Note the small stone carvings under the tall bamboo between the gallery and the main house. These are mourners at the death of the Buddha, collected by Hashimoto from all over Japan. Open daily 10 A.M.–5 P.M. Fee: ¥600. ¥200 extra for tea. *See map of Raku-tō, page 120.*

KAWAI KANJIRŌ MEMORIAL HOUSE. This is the home of the noted potter Kanjirō Kawai, who was one of the founders of the folk-art movement of the 1920s and 1930s. The movement was established to promote an interest in everyday Japanese crafts among the general populace who had rejected what they considered rough country products in favor of the new objects imported from the West. His home, workshop, and kiln are open to the public as a memorial to the life of this extraordinary man who excelled not only as a potter but as a poet, essayist, and designer. The giant climbing kiln Kawai used can also be seen behind the main building which he designed himself in the manner of a traditional farmhouse. Just five minutes southwest of Gojō and Higashiōji-dōri. Open 10 A.M.–5 P.M. Closed Mondays. Fee: ¥500. *See front end papers.*

NIJŌ JINYA. Located south of Nijo Castle, this "mystery house," with its secret passageways and trapdoors, was built in the mid–seventeenth century by a wealthy merchant named Yorozuya Hiraemon as an inn for *daimyō* (feudal lords) visiting the capital from the provinces. The twenty-four-room house has hidden staircases, concealed rope ladders, and even a secret tunnel under a pond in the garden. It graphically demonstrates the political intrigues of the Edo period when the shogunate resorted to the use of a special clan of ninja spies to maintain control over the provincial warlords. Nijō Jinya has been designated an Important Cultural Property, and tours are conducted daily by appointment only. Reservations can be made by calling (075) 821-9932 (in Japanese) or through the TIC. *See map of Raku-chū (north), page 42.*

ŌKŌCHI-SANSŌ. This exquisite villa is located in the middle of a bamboo forest atop Mt. Ogura in the Sagano district in the west of Kyoto. It is fifteen minutes on foot from the Togetsu Bridge at Arashiyama. Built by the late Denjirō Ōkōchi, one of Japan's greatest silent screen stars, the villa sits amid five acres of land surrounded by beautiful gardens with a breathtaking view of the entire city. For ¥800, guests will be served *matcha* and sweets in a court-yard below the magnificent building, after which they may stroll through the gardens, take a peek at the elegant main building with its curved shingled roof, and admire the magnificent view. Formal *kaiseki* luncheons (from ¥10,000) and dinners (from ¥25,000) are expensive, but guaranteed to be served in a magnificently appointed private room overlooking the most splendid view Kyoto has to offer. Open to the general public from 9 A.M.–5 P.M. for tea. *See map of Raku-sei, page 190.*

RAKUSHI-SHA. This is the thatched hut of Mukai Kyorai (1651–1704), a student of the famous wandering poet Bashō who is said to have written his *Saga Diary* here amid the persimmon groves and rice fields in the heart of Sagano. The hut is a twenty-minute walk from the Tōgetsu Bridge in Arashiyama. The path to Rakushi-sha leads through bamboo forests and out-of-the-way temples and shrines to an area that has been preserved as an area of scenic beauty. Many *minka,* or country houses, with their thatched roofs and rustic clay walls still remain in this area, one of the last remnants of rural Kyoto. Open daily 9 A.M.–5 P.M. Fee: ¥200. *See map of Raku-sei, page 190.*

Nishikikōji Street Market

A street market may sound like a peculiar place to go for therapy, but if the noisy buses and inscrutable contradictions of life in Kyoto start to drown you, wander in the direction of Nishiki. It has everything you need (and several things you don't) to restore flagging senses and revive the weary mind. The aroma of fresh-roasted tea, of ovens steaming with hot bean cakes, of skewered fish dripping with soy sauce over a charcoal grill (this latter pleasure admittedly reserved for Orientally adjusted noses). The sound of shopkeepers calling out a hearty welcome, of fishmongers touting the day's catch in boisterous tones—"*Oishii yo*"—"delicious!" Finally, the riot of color for which Nishikikōji, "Brocade" Street, earned its name—shiny red apples stacked in perfect pyramids beside equally impeccable towers of persimmons, green vegetables (some familiar, some obscure . . . fern fronds, *wasabi* root, and broccoli), clams, oysters, shrimp, more varieties of fish than you knew existed, freshwater and salt. Sprinkle with a few old shops selling knives and cookware, *geta* clogs, or pottery bowls and you have Nishiki, the liveliest street market in Kyoto.

Since the Middle Ages, this street has been the site of a public market for fish, produce, and saké. It was destroyed in the Ōnin War (1467–77), but was rebuilt in the late 1500s and has been a popular marketplace ever since. Today the shopkeepers of Nishiki still follow some of the customs of their early merchant ancestors, as can be seen in the careful specialization of shops. Shops selling freshwater fish never deal in fish from the sea. Egg shops don't sell chicken (and vice versa). Some shops sell only shellfish, and others specialize in eel or blowfish. This division dates to the guilds that were established in Kyoto in the thirteenth century for mutual protection and profit during the turbulent times. By the sixteenth century, this division had evolved into a strict system of government favoritism that gave particular merchants absolute monopolies on the goods they sold, including the right to pass on their trade to their descendants in exchange for taxes.

The merchants of Nishiki still work together in close cooperation with one another, and though competition exists, the almost endless variety of specialty items in the Japanese diet and the similarly endless throngs of eager customers (who continue to patronize the shops their grandparents did) makes for a harmonious atmosphere in one of Kyoto's oldest marketplaces.

Most of the shops on Nishiki are open by midmorning, and it is then that you'll find many of Kyoto's most lauded restaurateurs shopping for the special foods they need to prepare elaborate *kaiseki* meals. In the afternoon, the local housewives invade the market, and by 3 P.M. Nishiki is always crowded. Working people stop by on their way home, and most shops stay open until about 7 P.M.

Nishiki is one block north of Shijō-dōri and runs from Teramachi-dōri on the east to Takakura-dōri on the west (near Daimaru Department Store). It is four hundred yards long and the red, yellow, and green awnings overhead house 141 shops. Look for Aritsugu, the cutlery and traditional kitchenware shop, on the north side of Nishiki one block west of Teramachi. Farther east, on the corner of Fuyachō-dōri, is Jintora, a sweet shop that specializes in *kodai-gashi*, or old-style sweets. Over a dozen wooden cases with glass lids hold different-shaped sweets, each molded and colored in designs appropriate to the season—pine needles, maple leaves, plum blossoms, and hundreds more. About halfway between Fuyachō and Tominokōji, you'll find Tsunayoshi, a saké shop selling *ji-zake* (saké made in small villages all over Japan) and dozens of Fushimi saké from the local saké-producing area (see Day Trips to the Countryside; S4–S6, S9), some in gift sets of small painted bottles in specially made wooden boxes.

Dried beans, sea urchin jelly, cod roe, fish paste, chrysanthemums (both to arrange and to eat), seaweed, live eels, raw oysters, flakes of dried bonito for making soup, rice cakes, grilled squid . . . what more could you ask for?

Glossary

amazake, a sweet nonalcoholic drink made from saké lees

ayu, a small river fish that is a delicacy in western Japan

bonsai, miniature potted plants

cha-kaiseki. See *kaiseki.*

chanko-nabe, a hearty stew served in portions fit for sumo wrestlers

-chaya or *-jaya* (suffix), a shop that serves tea. See also *monzen-jaya*, *o-chaya.*

-chō (suffix), township

daimyō, provincial feudal lords

dango, balls of *mochi* served on skewers (*shinko dango*—the special type of *dango* served at Atago Shrine)

-dera. See *-tera.*

donabe, earthenware cooking pot

fu, wheat gluten

fusuma, sliding paper doors

futon, traditional folding bedding

-gawa. See *-kawa.*

geta, wooden clogs

Gion, the most famous old entertainment district and geisha quarter, east of the Kamo River

happi, workmen's coats

hashi-oki, chopstick rests

imobō, name of a dish of preserved fish and boiled potatoes (an old Kyoto specialty)

-jaya. See *-chaya.*

-ji (suffix), temple, See also *-tera.*

jingu, shrine

jinja, shrine

ji-zake, regionally produced saké (refers to saké made in limited quantities by small local breweries)

junmai-shu, 100-percent natural saké (no alcohol added)

kabuki, traditional Japanese drama

kaiseki (or *cha-kaiseki*), formal Japanese meal served with tea ceremony

kamaburo, literally "oven-bath"; refers to a clay-walled steam room shaped like an old country oven

kamado, old-style clay cookstove

-kawa or *-gawa* (suffix), river

kayabuki, thatched roofing

Kiyomizu ware, ceramics from the Kiyomizu district of Kyoto

koi, carp

komono, kimono accessories: handbags, sashes, etc.

-ku (suffix), ward

kura, family storehouse; saké brewer's warehouse

Kyō (prefix), refers to objects or

traditions of Kyoto (i.e., *Kyō-ryōri*, or Kyoto cuisine)

machi-nami, row houses
machiya, townhouse; refers to traditional city dwellings
maiko, apprentice geisha
maki-e, gold decoration on lacquerware
manjū, bean cakes
matcha, powdered tea-ceremony tea
miko, Shinto priestesses
mingei, folk art
minshuku, an inexpensive family-run inn
miso, soybean paste used in making soups and sauces
mochi, rice cakes
monpe, farmwomen's pants
monzen-jaya, a teahouse outside the gates of a temple. See also *-chaya*, *o-chaya*.

nabe, cooking pot. See also *donabe*.
nabemono, dishes stewed or boiled in a pot
nattō, fermented soybeans
netsuke, carved toggles attached to tobacco pouches or kimono sashes
ningyō, doll
Nō, traditional Japanese drama, which originated in the upper classes
noren, short curtain hung in the doorways of shops and restaurants indicating that the shop is open for business

obi, wide sash worn with kimono
o-chaya, literally "teahouse"; refers to places where geisha entertain their guests. See also *-chaya*, *monzen-jaya*.
oden, an assortment of ingredients such as potatoes, hardboiled eggs, and Japanese specialties like *kamaboko* (fish cakes) simmered in a light broth and served over a counter
o-hagi, a confection of rice and beans
o-kashi, sweets (*wagashi*, Japanese sweets; *yogashi*, Western sweets)
o-usu, the name for tea-ceremony tea as it is served in most Kyoto shops; (from *usui* meaning "weak" or "thin," as opposed to a thicker type which is also served in formal tea ceremonies)

Pontochō, an old entertainment district and geisha quarter on the west bank of the Kamo River

Raku (prefix), literally "capital"; used to refer to areas in Kyoto (i.e., Raku-chū, or Central Kyoto)
Raku ware, name of a type of pottery used in the tea ceremony which originated in Kyoto, usually black or red
rakugo, traditional storytelling
robata-yaki, a variety of fish, meat, and vegetables charcoal grilled and served at a counter
ryokan, a traditional Japanese inn
ryōtei, an expensive traditional restaurant

saké, rice wine
sashimi, raw fish
sencha, high-quality green leaf tea
sensu, folding fan. See also *uchiwa*.
shabu-shabu, thinly sliced beef quickly dipped in boiling water in a pot at the table and then dipped in a sauce
shaké. See *shaké-machi*.
shaké-machi, township or neighborhood of families connected with a local shrine
shamisen, three-stringed musical instrument
Shigaraki ware, ceramics from the

town of Shigaraki, southeast of Kyoto

shinkansen, bullet train

shinko dango. See *dango*.

Shinto, native Japanese religion that worships the spirit in natural things (gods of wind, fire, water, etc.)

shōji, white, translucent sliding paper doors and windows

shōjin ryōri, Japanese Zen-style vegetarian food

soba, buckwheat noodles

soboku, rustic; unpretentious

sōmen, thin white noodles served chilled in summer

sometsuke, blue painting on white porcelain background

sudare, reed or bamboo blinds

sukiyaki, thinly sliced beef sautéed in a slightly sweetened soy sauce

sushi, raw fish served with vinegared rice in a variety of forms

tansu, chests, cabinets

tanuki, a badgerlike animal with alleged magic powers to transform itself into different shapes; the ceramic mascot of the pottery town Shigaraki and of many Kyoto merchants

tatami, woven straw floor mats

teahouse. See *-chaya*, *monzen-jaya*. For "teahouse," see *o-chaya*.

-tera or *-dera* (suffix), temple. See also *-ji*.

TIC, Tourist Information Center

tofu, soft bean curd

tokonoma, recessed alcove in a Japanese home used to display objects, flower arrangements, and paintings

torii, gate to a Shinto shrine (often painted vermilion)

uchiwa, round flat fan. See also *sensu*.

ukiyo-e, woodblock prints depicting the "floating world" of entertainment

wabi, the elegance of simplicity, an aesthetic value of the tea ceremony

wagasa, Japanese paper umbrella

wagashi. See *o-kashi*.

wasabi, Japanese "horseradish"

yakitori, grilled skewers of chicken

-yama (suffix), mountain

yōgashi. See *o-kashi*.

yuba, skimmings from simmering soy milk

yudōfu, tofu simmered in a pot at the table, dipped in a sauce, and served with side dishes

yukata, cotton summer kimono

Yūzen textiles, a traditional resist-dyeing process in which colors are applied with a brush

zabuton, floor cushions

Shops by Type

ACCOMMODATIONS

Daimonji-ya   *inn (ryokan)*   C31 112
Gion Umemura   *inn*   E32 158
Heihachi-jaya   *inn (ryokan), restaurant*   N4 172
Hiiragi-ya   *inn (ryokan)*   C7 62
Hiraiwa   *inn (ryokan)*   C44 118
Inoue   *bed and breakfast (minshuku)*   W4 200
Iwanami   *inn (ryokan)*   E21 154
Kikaku-tei   *inn (ryokan), restaurant*   N5 175
Kinmata   *inn (ryokan), restaurant*   C17 92
Kiyomizu Sansō   *inn*   E35 159
Myōken-ji   *temple lodgings*   N14 188
Myōren-ji   *temple lodgings*   N12 187
Pension Kokyō   *inn, restaurant*   W6 201
Riverside Takase   *inn*   C43 117
Ryokan Yuhara   *inn*   C45 118
Saga no Sato   *bed and breakfast (minshuku), restaurant*   W7 201
Shiraume   *inn (ryokan), restaurant*   E4 130
Tama-ya   *inn (ryokan), restaurant*   S3 211
Tawara-ya   *inn (ryokan)*   C8 65
Terada-ya   *inn (ryokan)*   S10 213

CRAFTS AND TRADITIONAL GOODS

Aizen Kōbō   *indigo textiles*   C1 44
Aritsugu   *cutlery, kitchenware*   C36 114
Asahi-dō   *ceramics*   E38 160
Fujii Kei Shōten   *dolls*   E18 153
Fundō-ya   *footwear (tabi)*   C30 112
Gion Tanaka-ya   *footwear (geta)*   E24 155
Hinode-ya   *kimono*   N11 187
Hirata   *blinds*   E5 133
Hirata   *clay dolls, folk toys*   C46 118
Hōrai-dō   *tea, tea utensils*   C37 115

Hyōtan-ya *gourd flasks* E37 160
Ikawa Tategu-ten *paper-covered doors* C25 110
Jūsan-ya *combs* C18 95
Kagoshin *bamboo* E2 124
Kasagen *Japanese umbrellas* E27 156
Kazurasei *hair ornaments* E28 157
Komachi House *antique kimono* C24 110
Konjaku Nishimura *antique textiles* E17 152
Kotō-en *Shigaraki ware* W2 194
Kungyoku-dō *incense* C22 107
Kyō-ya Sudare *reed and bamboo blinds* C23 110
Kyūkyo-dō *incense, stationery, brushes* C29 112
Matsuda *antique Imari porcelain* E36 159
Miura Shōmei *lanterns* E29 157
Miyawaki Baisen-an *fans* C15 86
Monju *lacquerware* E26 156
Morita Wagami *handmade paper* C21 104
Naitō *brooms* C12 77
Nakamura Chingire-ten *textiles* E15 152
Nakanishi Toku Shōten *antique dolls* E3 127
Nijūsan-ya *combs* C42 117
Nishimura *woodblock prints* C14 83
Rakumi *happi, purses, accessories* C33 113
Rakushi-en *ceramics* E39 160
Saga Ningyō no Mise *Saga dolls, clay toys* W5 200
Saiun-dō *Japanese painting supplies* C9 68
Seika-dō *metalwork, pewter* C27 111
Seishō-dō Yamashita *tea utensils* N13 188
Tachikichi *ceramics* C35 114
Takumi *kimono accessories* C34 114
Tanka *Fushimi dolls* S1 205
Taruden *buckets and casks* N8 184
Tazawa Kobijutsu-ten *antiques* E14 152
Tsujikura *lanterns, umbrellas* C39 115
Yamato Mingei-ten *folk art* C16 89
Yamazoe Tenkō-dō *scroll paintings* E16 152

FOOD AND BEVERAGE SHOPPING

Fūka *wheat gluten* C3 50
Funahashi-ya *rice crackers* C13 80
Gekkeikan *saké brewery* S2 208
Hinode-zakari *saké* S6 212
Hōrai-dō *tea, tea utensils* C37 115
Ichiwa *rice cakes* N6 178
Ippō-dō *tea* C5 56
Iriyama Tōfu *tofu* C4 53

Isoda   *nattō*   N7 181
Murakami-jū   *pickles*   C20 101
Narita   *pickles*   N2 166
Shioyoshi-ken   *Kyoto confectionery*   C2 47
Shōtoku   *saké*   S4 211
Tama-no-hikari   *saké*   S5 212
Tsukimochi-ya Naomasa   *Kyoto confectionery*   C11 74
Yamamoto Honke   *saké*   S9 213
Yubahan   *yuba (soy milk "skin")*   C6 59

RESTAURANTS

Azekura   *buckwheat noodles (soba)*   N3 169
Azuma   *sushi*   S7 212
Fujino-ya   *tempura, kushikatsu kebabs*   C40 116
Hirano-ya   *restaurant*   E22 154
Hirano-ya   *sweetfish (ayu)*   W1 191
Ikkyū   *Buddhist temple food*   N10 187
Ikkyū-an   *Chinese-style temple food*   E9 145
Izujū   *sushi*   E30 157
Izusen   *Buddhist temple food*   N9 187
Kappa Nawate   *robata-yaki grill*   E19 153
Kinnabe   *one-pot cooking, inn (ryokan)*   E33 158
Kogō-an   *restaurant*   W9 202
Matsuno   *eel restaurant*   E23 155
Minokichi   *Kyoto cuisine*   E13 151
Minokō   *cha-kaiseki cuisine*   E7 139
Misoka-an Kawamichi-ya   *buckwheat noodles (soba)*   C10 71
Nakamura-rō   *restaurant*   E6 136
Nishiki   *kaiseki cuisine*   W3 197
Ōiwa   *kushikatsu kebabs*   C28 111
Okutan   *tofu cooking*   E1 121
Owari-ya   *buckwheat noodles (soba)*   C26 111
Rokusei Nishimise   *Kyoto "box lunch"*   E11 151
Sagano   *yudōfu restaurant*   W8 201
Sagenta   *sōmen noodles*   N1 163
Tagoto   *Kyoto "box lunch"*   C38 115
Takasebune   *tempura*   C19 98
Takochō   *oden stew*   E31 158
Torisei   *yakitori and saké*   S8 212
Yagenbori   *Kyoto cuisine*   E20 153
Yamatomi   *teppin-age, oden stew*   C41 116

SNACKS

Bunnosuke-jaya   *amazake (a sweet beverage)*   E8 142
Kagizen Yoshifusa   *Kyoto confectionery*   E25 155
Kanōshōju-an   *tea and sweets*   E12 151

Kasagi-ya   *sweets and tea*   E10 148
Rakushō   *tea and sweets*   E34 159
Suruga-ya   *tea and sweets*   C32 113

Alphabetical List of Shops

Aizen Kōbō   *indigo textiles*   C1 44
Aritsugu   *cutlery, kitchenware*   C36 114
Asahi-dō   *ceramics*   E38 160
Azekura   *buckwheat noodles (soba)*   N3 169
Azuma   *sushi*   S7 212

Bunnosuke-jaya   *amazake (a sweet beverage)*   E8 142

Daimonji-ya   *inn (ryokan)*   C31 112

Fujii Kei Shōten   *dolls*   E18 153
Fujino-ya   *tempura, kushikatsu kebabs*   C40 116
Fūka   *wheat gluten*   C3 50
Funahashi-ya   *rice crackers*   C13 80
Fundō-ya   *footwear (tabi)*   C30 112

Gekkeikan   *saké brewery*   S2 208
Gion Tanaka-ya   *footwear (geta)*   E24 155
Gion Umemura   *inn*   E32 158

Heihachi-jaya   *inn (ryokan), restaurant*   N4 172
Hiiragi-ya   *inn (ryokan)*   C7 62
Hinode-ya   *kimono*   N11 187
Hinode-zakari   *saké*   S6 212
Hiraiwa   *inn (ryokan)*   C44 118
Hirano-ya   *restaurant*   E22 154
Hirano-ya   *sweetfish (ayu)*   W1 191
Hirata   *blinds*   E5 133
Hirata   *clay dolls, folk toys*   C46 118
Hōrai-dō   *tea, tea utensils*   C37 115
Hyōtan-ya   *gourd flasks*   E37 160

Ichiwa   *rice cakes*   N6 178
Ikawa Tategu-ten   *paper-covered doors*   C25 110
Ikkyū   *Buddhist temple food*   N10 187
Ikkyū-an   *Chinese-style temple food*   E9 145
Inoue   *bed and breakfast (minshuku)*   W4 200
Ippō-dō   *tea*   C5 56

Iriyama Tōfu   *tofu*   C4 53
Isoda   *nattō*   N7 181
Iwanami   *inn (ryokan)*   E21 154
Izujū   *sushi*   E30 157
Izusen   *Buddhist temple food*   N9 187

Jūsan-ya   *combs*   C18 95

Kagizen Yoshifusa   *Kyoto confectionery*   E25 155
Kagoshin   *bamboo*   E2 124
Kanōshōju-an   *tea and sweets*   E12 151
Kappa Nawate   *robata-yaki grill*   E19 153
Kasagen   *Japanese umbrellas*   E27 156
Kasagi-ya   *sweets and tea*   E10 148
Kazurasei   *hair ornaments*   E28 157
Kikaku-tei   *inn (ryokan), restaurant*   N5 175
Kinmata   *inn (ryokan), restaurant*   C17 92
Kinnabe   *one-pot cooking, inn (ryokan)*   E33 158
Kiyomizu Sansō   *inn*   E35 159
Kogō-an   *restaurant*   W9 202
Komachi House   *antique kimono*   C24 110
Konjaku Nishimura   *antique textiles*   E17 152
Kotō-en   *Shigaraki ware*   W2 194
Kungyoku-dō   *incense*   C22 107
Kyō-ya Sudare   *reed and bamboo blinds*   C23 110
Kyūkyo-dō   *incense, stationery, brushes*   C29 112

Matsuda   *antique Imari porcelain*   E36 159
Matsuno   *eel restaurant*   E23 155
Minokichi   *Kyoto cuisine*   E13 151
Minokō   *cha-kaiseki cuisine*   E7 139
Misoka-an Kawamichi-ya   *buckwheat noodles (soba)*   C10 71
Miura Shōmei   *lanterns*   E29 157
Miyawaki Baisen-an   *fans*   C15 86
Monju   *lacquerware*   E26 156
Morita Wagami   *handmade paper*   C21 104
Murakami-jū   *pickles*   C20 101
Myōken-ji   *temple lodgings*   N14 188
Myōren-ji   *temple lodgings*   N12 187

Naitō   *brooms*   C12 77
Nakamura Chingire-ten   *textiles*   E15 152
Nakamura-rō   *restaurant*   E6 136
Nakanishi Toku Shōten   *antique dolls*   E3 127
Narita   *pickles*   N2 166
Nijūsan-ya   *combs*   C42 117
Nishiki   *kaiseki cuisine*   W3 197
Nishimura   *woodblock prints*   C14 83

Ōiwa   *kushikatsu kebabs*   C28 111
Okutan   *tofu cooking*   E1 121
Owari-ya   *buckwheat noodles (soba)*   C26 111

Pension Kokyō   *inn, restaurant*   W6 201

Rakumi   *happi, purses, accessories*   C33 113
Rakushi-en   *ceramics*   E39 160
Rakushō   *tea and sweets*   E34 159
Riverside Takase   *inn*   C43 117
Rokusei Nishimise   *Kyoto "box lunch"*   E11 151
Ryokan Yuhara   *inn*   C45 118

Saga Ningyō no Mise   *Saga dolls, clay toys*   W5 200
Saga no Sato   *bed and breakfast (minshuku), restaurant*   W7 201
Sagano   *yudōfu restaurant*   W8 201
Sagenta   *sōmen noodles*   N1 163
Saiun-dō   *Japanese painting supplies*   C9 68
Seika-dō   *metalwork, pewter*   C27 111
Seishō-dō Yamashita   *tea utensils*   N13 188
Shioyoshi-ken   *Kyoto confectionery*   C2 47
Shiraume   *inn (ryokan), restaurant*   E4 130
Shōtoku   *saké*   S4 211
Suruga-ya   *tea and sweets*   C32 113

Tachikichi   *ceramics*   C35 114
Tagoto   *Kyoto "box lunch"*   C38 115
Takasebune   *tempura*   C19 98
Takochō   *oden stew*   E31 158
Takumi   *kimono accessories*   C34 114
Tama-no-hikari   *saké*   S5 212
Tama-ya   *inn (ryokan), restaurant*   S3 211
Tanka   *Fushimi dolls*   S1 205
Taruden   *buckets and casks*   N8 184
Tawara-ya   *inn (ryokan)*   C8 65
Tazawa Kobijutsu-ten   *antiques*   E14 152
Terada-ya   *inn (ryokan)*   S10 213
Torisei   *yakitori and saké*   S8 212
Tsujikura   *lanterns, umbrellas*   C39 115
Tsukimochi-ya Naomasa   *Kyoto confectionery*   C11 74

Yagenbori   *Kyoto cuisine*   E20 153
Yamamoto Honke   *saké*   S9 213
Yamato Mingei-ten   *folk art*   C16 89
Yamatomi   *teppin-age, oden stew*   C41 116
Yamazoe Tenkō-dō   *scroll paintings*   E16 152
Yubahan   *yuba (soy milk "skin")*   C6 59

Selected Bibliography

Condon, Camy and Kimiko Nagasawa. *Kites, Crackers, and Craftsmen*. Tokyo: Shufunotomo, 1981.

Engle, Heinrich. *The Japanese House*. Tokyo: Tuttle, 1964.

Japan Travel Bureau. *Travel Guide: Kyoto*. Tokyo: Japan Travel Bureau, 1984.

Kondō, Hiroshi. *Saké: A Drinker's Guide*. Tokyo: Kodansha International, 1984.

Massy, Patricia. *Sketches of Japanese Crafts*. Tokyo: Japan Times, 1980.

Morse, Edward S. *Japanese Homes and Their Surroundings*. Tokyo: Tuttle, 1982 (original edition, 1885).

Mosher, Gouverneur. *Kyoto: A Contemplative Guide*. Tokyo: Tuttle, 1978.

Nitchi Map-Publications. *Japan Solo: A Practical Guide for Independent Travelers*. Tokyo: Nitchi Map-Publications, 1985.

Plutchow, Herbert E. *Historical Kyoto*. Tokyo: Japan Times, 1983.

———. *Introducing Kyoto*. Tokyo: Kodansha International, 1979.

Ponsonby-Fane, R. *Kyoto: The Old Capital of Japan (794–1869)*. Tokyo: Ponsonby Memorial Society, 1956.

Richie, Donald. *A Taste of Japan*. Tokyo: Kodansha International, 1985.

Sansom, George. *A History of Japan*. Tokyo: Tuttle, 1981.

Steward, Harold. *By the Old Walls of Kyoto*. Tokyo: Weatherhill, 1981.

Thomas, A. F. *Commercial History of Japan*. Tokyo: Yuhodo, 1936.

Treib, Mark and Ronald Herman. *A Guide to the Gardens of Kyoto*. Tokyo: Shufunotomo, 1983.

Yamaguchi, K. M. *We Japanese*. Tokyo: Fujiya Hotel, 1964.

Acknowledgments

I would like to express my deepest thanks, first of all, to Yōko Yoshikawa, who has been an invaluable assistant from the days when this book was just another crazy-idea. Herself belonging to an old Kyoto family, she apologized to, pleaded with, and pampered many of the shopkeepers in this book on my behalf (teaching me how to say yes when I mean no, and other nuances of Kyoto-ese, in the process). Without her capable research assistance and support through interviews, this book would still be in the crazy-idea basket.

Thanks also to Rieko Iwaki, Mikiko Murata, and Mayumi Mizuguchi for their research assistance; to those who gave away their favorite (and occasionally secret) shops, especially to Philip Meredith and Joseph Justice (who dragged me all over Muromachi in search of the roots of *Kyō-ryōri*, a cuisine at which he has become an artist); to Kenkichi and Ayako Kuroda, Toshitaka Kawai, Hirotoshi Kuwano, and Kazuko Saitō, who taught me how to think Japanese; to Drs. Yoichi and Yoshiko Nagayama for their unfailing moral support; to Claire Gallian, a student of the history of Japanese architecture at Kyoto University, who offered much valuable information on *machiya* and made sure I got my *daidokoro* and my *toriniwa* in the right places.

Many thanks to Lucy Birmingham, for beautifully executing a very tough photographic assignment; to Kenneth Hamm, for photos of Isoda and Sagenta; to Tsuyoshi Ito, for photos of *machiya*; to Yūkō Okada for his wonderful *sumi-e* drawings; and to the many shopkeepers who allowed me to use old photographs from their family albums.

Thank you, Donald Richie and Yasuo Kitazawa, for adding a touch of class to the manuscript. To the staff at Kodansha International for building something livable out of rough timbers and dangling participles; to David Jack and the staff of the *Kansai Time Out*, in which my *"Oideyasu"* series on old Kyoto shops first appeared; to Tom Chapman and Greg Starr at Emphasis, Inc., in whose magazine, *Winds*, a portion of the material in this book was originally published in a slightly different form . . . thank you.

To the shopkeepers of Kyoto who opened their doors and hearts to this foreigner, *"Ōkini."*

And last, but most of all, to Stephen Futscher, who first suggested that I might believe in myself.